CONTEMPORARY CONTINENTAL THEOLOGIANS

S. PAUL SCHILLING

CONTEMPORARY
CONTINENTAL
THEOLOGIANS

ABINGDON PRESS • NASHVILLE • NEW YORK

CONTEMPORARY CONTINENTAL THEOLOGIANS

Copyright © 1966 by Abingdon Press

Library of Congress Catalog Card Number: 66-10854

SET UP, PRINTED, AND BOUND BY THE
PARTHENON PRESS, AT NASHVILLE,
TENNESSEE, UNITED STATES OF AMERICA

To
Mary

PREFACE

American Christians who seek to understand and communicate the gospel can find both stimulation and enlightenment through an acquaintance with contemporary European theology. Occasionally a strong plea is made for theologizing which is distinctively and indigenously American rather than bound to issues and methods determined by Continental thinkers. The demand for original theological labor should be heeded: American theology dare not be merely a pale copy of something "made in" Basel, Marburg, or Lund. It is responsible for making its own contribution to the total theological enterprise. It cannot do this, however, if it ignores the creative work which continues to be done on the other side of the Atlantic. Theological isolationism is no more commendable than the political variety. Moreover, American church life as a whole will be impoverished unless pastors, teachers, theological students, and thoughtful laymen in general are informed about and responsive to the most vigorous present-day movements in Christian thought wherever they are found. It is therefore imperative that serious-minded Christians in the United States come to grips with the problems being raised by European thinkers, while at the same time accepting responsibility for theological inquiry of their own.

The present book is an attempt to further this double process. It is an interpretation of the main trends in systematic theology on the Continent of Europe today. It expounds, compares, and evaluates the thought of eleven living theologians representing three Protestant movements, Roman Catholicism, and Eastern Orthodoxy. Each of the first eleven chapters

7

seeks to present as objectively as possible the main emphases of one thinker, then to comment critically on some of the important issues which he raises. Chapter 12 endeavors to compare and contrast the central ideas encountered in the investigation. Here the focus shifts from theologians to the topics which concern them. The intent of this twofold procedure is to do justice to the integrated thought of individual thinkers while shedding light on their relations to one another, and thus on the contemporary theological landscape as a whole.

The total situation is marked by both complexity and fluidity. Protestants, Roman Catholics, and Orthodox of course remain divided on crucial historic issues, though at certain points they are attaining greater understanding and harmony, in Europe perhaps even more than in the United States. Continental Protestant theology is far from being the unity which American Christians have frequently supposed. Side by side with broad agreements, wide diversity and sharp opposition in important doctrinal areas are evident, and unexpected relationships and influences sometimes appear. On occasion a particular Protestant theologian may find himself closer to a particular Catholic thinker than either may feel to a colleague of his own communion. French Catholics, for example, have manifested greater interest in Bultmann's thought than have French Protestants, while two of the most perceptive and appreciative critical interpretations of Barth's theology have been written by German Catholics. Though Barth's influence remains powerful in Germany, Switzerland, Holland, and France, it is relatively small in Scandinavia. In Holland Calvinistic conservatism continues predominant in spite of the impact of newer ways of thought. Analytical or linguistic philosophy, insignificant in its effect on German Protestant thought, has exerted important influence on several theologians in Sweden and Denmark, while existentialism, influential in Denmark and Germany, has made little headway in Sweden. Profound disagreements are apparent between Christian existentialists and confessional Lutherans in Germany and Denmark. Norwegian theology is marked by a pietism notably lacking elsewhere. Hardly any Continental theologian today would call himself a liberal, yet most are committed to the historical-critical study of the Bible, and liberal attitudes and positions find active—if minority—representation. Deep-seated differences appear with respect to the relation between Christianity and communism and with regard to the problem of Christian social responsibility in general.

Nevertheless, amid these and other diversities the repeated appearance of certain constellations of ideas makes possible the identification of a number of theological movements or tendencies. Theologians can within broad limits be grouped according to the different ways in which they confront basic contemporary issues. They are not shadow-boxing or playing intellectual games but striving earnestly to clarify for men today the meaning of the Christian revelation and the faith which it calls forth.

Of particular concern to Protestant thinkers are such problems as man's knowledge of God, the principles which should guide our understanding of the Scriptures (hermeneutics), the place of Jesus Christ in faith, the connection between faith and history, the nature or existence of man, the relation between self-understanding and the reality of God, salvation and the way to its attainment, the relation of gospel and law, the proclamation of the gospel, the nature and mission of the church and its ministry, the ethical and social responsibility of the Christian and the church, and the eschatological hope. Ordinarily the answers which a theologian gives to questions like these spring from a basic orientation which he shares with other thinkers. In the present theological situation three major orientations are discernible, hence three main groups of Protestant theologians. These may be broadly characterized as follows:

1. Theologians of the Word of God, whose perspective is predominantly Barthian. Among these, in addition to Karl Barth himself, are such German-speaking theologians as Ernst Wolf (Lutheran) and Otto Weber (Reformed) of Göttingen, Hermann Diem of Tübingen, Helmut Gollwitzer of Berlin, Karl Gerhard Steck of Frankfurt, Walter Kreck of Bonn, Wilhelm Niesel of Wuppertal, H. H. Wolff of the Ecumenical Institute at Bossey, and Heinrich Ott of Basel. For writers like these the monthly journal *Evangelische Theologie* (*Evangelical Theology*) provides a frequent medium of expression. Thinkers in other lands who represent a more or less Barthian point of view include Josef L. Hromádka of Prague, Jean Bosc (Reformed) of the Faculté Libre de Théologie Protestante in Paris, Roger Mehl of Strasbourg, Jacques Ellul of the law faculty at Bordeaux, Jean-Louis Leuba of Neuchâtel, Switzerland, and N. H. Söe of Copenhagen.

2. Theologians who are influenced decisively or conspicuously by existentialist modes of thinking. These include in varying degrees Rudolf Bultmann of Marburg, Friedrich Gogarten of Göttingen, Gerhard Ebeling of Zürich and Tübingen, Ernst Fuchs of Marburg, Knud E. Lögstrup of Aarhus in Denmark, and in some respects Emil Brunner of Zürich. The ideas of these men often appear in the quarterly *Die Zeitschrift für*

Theologie und Kirche (*Journal for Theology and Church*), selections from which are now published in an annual English edition.

3. Theologians who find either in the Lutheran confessions or Luther himself definitive guidance in interpreting the faith of the Scriptures. Typical of this group are Peter Brunner and Edmund Schlink of Heidelberg, Wilfried Joest and Walter Künneth of Erlangen, Ernst Kinder of Münster, Wolfhart Pannenberg of Mainz, Gerhard Gloege of Jena, East Germany, Theobald Süss of the Faculté Libre de Théologie Protestante in Paris, Regin Prenter of Aarhus, Denmark, Gustaf Wingren of Lund, Sweden, and Nils A. Dahl of Oslo, Norway. These and other Lutherans cooperate in the publication of the quarterly journal *Kerygma und Dogma,* the very title of which constitutes an implicit polemic against the Bultmannian orientation of the five-volume symposium *Kerygma und Mythos* (ed. Hans-Werner Bartsch). Another vigorous journal, *Position Luthérien,* is published by the French Lutherans.

It should be emphasized that these groupings represent rough classifications rather than organizations. They are in no sense mutually exclusive "schools," and overlap in various ways. Their German-speaking representatives in particular spring from common backgrounds in the dialectical theology of the twenties and the confessing church of the thirties and forties. Lutherans no less than Barthians are theologians of the Word. Ernst Wolf, a Barthian, and Gogarten and Ebeling, more friendly to existentialist attitudes, agree in regarding the outlook of confessional Lutheranism as too traditional, yet all three think of themselves as genuinely Lutheran, and all have made important contributions to Luther-research. Yet in spite of these somewhat blurred distinctions the three groups do represent different tendencies, movements, or streams of thought, and they will be so treated in this volume.

Side by side with these movements are others which are less extensive and influential but nonetheless vigorous. Also active are many individual scholars whose standpoints cannot be readily classified but who are making important independent contributions or building bridges between opposing positions. In Germany, for example, a considerable number of thinkers deeply cherish the values of historic Lutheranism but are somewhat critical of traditional Lutheran confessionalism. The names of Paul Althaus of Erlangen, Helmut Thielicke of Hamburg, Carl-Heinz Ratschow of Marburg, and Heinrich Vogel of the Humboldt University of East Berlin come readily to mind. A comparable attitude is found in K. E. Skydsgaard of Copenhagen, and in Gustaf Aulén and Anders Nygren of Lund, both of whom have contributed significantly to the Luther-renaissance in Sweden. In Holland a conservative Calvinistic biblicism is ably represented by G. C. Berkouwer of Amsterdam, who has also written an interpretation of Barth's theology which is appreciative as well as incisively critical, and by Hendrikus Berkhof of Leiden.

Emil Brunner, a co-founder of the dialectical theology who broke with Barth on the issue of revelation in creation and history, stresses the personal coming of God to man in Jesus Christ, locates the distinctively human in man's I-thou relation to God requiring his response in either faith or revolt, and grounds ethics in the divine command and the orders of creation. Receiving increasing attention is Fritz Buri of Basel, who in the context of the liberal eschatology of Albert Schweitzer and Karl Jaspers' philosophy of existence sees Christian faith as the encounter of the innermost existence of man with the transcendent God self-revealed in Jesus Christ. From within the Barthian movement Heinrich Ott of Basel has attempted not only to mediate between Barth and Bultmann but also to correlate with Barthian thought certain emphases of the later Heidegger. Paul Ricoeur of the Sorbonne has undertaken from a philosophical perspective a reinterpretation of theological themes such as sin and guilt, and is seeking to remove the opposition between Greek and Christian thought. Other independent theologians actively interested in the philosophy of religion are Sören Holm of Copenhagen and Axel Gyllenkrok of Uppsala. These examples offer further indication of the range and variety of contemporary tendencies in Protestant theology.

Roman Catholic and Orthodox thinkers are making critical and creative contributions which deserve far more attention than can be given in this volume. Representative of German-speaking Catholic systematicians are Romano Guardini, Karl Rahner, Michael Schmaus, and Gottlieb Söhngen of Munich, Karl Adam and Hans Küng of Tübingen, Heinrich Schlier of Bonn, Rudolf Schnackenburg of Würzburg, Karl Schumann of Münster, Hans Urs von Balthasar of Basel, and Otto Karrer of Lucerne. Outstanding among French and Belgian Catholic theologians are Yves M.-J. Congar of Strasbourg, Jean Daniélou of Paris, Henri de Lubac of Lyons, and Albert Dondeyne of Louvain. Protestants may be particularly interested in the views held by these men in such doctrinal areas as Christology; Mariology; anthropology; the divine-human nature, catholicity, apostolicity, and renewal of the church; the sacraments; the status of the laity; Scripture and tradition; the salvation of non-Catholics; eschatology; and the bases of ethical decision.

Unfortunately, relatively little of the work of the Eastern Orthodox thinkers of Europe is available in western languages. However, representative expressions are found in the writings of Paul Evdokimov and Boris Bobrinskoy of St. Sergius Institute, Paris, Pangiotis I. Bratsiotis of the University of Athens, and Nikos A. Nissiotis of the Ecumenical Institute at Bossey. These theologians devote serious attention to such questions as the Trinity, pneumatology, man and his restoration, the catholicity and sacramental life of the church, eucharistic worship, the relation between clergy and laity, scriptural revelation and tradition, the church's mission to the world, and the relation of Orthodox uniqueness to Christian unity.

The problem of choosing for special study a few of the many highly qualified theologians listed above is a baffling one. No two interpreters would make the same selection, and any list is bound to raise questions regarding both inclusions and omissions. However, the choices made have grown out of extensive library research, personal consultations with thirty-six theologians in seven European countries, and many discussions with colleagues in America. They are believed to be truly representative of the most competent and influential thinking now being done on the Continent and of the themes now commanding primary attention.

In view of spatial limitations, I believe that the best picture of the total situation in Protestant theology will be gained if attention is concentrated on representatives of the three main movements described. Since I am myself a Protestant and the potential readership is no doubt also chiefly Protestant, major consideration is given to these Protestant tendencies. However, in these days of a new and cherished openness among the Christian communions it seems imperative to include examples of the penetrating investigations of Catholic and Orthodox thinkers. Yves Congar and Karl Rahner, because of the depth and scope of their writings and their profound influence on the Second Vatican Council, seem obvious choices. Nikos Nissiotis, in spite of his relative youth, is probably communicating the meaning of Orthodox faith to Protestants and Roman Catholics in the West more effectively than any other representative of his tradition.

Critical readers will wonder at the absence from the Protestant listing of a number of thinkers of outstanding merit. Such omissions I equally regret, but they are unavoidable, and they have not been governed by chance. Some systematicians have divided their attention between doctrinal studies and related areas such as exegesis, hermeneutics, ethical and political questions, or preaching, hence have been occupied with the central problems of systematic theology somewhat less than most of the theologians here interpreted. Others who have made conspicuous contributions in the past are now declining in influence. Still others are promising younger men whose major productivity lies ahead. It remains true that strong cases could be made for different selections. Nevertheless, the eight men selected I believe to be worthy and typical representatives of contemporary Protestant thought.

These chapters seek to present thinkers and ideas as accurately and fairly as possible. They would not achieve their purpose, however, if they stopped with impartial reporting. The theologians dealt with are struggling with living issues, most of which at heart concern ordinary, garden-variety Christians as well as professional scholars. The thoughtful reader will therefore inevitably find himself taking sides, raising questions, and responding to views encountered with ideas of his own. To encourage and facilitate this process, each chapter adds to its exposition a critique which explores typical problems raised and examines strengths and weaknesses as I see them. In this way, it is hoped, the reader will be drawn into active participation in an absorbing conversation, and gain not only clearer understanding of the thought of others but also deeper awareness of the directions in which he himself desires to move, and why. A genuinely theological discussion should be not a laboratory for the anatomical dissection and classification of fixed ideas, but a launching pad for journeys of new and exciting discovery.

The critical comments will be guided mainly by three criteria. First, is the theologian under consideration consistent within his own perspective? Is a given affirmation self-consistent and likewise harmonious with other assertions of the same thinker? Are his methods and conclusions in keeping with his avowed or implicit presuppositions? Are his real assumptions the same as the ones he acknowledges? Secondly, are his ideas in accord with the central thrust of the biblical witness to the salvation offered to men by God in Jesus Christ? Most of these theologians accept in some form the normative authority of the Scriptures. It is therefore appropriate to examine the relation of their positions to biblical teaching. This does not mean inquiring in proof text fashion whether a given concept is "in the Bible," but asking rather how far it is consistent with the fundamental emphases derivable from careful study of the Bible as a whole. Thirdly, is the interpretation advanced capable of being intelligibly related to relevant knowledge gained from secular sources? This does not mean making science or philosophy the norm of Christian belief. It does assume that the gospel must somehow make connection with the total life and thought of the men to whom it is addressed, who must be appealed to and re-created as whole persons.

In offering my criticisms I wish above all else to be fair. I make no claim to either pontifical authority or completely unbiased detachment, and know only too well how impossible it is to rise above all subjective interests. My own presuppositions will doubtless make their influence felt. Nevertheless, I will strive honestly to be as objective as possible. If what is intended as forthrightness sometimes sounds like dogmatism, I ask the reader to remember that the qualification "It seems to me that . . ." is always implied when a judgment is passed.

Many of the published works of the theologians here investigated are now available in English. Where this is the case, quotations and other references ordinarily cite the English editions, so that the passages referred to can readily be consulted by the English-speaking reader. I have myself translated passages quoted from German and French works not accessible in English.

Work on this volume was begun during leave granted by Boston University School of Theology in 1959-60, and with the support of a Faculty Fellowship of the American Association of Theological Schools. Profound gratitude is extended to both institutions. Thanks are due also to the library staff of the University of Heidelberg, research headquarters during the sabbatical year, for making books and study space so readily available. I can never adequately express my indebtedness to the many Continental theologians whose hospitality and guidance, graciously extended to a stranger from abroad, have given to the interpretations here offered a foundation in cherished personal acquaintance.

Professor Nils Ehrenstrom of Boston University has read the entire manuscript and offered discriminating critical comments. Others who have given valuable aid through reading critically portions of the manuscript, participating in the research, or proofreading, include Professors Paul K. Deats, Joseph C. Weber, and Catherine Gunsalus, Dr. William D. Ellington, and T. Edward Damer. All these contributions are acknowledged with deep appreciation.

Most of all I am indebted to my wife, who has painstakingly typed the manuscript and rendered indispensable assistance in proofreading and indexing, and whose counsel and support have been unfailingly helpful.

S. PAUL SCHILLING

Newton, Massachusetts
May 31, 1965

CONTENTS

PART ONE: PROTESTANT THEOLOGY

PART ONE: PROTESTANT THEOLOGY

Section I: Theologies of the Word of God

1. KARL BARTH

Karl Barth began his theological pilgrimage as a liberal. However, the shattering events in Europe during and after World War I and his own agonizing search for a positive gospel to preach combined to produce a radical change. He was deeply troubled by the support given the war policy of Wilhelm II by the German church, including most of his own theological teachers. Behind such accommodations to political conservatism, nationalism, and militarism, he saw operating an extreme form of Luther's separation of the temporal and spiritual realms, which assumed it to be the duty of the Christian to give unquestioning obedience to temporal authority. Even more, he saw a theology which focused attention not on the gospel but on statements concerning Christian self-awareness, depriving men of a reliable norm and inviting uncritical adjustment to passing human opinions and changing social forces. With no clear object or content beyond itself, such faith afforded little protection against external pressures. Out of such reflections came Barth's famous *Epistle to the Romans* and the beginning of a theological revolution.

Developments in Barth's Theology

Three main periods may be identified in Barth's postliberal theological development: (1) the decade beginning in 1919 with the publication of his work on Romans; (2) a period of transition from the late twenties to the appearance in 1931 of his *Anselm: Fides Quaerens Intellectum;* and (3) the decades marked by the writing of the successive volumes of his monumental *Church Dogmatics.*

1. In the first period Barth's thought, primarily critical and corrective in intent, was dominated by his reaction against the then-ruling theological tendency which, rooted in Schleiermacher, focused major attention on man's religious experiences. Barth sought to shift the focus from the "religious man" to the divine Word witnessed to in the Bible. Theology must begin with the miracle of God's gracious self-disclosure, and center in the subject rather than the object of revelation. God's Word to man is not founded on or implicit in Christian faith; it is rather the source of faith. As Kierkegaard declared, there is an infinite qualitative difference between time and eternity. Finite sinful man standing under the divine judgment can by his own reason make only contradictory statements about the wholly other God. Each assertion may prompt a negation. True and saving knowledge of God occurs therefore only when God in his freedom and lordship acts in Jesus Christ to disclose himself to man.

2. This dialectical or crisis theology proved to be but a necessary prologue to Barth's own positive dogmatics. In critical confrontation with liberalism, philosophy, and Roman Catholic thought he gradually clarified his presuppositions and worked out what were to him the central implications of the ancient and Reformed traditions. This process culminated in 1931 in his book on Anselm, in which he cast aside the last vestige of philosophical and anthropological support and asserted the "noetic rationality of faith." [1]

In this work Barth shows that Anselm's so-called ontological argument, that "God cannot be thought of as not existing," is not really a rational proof in which understanding demonstrates the validity of faith, but at heart a process in which faith, confronted by God's reality, seeks understanding. The "proof" begins with the knowledge of God whose existence it wants to know. "God gave himself as the object of [Anselm's] knowledge and God illumined him that he might know him as object." Out of

[1] "How My Mind Has Changed," *The Christian Century*, LVI (1939), 1132.

this double action springs human faith, which then in a spirit of prayer inquires into the meaning for man's life of the God who is self-revealed, believed, worshiped, and obeyed. *"Credere* is the presupposition of *intelligere."* [2] But prior to man's belief is God's self-communication.

Here appears an early form of the "analogy of faith" which Barth has strongly stressed in recent decades, in opposition to Thomas Aquinas' "analogy of being." Here emerges also the christological orientation which has become determinative. God has actually revealed himself in his Word. Therefore, when men truly receive this Word, they know God. The being who in Jesus Christ is God for us is the eternal triune being of God himself. Hence it is not enough to stress the hiddenness of God or the inability of man to predicate any qualities of him. Rather we must affirm a genuine correspondence between him and his creatures. By analogy, therefore, we can move from our revealed knowledge of God, given in faith, to understanding of man and other created things.[3]

3. From this perspective Barth was ready to undertake the construction of his own systematic theology, which is still unfinished. Concerning his purpose in this colossal work[4] Barth himself writes:

I had to learn in those years [1928-38] that Christian doctrine must be exclusively and consistently in all its affirmations directly or indirectly doctrine of Jesus Christ as the living Word of God spoken to us, if it is to be worthy of its name and edify the Christian church in the world. . . . My new task was to think through again and express everything I had said before in a different way, as a theology of the grace of God in Jesus Christ.[5]

This movement toward the complete dominance of Christology in Barth's thought was strengthened by his participation in the German church struggle. The rise of Hitler to power was accompanied by the spread of the German Christian movement, which sought to retain the

---

[2] *Anselm: Fides Quaerens Intellectum: Anselm's Proof of the Existence of God in the Context of His Theological Scheme,* tr. Ian W. Robertson (Richmond: John Knox Press, 1960), pp. 166, 171, 24. Barth points out that the opening sentences of *Proslogion 2* and the closing portion of *Proslogion 3* have the form of address to God, and concludes that the whole inquiry is intended to be understood as carried out in prayer, with the reality of God assumed. *Ibid.,* p. 150.

[3] This *analogia fidei* is the opposite of the ordinary understanding of analogy. In Barth's view we cannot move from self-understanding to the knowledge of God, since apart from revelation we do not really know ourselves.

[4] *Church Dogmatics* I/1–IV/3, eds. G. W. Bromiley and T. F. Torrance (Edinburgh: T. and T. Clark, 1936-62). Hereafter this work will be designated by the abbreviation CD. The German *Kirchliche Dogmatik* (Zollikon-Zürich: Evangelischer Verlag, 1932-59) now comprises 12 part-volumes totaling 8,719 large pages.

[5] "Parergon," *Evangelische Theologie,* VIII (1948), 272.

outer trappings of Christianity while perverting its reality into a religious version of Nazi ideology. Marked by intense nationalism, racialism, and anti-Semitism, it demanded that the churches recognize National Socialism as divine revelation and modify their belief and practice accordingly. This dangerous threat to evangelical Christianity aroused the courageous opposition of many Christians, especially pastors and teachers, who became the "Confessing Church." A historic rallying point for the leaders of this group was the Barmen Synod of May, 1934. Based in its essential points on the work of Barth, the famous Declaration which resulted affirmed Jesus Christ to be the one Word of God, and vehemently rejected "the false teaching that the church can and must recognize yet other happenings and powers, images and truths, as divine revelation," and "that there are areas of our own life in which we belong not to Jesus Christ but another Lord." [6]

The *Church Dogmatics* aims to be christocentric reinterpretation of the whole of Christian doctrine. Inevitably an undertaking so large and fundamental, covering almost three decades, reflects significant changes in Barth's thought, even within the successive volumes themselves. He himself regards such alterations as consistent developments rather than discrepancies. For instance, he writes in introducing his second part-volume on the doctrine of reconciliation:

There is no break with the basic view which I have adopted since my parting from Liberalism, but only a more consistent turn in its development. To make this clear, I had to give particularly careful expression to the christological section which stands at the head and contains the whole *in nuce,* speaking as it does of the humanity of Jesus Christ.[7]

The more important changes will be indicated in the account which follows.

Major Doctrinal Emphases

No brief exposition can do justice to the whole of Barth's theological system. The most that can be hoped for is an accurate interpretation of his dominant motif and its expression in selected areas of his thought. We begin, therefore, with the christological center.

---

[6] *Die Religion in Geschichte und Gegenwart* (3rd ed.), I, 873-79.
[7] CD IV/2, x.

The Centrality of Christology

For Barth the crucial text in the New Testament is John 1:14, but he confesses that he did not do justice to it in his work on Romans.[8] In Jesus Christ we have to do with "the eternal beginning of all the ways and works of God." [9] He is the "ground, content, and object" of Christian faith.[10] "The Christian religion is the predicate to the subject of the name of Jesus Christ." [11] Apart from him, therefore, no statement is theologically correct or justified.[12] All Christian doctrines must be interpreted in the light of the incarnation.[13]

In Barth's view the Chalcedonian two-nature doctrine formulates truly the meaning of the New Testament assertions concerning Jesus Christ. God the Son exists eternally in the unity-in-distinction of his divine and human essences. In Jesus Christ this eternal Word is actualized in a human-divine life in earthly history, thus becoming the Word of reconciliation addressed by God to man. In this act of free and sovereign love— the whole of the life, death, and resurrection of Jesus Christ—God makes his own the lost cause of man, who in sin has denied his Creator and spoiled his creaturehood. Thus the broken relation is restored. Man's salvation becomes possible because God in the reconciled God-man has become what man is. Jesus Christ is at once the Lord as Servant, God who has abased himself to man's low status; and the Servant as Lord, man who is exalted to the status of God.[14] In him two great movements are carried out, "the one from above downwards and the other from below upwards, but both grounded in His person in the union of its true deity and true humanity." [15]

In the cross and resurrection of Jesus Christ, both events in history, God identifies himself with man's sin, permits himself to be judged in man's place, transforms man's condition from within, and conquers sin and death. Thereby he opens the way to man's justification and sanctification, which are effected through faith within the faithful community created and

[8] CD I/2, 50, 123. This part-volume contains twelve references to John 1:14, many more than to any other New Testament passage except Matt. 28:20, cited eight times.

[9] CD IV/2, 31.

[10] *The Humanity of God,* tr. John Newton Thomas and Thomas Wieser (Richmond: John Knox Press, 1960), p. 30.

[11] CD I/2, 347.

[12] CD III/1, 3.

[13] CD II/1, 319 f.

[14] CD I/2, 122; IV/1, 5 f.; IV/2, 3, 50, 62, 84-87; IV/3, 3-5, 532 f.

[15] CD IV/3, 4; IV/2, 62.

empowered by the Holy Spirit—"the power in which Jesus Christ attests Himself." Thus is fulfilled the covenant based on God's eternal election of man, whereby God graciously determines himself to be man's God and man to be God's man.[16]

The Knowledge of God

1. Revelation and Reason. Jesus Christ is the sole disclosure of God to man, "the one and only light of life." [17] Barth therefore rules out "the sorry hypothesis of a so-called 'natural theology,' " which he defines as "a knowledge of God given in and with the natural force of reason and to be attained in its exercise." Man as such has no capacity to know God. Natural theology can yield only abstract conclusions concerning God's existence as Supreme Ruler and man's general responsibility to him. It cannot discover the real God who acts in Jesus Christ by the Holy Spirit for man's salvation, and who is related to man through a personal covenant of grace.[18] There may be "other realities and forces," such as philosophies of nature, history, society, and ethics, which are worthy of the consideration and respect of the Christian community. However, these represent not revealed knowledge of God but human conceptions subject to correction and revocation. Therefore the church cannot derive from them any part of its proclamation or include them in its one witness.[19]

Barth does recognize the existence in the secular sphere of "true words" which agree with the one Word proclaimed by the Bible and the church and can be materially tested by it, though they are of a very different order. Jesus Christ is sovereign of the periphery as well as the center of the circle constituted by his Word; hence we may expect some attestations of his lordship which are not alien to his revelation, but to a degree illumine it and make it more concretely evident. However, such words are true only as they point to their origin in Jesus Christ, and to the extent that he "declares Himself in them"; and they are seen to be true only in the light shed through faith in him.[20]

Natural theology is closely associated in Barth's thought with the Roman Catholic doctrine of the *analogia entis*. According to this, despite their differences man and God can both be comprehended under the idea of

[16] CD IV/1, 648; IV/3, 3 f., 298, 312; *Evangelical Theology*, tr. Grover Foley (New York: Holt, Rinehart and Winston, 1963), p. 29.
[17] CD IV/3, 86, 99-104, 135.
[18] CD IV/3, 117 f., IV/1, 45; cf. II/1, 47, 168, 173, 177 f.
[19] CD IV/3, 837 f., 849.
[20] CD IV/3, 115, 122-25, 130, 163-65.

being. Since we know from our own nature to some extent what being is, we can conceive of God as the most real being, and thus gain a general knowledge of him apart from revelation. Assuming "a union of man with God existing outside God's revelation in Jesus Christ," we argue from what we know of man to conclusions concerning God.[21] Barth raises two chief objections to this procedure. (1) Seeing both man and God from below, instead of from above in the light of Jesus Christ, it simply articulates what man himself is and creates God in man's image. But our finite human understandings of lordship, creation, reconciliation, and redemption cannot make accessible to us the being of one who is Lord, Creator, Reconciler, and Redeemer in an infinite sense.[22] (2) It implies a cleavage in God between his being which is abstractly held to be "naturally" knowable and his action on us which is known only by revelation. It falsely postulates a previous creative work of God the Father separate from the reconciling activity of God the Son.[23]

For the analogy of being Barth substitutes an analogy of relation or faith. We can speak truly of God only from a faith-relationship to him based on his self-revelation in Jesus Christ. From this perspective there is in spite of all diversity a correspondence between the relation of God to man and the prior relation of God to himself. Within his own nature God is the interrelatedness of Father, Son, and Holy Spirit, and he is related to man as Lord, Creator, Reconciler, and Redeemer. The eternal love with which Father and Son love each other is also the love which is addressed by God to man—as perfectly portrayed in John 17.[24] The I-thou relationship within God is thus determinative for the relations between God and man (Father-son) and between human beings (parent-child, man-woman, etc.). Man is the image of God, and human as well as divine existence is existence in the vis-à-vis of I and thou, existence in encounter.[25] In "analogy and correspondence" to the Son of God, we see that we may become sons of God and brothers to each other.[26]

Man's proper relation to the knowledge of God given him from above is one of *acknowledgment*.[27] His role is to stand before God, listen attentively to the divine Word, and receive and repeat what he hears. The revelation

---

[21] CD II/1, 79-85, 168, 243.
[22] CD II/1, 165, 168, 75-79.
[23] CD II/1, 83 f.; III/2, 157.
[24] CD III/2, 220 f., 323.
[25] CD III/2, 203; III/3, 49 f., 421 f.; III/1, 185.
[26] CD IV/3, 532 f.
[27] CD I/1, 213.

is self-authenticating, so man need not and may not examine its truth. He has no place from which to ask whether Jesus Christ really is the true Word. Indeed, to claim the competence to put such a question is *ipso facto* to deny the revelation.[28] The Christian understands the truth of God to the degree that he places himself within the divine presence and heeds the divine summons. He grows in understanding by repeated encounters, within the Christian community, with God himself.

This does not mean that our knowledge of God makes no use of reason. It is real knowledge, and as such has a rational character. Since the gospel is really understood only by those who open themselves to it, it is "not generally knowable." However, "it is generally intelligible and explicable. For its content is rational and not irrational." [29] Man's response to the revelation involves "an awakening and enlightening of the reason." The answer of each individual must be a logical answer appropriate to "the logical attitude of God." It requires him to think as he has never thought before. Furthermore, like the apostles the Christian today must explicate his faith in the process of witnessing to it. This requires the fullest possible use of his reason.[30]

2. Encounter with Reality. Barth's christocentric understanding of man's knowledge of God has resulted in several important modifications of his earlier thought.

a. The dialectical character of his theology has been considerably moderated. In the light of the incarnation, man can make statements about God and man in relation which rise above contradiction and express positive and rational truth. This change is illustrated by the very existence of the *Church Dogmatics*, a systematic exposition of the church's convictions concerning the Word uttered in Jesus Christ.

b. Barth no longer holds to "the eternal qualitative distinction between time and eternity." In the *Epistle to the Romans* he stressed "the chasm which separates God and man," and wrote approvingly of the alternative, "either ascent of man toward God or God's condescendence to man." [31] He now attacks this antithesis as false.[32] The incarnation makes the idea that God is wholly other "untenable, and corrupt and pagan." Here he

---

[28] CD IV/3, 72 f., 161.
[29] CD IV/3, 849.
[30] CD IV/2, 312-14; cf. IV/3, 785; II/1, 211.
[31] *Epistle to the Romans*, 6th ed., tr. Edwyn C. Hoskyns (London: Oxford University Press, 1933), p. 142.
[32] CD IV/2, 827, 740 f., 747.

becomes temporal without ceasing to be eternal.[33] His call to man in Jesus Christ is "a genuine, concrete, historical event in time." [34]

Writing of "the humanity of God," Barth insists that his earlier stress on God's divinity, though necessary to correct the one-sidedness of liberal theology, was only half right, yielding a God almost as remote and abstract as the God of the philosophers.[35] The world is different from God, but he *affirms* it; in all his absoluteness he is free love, entering into fellowship, with his own, and making himself "solidaristic" with the world. He is emphatically immanent as well as transcendent.[36]

c. Barth has abandoned the attempt to interpret theology in existentialist terms. He admits "a good deal of unwitting responsibility for introducing existentialist philosophy into theology." He concedes that existentialism has been a useful negative instrument in criticism, polemics, demythologizing, and the like. He agrees that the reconciliation accomplished in Jesus Christ must be real *for me* and *for us*. "We are those who are eternally loved and elected by God in Jesus Christ." [37]

Beyond this, however, Barth cannot see that existentialism in theology has produced or can produce "positive results worth mentioning." [38] In fact, it is a development of the anthropocentric tendency exemplified by Schleiermacher and the pietism and rationalism of the eighteenth century. In this perspective the call of God becomes little more than "the monologue of the Christian concerning his faith." [39] But Christian existence is much more than a reality *pro me*.[40] "The Holy Spirit is the Lord and Master of the Christian spirit and not simply identical with it." The gospel has to do with the objective act of the real God to redeem mankind. However, it is false to separate the objective and subjective aspects of the Christian message. Its content "is neither an isolated man nor an isolated God, but God and man in their divinely established and effective encounter." [41]

The Scriptures: Authority and Interpretation

The authoritative witness to the revelation in Jesus Christ, hence the abiding assurance that sinful man can be confronted ever anew by the

[33] CD IV/1, 186-88.
[34] CD IV/3, 499.
[35] *The Humanity of God*, p. 45.
[36] CD IV/1, 187.
[37] CD IV/3, 106-7.
[38] CD III/4, xii-xiii.
[39] CD IV/3, 498; cf. I/1, 159.
[40] CD IV/3, 567 f.
[41] CD IV/3, 498.

gracious God, is found in the Scriptures. The Word "waits for us in the words of prophets and apostles," who spoke from their direct confrontation with God. Their testimonies were collected, handed down, and canonized by the Christian communities of the first four centuries as the faithful record of what they saw, heard, and proclaimed. Therefore the Bible has a unique authority which far exceeds that of any later tradition controlled by an ecclesiastical office. It is "the source and the guiding-principle of all Christian doctrine and exposition." [42] The Word written is the surest pointer to the Word revealed and the firmest foundation for the Word preached. [43]

To discover what the Bible means we need not look beyond the Bible itself; in fact, we shall be misled if we do. The guiding principle of hermeneutics is that Scripture is the interpreter of Scripture. A given text is to be understood "only with reference to and in the light of its theme." [44] "These writings, as God's Word in human words, expound themselves, are in themselves—i.e., in the coherence of the so differentiated and complex reality given them by their common subject—everywhere perfectly clear and transparent." [45]

However, this self-expounding clarity is realized only as the reader becomes actively involved in the service of the exposition. This means seeking to understand the meaning of a text in terms of the conceptual world of its author, then to reproduce its intention within the perspective of the exegete's own time. More particularly, it means reflecting on and assimilating the passage in grateful remembrance of previous hearings of God's Word and joyful anticipation of new hearings. Normally this entails three stages: *explicatio* (explanation), *meditatio* (reflection), and *applicatio* (appropriation). [46]

Barth is convinced that only deformation of the gospel can result if interpretation is guided, as in Bultmann's hermeneutics, by alien presuppositions such as the "Christian understanding of human existence" or the interpreter's prior understanding of the subject. [47] Who can have a prior

---

[42] *Against the Stream*, tr. Mrs. E. M. Delacour and Stanley Godman (London: SCM Press, 1954), p. 220; *Evangelical Theology*, pp. 30-32, 34-36; *God Here and Now*, tr. Paul M. van Buren (New York: Harper & Row, 1964), p. 55; CD I/1, 98.

[43] For Barth's illuminating discussion of these three interrelated forms of the Word, see CD I/1, 98-140.

[44] CD I/2, 493.

[45] *God Here and Now*, p. 52.

[46] *Ibid.*, pp. 52-54; CD I/2, 722-40.

[47] CD III/2, 445 f.; IV/3, 820-22. Cf. Rudolf Bultmann, *Essays Philosophical and Theological*, tr. James C. G. Greig (New York: The Macmillan Company, 1955), pp. 256-61.

understanding of the true God disclosed in Jesus Christ? Barth also refuses to admit the competence of historical-critical study to go "behind"
the given New Testament writings to explore questions of historical authen-
ticity. "We can only know and confess" the self-revelation of Jesus Christ
as attested and expounded by the apostles, its direct witnesses. Barth's
exegesis therefore concentrates on the words of the text itself, seen as a
part of the canon and hence as normative for Christian doctrine.[48]

Gospel and Law

Approaching the content of the Bible christologically, Barth reverses the
traditional opposition and order of law-gospel in favor of the synthesis of
gospel and law. As creation is to be understood only in the light of redemption, so the law must be seen in the light of the gospel, the old man in the
light of the new man who has encountered Jesus Christ.[49] The sole task
of the church is to bear witness to the will of God in opposition to sin.

The law itself is basically the gospel in concrete form, the opportunity of
sanctification given to man through his election as God's covenant-partner.
It is a promise of the kind of conduct to which the gospel frees and leads us.
The gospel is prior in that the command of God which requires our
obedience presupposes and springs out of the relationship in which we
already belong to him. Instead of commanding, "You shall, so that you may
receive my grace," God declares, "You may and will, because you have my
grace." Even in judgment he judges us as his own, in order to free us for
eternal life under his lordship.[50] In this context, Barth holds that when
the New Testament portrays the law as brought to an end by Christ it
means not God's real law but the law as legalistically misunderstood by
man.

Man and Sin

Taking as his "one Archimedean point" of reference the union of humanity and divinity in Jesus Christ,[51] Barth has arrived at a much more
affirmative view of man than the one he held in his Epistle to the Romans.
There he described sin as "the pre-supposition which underlies every human
event and conditions every human status," "the characteristic mark of
human nature as such." Now he declares, "Jesus Christ is the essential

---

[48] CD IV/2, 38 f., 122 f., 149 f. A good example of Barth's exegetical method is Christ and
Adam, tr. T. A. Smail (New York: Harper & Brothers, 1956), an exposition of Romans 5:12-21.
[49] CD III/2, 204-6.
[50] CD III/2, 509-12, 632, 689 f., 733.
[51] CD III/2, 132-36; IV/1, 389.

truth about the essential nature of man, and even sinful man is still essentially related to him." [52] Barth has shifted the emphasis from judgment (*krisis*) on man's old being to the reality of the new being in Christ. He has compressed his doctrine of man into an almost Hegelian triad which provides a useful outline for our exposition: the one human subject is "a creature, a sinner, and a sinner saved by grace." [53]

1. Man is created by God to be God's covenant-partner. To be a man means primarily to be chosen, summoned, awakened, and claimed by the Word of God. Since the Son of God is true man, man as such, the determination of all men is to be his brothers and therefore God's children. [54] In creating man God chose the good and gave it being; to be truly human, therefore, is to affirm gladly what God has chosen as good. When man sins he actualizes that which has no being, because it is the possibility which God did not choose to create. In this sense sin is an "ontological impossibility," while the doing of God's will is man's only way of realizing his ontological possibility. In the capacity granted him by God he "cannot" sin. His true nature is to be with God and his fellow man; godlessness is thus a mode of being contrary to his humanity. [55]

2. Nevertheless, man does sin, absurdly affirming what God has negated, and calling good what God has not chosen. Though there is no basis for such a choice in his creaturely nature, he tries to find his essence by denying both God and himself in "irrational and inexplicable apostasy." He thus perverts the good work of God, choosing "his own impossibility." The corruption is "radical and total." Whether in pride, sloth, or falsehood, [56] he sins at the very center of his being and therefore in his whole being. The one whole man whom God created to be his covenant-partner has become his enemy. As a result, man lives in contradiction between his original determination for God and his own rebellious determination against God. By opposing the divine will he actualizes "nothingness," loses his true identity, and introduces chaos into creation. [57]

3. Even in sin, however, man is not outside the realm of God's grace. He is relatively but not absolutely godless. He cannot negate God's cove-

---

[52] *Romans*, pp. 167, 173; *Christ and Adam*, p. 86.

[53] CD III/2, 275.

[54] CD III/2, 146, 150, 203, 265, 685; III/4, 337; IV/3, 369.

[55] CD III/2, 136, 142, 146; IV/2, 494 f.; cf. III/2, 273-75.

[56] Barth discusses these three chief forms of sin in contrast to Jesus Christ as servant, Lord, and witness—his priestly, royal, and prophetic works. CD IV/1, 358-513; IV/2, 378-498; IV/3, 368-480.

[57] CD III/2, 136, 274 f., 266; III/3, 353; IV/1, 492-95; IV/2, 495; IV/3, 448-63.

nant relationship with him or cease to be a man whose nature is freedom for God. He is a lost sheep, but he is not lost to the seeking Shepherd. He is totally sick, but not dead, and the Healer does not reject him. Though he is in bondage to sin, his real nature is maintained by God, whom he cannot make a "manless" God. He hears the No of God's judgment, but it is still God's eternal Yes. His sins are conquered by God's reconciling grace in Jesus Christ, and he is led through pardon and conversion to a new existence. Even "the final deliverance of all men" is a real possibility.[58]

Barth's christocentric view of man supports an increasingly positive attitude toward human culture. He now finds real continuity between Greek-heathen and Christian humanism, and sees in all culture opportunities for fulfillment of the gifts of God. The artists have an important contribution to make in interpreting the ethical situation with which the theologian deals. In particular Barth evidences deep appreciation for the poetry and dramas of Goethe and the music of Mozart. Because of God's reconciliation of the world to himself through Jesus Christ, "the world and every man has . . . received a new and positive determination." [59]

The Church

The reconciling action which calls man into the new life of sonship to God at the same time calls him into the church, "the living community of the Lord Jesus Christ." As the body of Christ, the church exists to carry forward in earthly history the ministry of his prophetic Word. Enlightened and empowered by his Holy Spirit, it is sent to testify to Jesus Christ before all men, to call them to him, to proclaim that the covenant between God and man fulfilled in him is the ultimate meaning of their history, and to make known that his future manifestation is already their ground of hope.[60]

As the fellowship of those who have been gathered by Jesus Christ and are participants in the salvation wrought by him, the church enjoys a rich internal life. However, it is not an end in itself. Barth criticizes the classical definitions of the church for their lack of a basic sense of responsibility for the world ouside. The true community of Christ, like its Lord, is sent into the world, and exists for the world. In this society "it is given to men to see and understand the world as it is, to accept solidarity with it, and to be pledged and committed to it." In grateful response to the fact

---

[58] CD III/2, 274 f.; IV/1, 46-49, 69, 481-84; IV/2, 486, 499; IV/3, 270-74, 477 f., 674-76.
[59] CD IV/3, 299 f.
[60] CD IV/3, 681, 729, 759; God Here and Now, pp. 62, 67.

that Jesus Christ has confessed the church and continually does so, it confesses him before the world.[61]

The church's ministry consists of the declaration, explication, and application of the good news of God committed to it. It may take the form
of either speech or action. As speech, this ministry includes worship, preaching, instruction, evangelization, mission, and theology. As action, it comprises prayer, the cure of souls, the personal lives of charismatic individuals,
the diaconate or service to those in special need, prophetic action, and fellowship. All these ministries involve responsibility on the part of the whole
community, lay as well as clerical. The members of the body have different
gifts and commissions, but no Christian is ever "off duty." [62]

Ethical and Social Responsibility

Contrary to a belief still widespread in America, Barth has always manifested an active ethical and social interest. As a Swiss pastor he was a Socialist before he was a dialectical theologian. Included in a collection of lectures
published in 1924 are two on "The Christian's Place in Society" (1919)
and "The Problem of Ethics Today" (1922).[63] We have already noted his
vigorous part in the German church struggle against Hitler. A number
of the essays in *Against the Storm*,[64] representing the period 1946-52, deal
with social issues. Since World War II he has sought to advance understanding between East and West. This whole trend reaches its clearest theological
expression in the later volumes of the *Church Dogmatics,* as Barth explicates the meaning of the incarnation for Christian ethical responsibility.

As God in Christ calls man to himself as his covenant-partner, he directs
him also to his fellow man. He who is himself trinitarian, God in relationship, wills that man should find fulfillment in relationship with both God
and his fellows. At the very center of his being he is related to the being
of the thou, "under his claim and . . . constituting a claim upon him."
Thus human being *is* being in encounter with the thou. "Humanity, the
characteristic and essential mode of man's being, is in its root fellow-
humanity. Humanity which is not fellow-humanity is inhumanity." [65]

In the perspective of God's redemptive act in Jesus Christ, every man's
existence "belongs to God," and is "His loan and blessing"; it should there-

---

[61] CD IV/3, 764-68, 773 f., 780, 786-90, 800.
[62] CD IV/3, 843-901; III/4, 489 f.
[63] *The Word of God and the Word of Man,* tr. Douglas Horton (London: Hodder and Stough-
ton, 1935).
[64] (London: SCM Press, 1954).
[65] CD III/4, 116 f.; III/2, 247.

fore be treated with respect. Human life as such is "the matter about which God is concerned and therefore man must also be concerned in His service." If Christians "renounce their solidarity with non-Christians," they endanger their own being as Christians. All who exist in conditions of bondage "are still our fellows, indeed, our brothers as men who like ourselves are reconciled to God." Jesus Christ is *every* man's brother and God is *every* man's Father; this becomes for Barth the basis of all Christian concern for human worth and rights.[66]

The same considerations summon the church to responsible social action. God calls men into a community which is commissioned to embody in speech and action his love for men. With its proclamation of the gospel it must "summon the world to reflect on social injustice and its consequences" and to act to correct them. The ministry and the Christian community "become dumb dogs, and their service a serving of the ruling powers, if they are afraid to tackle at their social roots the evils by which they are confronted in detail." The gospel is relevant to "the particularly critical times and situations" of today, and the church dare not be neutral. Barth champions an "evangelical radicalism" as against the "unevangelical conservatism" which transforms the good news into a "pseudo-Gospel." [67]

What, then, constitutes "the good" for the Christian, and where does he find ethical guidance? In Barth's view the gospel offers no rules, but provides something more basic. The Christian ethical life is the fruit of man's saving encounter with God's mercy manifested in Jesus Christ. It is man's grateful acknowledgment that he both needs and shares in this mercy, his daily new response to the gracious lordship of Christ. Good human action is that which corresponds to the act of God in humbling and giving himself for the sake of men, action "in which man is thankful for God's grace." Christian ethics, therefore, "is the imperative of the indicative of Christian dogmatics." [68] It is epitomized in II Cor. 5:19-20.

Eschatology

Though the salvation effected in Jesus Christ intimately concerns human existence here and now, it is profoundly eschatological. The gospel promises the eternal fulfillment of God's redemptive purpose for men through the real *parousia* or coming again of Jesus Christ. The *eschaton* is the last time, the time of human history which is moving toward the end appointed in

---

[66] CD III/4, 340; IV/3, 340, 346 f.; *The Humanity of God*, p. 53.
[67] CD IV/3, 780, 816, 818 f., 892 f.
[68] *God Here and Now*, pp. 88 f., 93.

the death of Jesus Christ. Barth insists that the New Testament knows only *one* return of Jesus after his earthly life, though it occurs in various times and forms. Christ is manifested to his people in the Easter event, the resurrection; in the impartation of the Holy Spirit, at Pentecost and repeatedly throughout history; and in his final return in glory and universal judgment. The first two occurrences point irreversibly toward the third which completes them, but they all comprise a single event which brings the entire temporal process to its divine goal. Eschatological time, then, is the whole movement from the beginning of the final revelation to its completion.[69]

History continues after the Easter appearance of the living Lord so that his saving Word may be proclaimed and received by men. To this end he called into existence his church, which is commissioned to attest his lordship to the world and call men to repent and enter his service. Thus the church itself is "the eschatological fact *par excellence*"; it exists in anticipation of the final fulfillment of God's redemptive action. In this way Christians participate even now in the coming of Christ who is their hope. But the community lives in expectation of the judgment as well as the glory to come. Its present life and action are weighed in the balances of Christ's future, according to the measure in which it discerns his presence in those who need help here and now—the hungry, thirsty, naked, and imprisoned of Matt. 25:31-46—and acts accordingly.[70]

Critique

To evaluate fairly in a few pages a theology as complex and wide-ranging as Barth's is at least as difficult as to give in brief compass an accurate and balanced exposition of his thought. However, both the views he holds and the decisive manner in which he advances them inevitably stimulate critical reflection on the issues raised. Such reflection may be furthered by brief mention here of typical elements of strength and difficulty.

Values

1. Barth's christological reinterpretation of the whole of Christian doctrine has made distinctive, illuminating, and fruitful contributions at many points, notably with reference to the knowledge of God, the relation

---

[69] CD I/1, 530 f.; III/2, 468, 486 f., 490, 497; IV/1, 120 f.; IV/3, 293-96, 313, 317-20, 333 f., 915.

[70] CD III/2, 505-8, 623; IV/1, 662; IV/3, 321-63, 464 f., 684, 903-28; *God Here and Now*, p. 46.

of gospel to law, the nature of man, the church, and ethical and social responsibility. For the sake of consistency with his incarnational perspective
he has modified his early dialectical emphasis, repudiated the "infinite
qualitative difference" between God and man, abandoned his previous
existentialistic orientation, and adopted a realistically affirmative view of
man. Such changes illustrate Barth's refreshing advocacy of a "pilgrim
theology," one which is always open to new understandings of divine revelation.

2. In full accord with the New Testament, he makes unmistakably plain
the sovereignty of God in both judgment and grace, and the primacy of
the divine initiative in revelation and salvation. Ultimately we know God
only because he chooses to reveal himself. Apart from his own self-
communication no amount of human search would yield truth concerning
him. Similarly, the repentance and faith which signal the sinner's turn to
God are a response to the reconciling action by which God seeks to restore
him to the covenant-partnership for which he was created. The new relation to God is a gift which we gratefully receive, not a reward which
our effort deserves.

3. Barth's insight gained from his study of Anselm, and worked out
in the Church Dogmatics as the analogy of relation or faith, has shed
valuable light on the cognitive significance of faith. We do not argue our
way from human existence without God to belief in God's existence. Instead, in faith we find ourselves in the presence of the God to whom we
are already related. As we repeatedly open ourselves to his disclosures and
respond in trustful commitment, we receive deepened understanding and
assurance. The faith-relationship enables us to see ourselves as God's children and each other as brothers.

4. Barth's incarnationally grounded view of human nature recognizes
realistically both the appalling depth of sin and the positive possibilities of
man as a child of grace. Barth lays the emphasis where the gospel lays it,
finding the essential truth concerning man not in his sinfulness but in
relation to Jesus Christ. He sees clearly the radical corruption involved in
man's denial of both God and his own true identity, but just as plainly
the persistence of fundamental human nature even in sin, which cannot
make void God's covenant with man. By the grace of God, therefore, man
can be redeemed and become a new creation.

5. In his insistence that humanity as related to God in Jesus Christ is
fellow-humanity, Barth provides firm theological foundation for social
responsibility on the part of both individual Christians and the church. In

view of his writings of the past several decades it is difficult to justify John Macquarrie's reference to Barth's "apparent indifference to secular concerns," or Reinhold Niebuhr's accusation that he is guilty of "transcendental irresponsibility." [71] Actually, Barth calls vigorously for Christian action against social evil. It is true that he finds in the gospel no direct guidance for concrete ethical decisions, being content to affirm that the Christian, in gratitude for God's grace, should always follow the course which best corresponds to God's self-giving love. Such a norm is quite general, yet it does go to the heart of the Christian ethical life, and when taken seriously it provides the necessary perspective within which more specific criteria may be determined.

Difficulties

1. It is difficult to harmonize the dominance of Christology in Barth with the claims of a fully trinitarian view of God. He definitely espouses a modalistic trinitarianism, but it is questionable whether he preserves the uniqueness of the Father and the Holy Spirit or their full equality with the Son. Directly or indirectly, Barth maintains, all Christian doctrine must be exclusively doctrine of Jesus Christ. Thus it is the gracious election of man in Jesus Christ which makes creation possible and necessary; he is the "meaning and purpose" of creation and also of God's preservation and government of what he has created. Moreover, God's covenant with man begins as well as centers and culminates in Jesus Christ.[72] Likewise, the Holy Spirit is the attesting, quickening, and enlightening power of the living Jesus Christ, "the power of God proper to the being of Jesus Christ" in relation to his community. Conversely, Jesus Christ is "the Subject" who acts in and through the Spirit to cause his church to exist.[73] Barth is rightly concerned to avoid a separation between God as Creator and God as Redeemer, and likewise to oppose the conception of the Holy Spirit as an independent force intervening between the living Christ and men. However, his controlling christological perspective tends to obscure the differentiations within the divine unity, resulting in a contraction of trinitarian faith.

2. If Barth's analogy of relation is taken as a genuine analogy, it calls into question either the unity of God or the individuality of men. Referring

[71] John Macquarrie, *Twentieth Century Religious Thought* (New York: Harper & Row, 1963), p. 324.

[72] CD III/4, 39 f.; IV/3, 137; III/2, 43.

[73] CD IV/1, 648; IV/3, 758 f., 502 f., 293-96, 351.

to the interrelatedness of Father, Son, and Holy Spirit and the love between Father and Son, Barth speaks of an I-thou relation as characteristic of the divine nature. He then takes this as determinative for the relations between God and man and between human beings (e.g., father-son, man-woman, brother-brother). Like God, man exists in encounter, in the vis-à-vis of I and thou. However, if the I-thou relation in God is really the model for what we know of that relation on the human level, it seems to imply a tritheism which Barth obviously rejects, since for him the three "Persons" are not individuals but modes of being within one divine Person. But if on the contrary human persons are seen in analogy to the Trinity as modes of being within one humanity, what happens to the concrete singularity of human personality? Do not finite individuals become simply different forms of activity of one human whole? Barth can avoid this dilemma only by changing the meaning of his relational terms when he moves from God to man. But in this case the analogy no longer holds true.

3. There is a serious question whether the incarnational center of Barth's theology does not itself invalidate his rejection of natural theology. In his view God's action in Jesus Christ *makes known* his solidarity with men. If the knowledge thus conveyed is true, then the act is ontologically as well as epistemologically significant; God really *is* closely related to men. The incarnation does not bring this to pass, but brings to light an already existing situation. No man is really without God.

Barth himself is quite explicit about this: Godlessness is "an ontological impossibility for man." There is a continuity of the truly human in created man and the reborn man of faith, a correspondence between the human and the divine which sin could not destroy. Recognizing that God became man, we see all men as beings in whom God's Word exists, even though they may be unaware of it.[74] Is it not clear that for Barth God's grace as disclosed in Jesus Christ is operative in all men? If so, there is no such thing as the "natural man," in the sense of a man left wholly to his unaided intellectual and spiritual resources. But then the ground for Barth's devaluation of natural theology disappears.

At times he seems on the verge of acknowledging this. He recognizes that in the perspective of the cross "all men and all creation . . . are ordained to be the theaters of His glory and therefore to be the recipients and bearers of His Word." Consequently persons enlightened by God's self-revelation

[74] CD III 2, 136, 148-50; IV 3, 299 f., 340; *The Humanity of God*, pp. 53, 59 f.; *Christ and Adam*, p. 86.

in Christ may hear in the secular realm "true words" which root in, agree with, and attest the one true Word. Yet Barth explicitly distinguishes such utterances from the unilluminating insights which are attainable through "the natural force of human reason" by persons "outside the circle and ministry of God's Word." [75]

However, on Barth's own incarnational premises it may be asked whether any man is really outside that circle. The truth that all men are recipients and bearers of God's Word may be disclosed only to Christians, but it is nonetheless true, and it has cognitive as well as ontological implications for non-Christians. In fact, in the light of this truth it seems impossible to dismiss "natural reason" as a purely human enterprise. All of man's thinking occurs within the context of the creative, redemptive, sustaining, and potentially revelatory activity of God. If God is as actively present in the whole of human life, and in every man, as Barth's theology of the Word affirms him to be, the earnest inquiry of the humble, receptive seeker may be expected to yield some truth about him.

In this perspective the analogy of being so scorned by Barth regains cogency, since human personality *as upheld by God* may rightly be expected to yield some clues to the divine character and will. The partial insights thus gained should be seen not as substitutes for or competitors of the fullness of the revelation in Christ, but rather as standing in a preparatory, and to a degree confirmatory, relation to that revelation.

It can hardly be soundly denied that many persons have some knowledge of God without conscious knowledge of Jesus Christ. However, this does not mean that they have relied on their own purely human resources. Rather, the capacity for such knowledge is itself a gift of God's prevenient grace. It may also be seen as a remnant of the *imago dei,* distorted but not erased by sin. Man's total quest for God is a response to the prior activity of God in him. The truth granted him results not from his own unaided efforts, but from human life and thought which at every point are dependent on and supported by the self-disclosing action of God.

4. A related objection must be raised respecting Barth's unwillingness to grant a critical function to human thought in the revelatory process. Man's role is to stand before God, to listen to his Word, and to acknowledge, receive, and bear witness to it. For him to ask whether Jesus Christ is the true light is falsely to presume that he possesses a light of his own which qualifies him for such queries, and thus in effect to deny the revelation.

[75] CD IV/3, 116 f.

Instead of questioning he is questioned by the Word—as to whether he is receiving it in a way which corresponds to its self-witnessing declarations.

Actually, however, the raising of critical questions about revelatory events need not mean that we are replacing divine illumination with a pretended human insight. It may signify rather that we are taking seriously the implications of Barth's view, based on the incarnation, that God's Word is at work in us, and is using our God-given mental faculties in the service of his truth.

We must also recognize that the divine Word comes to us mixed with and in the form of human words. As soon as revelation is received by man, it is cast in the thought-patterns and language of the recipient and inevitably becomes subject to the distortion and error which characterize all finite knowledge. Divine disclosures are known to us only as they are apprehended and colored by our human understanding. One result of this circumstance is found in the widely divergent interpretations given by persons who believe they are declaring the self-authenticating Word of God attested by the Scriptures. Hence we have not only the right but the obligation to scrutinize all revelation claims—to "test the spirits to see whether they are of God" (I John 4:1). When we inquire into the truth of revelation we are not calling on God to defend himself before the bar of human reason, but asking for the credentials of human claims to speak for God. We are not doubting or questioning God, but examining the validity of human judgments about him.

5. Barth's hermeneutics allows dogmatic considerations to restrict unduly the scope of historical-critical investigation of the Scriptures. Viewing the canon as a unified, closed dogmatic whole grounded in God's action in Jesus Christ, Barth regards it as outside the province of factual historical research. Jesus Christ in his self-revelation is the basic text attested and expounded by the apostles in the New Testament. The *truly historical element* is thus to be found in the unity and continuity of the biblical texts themselves. They should be impartially and painstakingly investigated, but not subjected to criticism based on a nonbiblical conception of history. The sole aim of biblical scholarship is the interconnected exegesis of the canonical writings which attest the Christ-event. We cannot go behind the texts to raise questions of "historical" genuineness which are irrelevant to the history with which they deal, and which is in rather than behind them.[76]

[76] CD I/2, 474 f.; IV/2, 122-24, 149 f.

Two questions may be raised about this position. First, it fails to recognize sufficiently that the biblical canon is the result of a long process of historical development, and therefore cannot legitimately be excluded from critical examination. Full understanding of a given text requires the best attainable knowledge of its background and genesis as well as its present relation to other texts. Secondly, Barth has no satisfactory explanation for the theological differences and inconsistencies disclosed by careful historical-critical exegesis of the New Testament writings. The conflicts which appear on important issues make it impossible to merge historical with dogmatic truth.[77]

Barth's attitude has contributed substantially to the cleavage recently evident on the Continent between exegesis and dogmatics. Few theologians have been more concerned to resolve the impasse than Hermann Diem, whom we shall consider next.

[77] See Ernst Käsemann, "Begründet der Neutestamentliche Kanon die Einheit der Kirche?" *Exegetische Versuche und Besinnungen* (Göttingen: Vandenhoeck und Ruprecht, 1960), pp 214-23; P. Vielhauer, "Zum 'Paulinismus' der Apostelgeschichte," *Evangelische Theologie*, X (1950-51), 1 ff.

2. HERMANN DIEM

Among the theologians most positively influenced by Karl Barth, possibly none has addressed himself more vigorously to the central issues in the current theological debate than Hermann Diem of Tübingen. A Lutheran, Diem has the exceptional distinction of having been named to a German university professorship in middle age, directly from the pastorate, without the usual requirement of "habilitation" through a postdoctoral dissertation. He is the author of a three-volume work, *Theology as Churchly Science*, several important studies of Kierkegaard, and a multitude of briefer writings on a wide variety of subjects. Most valuable for our purposes is his *Dogmatics*,[1] which is Volume II of the first-mentioned publication, and several shorter essays.

The Present Situation in Theology

Diem's point of departure is the double threat to dogmatic theology represented successively by historicism on the one hand and existentialism

---

[1] *Dogmatics: Its Way Between Historicism and Existentialism*, tr. Harold Knight (Philadelphia: The Westminster Press, 1959) (*Dogmatik: Ihr Weg zwischen Historismus und Existentialismus*, [1955] 1957). Volumes I and III, both untranslated, are respectively *Theologie als kirchliche Wissenschaft* (*Theology as Churchly Science*), 1951; and *Die Kirche und ihre Praxis* (*The Church and Its Practice*), 1963. All three German volumes are published by Chr. Kaiser Verlag, München.

on the other. Both regard dogmatics as superfluous or impossible, though for radically different reasons. Historicism is best exemplified by Ernst Troeltsch, who extended the line of development which began with Lessing's famous dictum, "Contingent truths of history can never provide proof of the necessary truths of reason." In this spirit Troelsch himself declares, "The historical serves as illustration, not as demonstration of faith."

The historical person of Jesus is for Troeltsch socially and psychologically necessary if the Christian cult is to be propagated and maintain its power. Piety cannot remain vital if it springs merely from the inner life of the individual and has no historical or social connections. Hence the Christ must be placed in the center as a necessary cultic symbol. However, this is not a dogmatic or doctrinal affirmation based on an objective action of God in history for man's salvation. The symbolic figure of Christ must be firmly grounded in fact, and it must be possible to establish the historicity of Jesus' life and teachings by historical-critical methods. But the historical data afford no basis for conclusions which might claim to be ultimate or abiding truths. Christianity is "a religious idea or principle," not a faith centering in a historical redemption. The historical element was "no more than the means of introducing the Christian idea into history." [2] There is no inner necessity about it, and it provides no foundation for affirmations about God or his relation to man.

When Troeltsch was expressing opinions like these, the first edition of Albert Schweitzer's *Quest of the Historical Jesus* had already appeared, but few realized fully the negative implications of Schweitzer's research. Noting this, Diem writes,

The radical dissolution of dogmatics resulting from the challenge to theology represented by the historical method was taken to its extreme conclusion by Troeltsch at the very moment when historical criticism itself was prepared to declare the bankruptcy of its own attempt to establish the historical reality of Jesus. Hence it is not astonishing that Troeltsch marked a terminal point in the history of theology from which there could be no further progress in the same line of development.[3]

Diem finds a second—and currently much more dangerous—threat to dogmatics among the theologians of the school of Bultmann. Strongly in-

[2] Ernst Troeltsch, *Die Bedeutung der Geschichtlichkeit Jesu für den Glauben* (Tübingen: J. C. B. Mohr [Paul Siebeck], 1911), pp. 6-34; *Gesammelte Schriften* (Tübingen: J. C. B. Mohr [Paul Siebeck], 1922-25), II, 431, 500 f., 514-16.

[3] *Dogmatics*, pp. 8 f.

fluenced by Kierkegaard and Heidegger, they are primarily concerned not
with the factuality of historical events but with their significance for human existence. This position regards as all important the concrete decisions
of faith leading to authentic existence. Hence it radically suspects all dogmatic pronouncements—regardless of their claim to objective validity—
if they cannot demonstrate their bearing on such decisions. Bultmann's
aim is to extract the kerygma or proclamation of the early church from
the New Testament writings, and so to interpret it that it challenges the
hearer to the decision which makes possible his self-fulfillment. All theological tasks converge toward this goal. There is therefore no occasion for a
distinction between biblical and dogmatic theology. Moreover, it is both
impossible and unnecessary to systematize in normative and final fashion
the understanding of God, man, and the world which arises from faith.

The biblical exegete brings to his examination of the text an understanding of existence which makes plain the truth of the text while at the same
time being itself illuminated and criticized by the message of the self-inter-
preting text. From this reciprocal process arise valid criteria for judging
between life-giving preaching and superstition. Hence the definitive
theological work is done not by the dogmatician but by the scriptural
exegete who practices this hermeneutical method. Responsibility for finding
theological truth is thus shifted from dogmatics to hermeneutics. Sound
exegesis renders dogmatics superfluous.[4]

Side by side with this suspicion of dogmatic theology has emerged in
many dogmaticians a mistrust of exegesis pursued on existentialist lines.
The presuppositions of such exegesis are felt to involve a surrender of the
claim of the Christian faith to objective and universal truth, hence to be-
tray the essence of the biblical message. As a result of these developments
a deep cleavage is now apparent. W. Janasch records his impression "that
dogmatic theologians and New Testament critics have two quite different
New Testaments before them." [5] The former regulate their exegesis by dogmatic principles, and the latter, rejecting all dogmatics, content themselves with a one-sided critical exegesis. As Ernst Käsemann points out,
the New Testament scholars, in spite of their reaction against a merely
historical approach, carry on their work in full continuity with historical
criticism. On the contrary, systematic theologians tend to ignore or attack
the insights, methods, and conclusions of exegesis, to bypass the problems

---

[4] Rudolf Bultmann, *Theology of the New Testament*, II, tr. Kendrick Grobel (New York:
Charles Scribner's Sons, 1955), 237 f., 240 f.; Diem, *Dogmatics*, pp. 25, 33, 70-72.

[5] *Theologische Literaturzeitung*, LXXVI (1951), 5.

of historical criticism, and to uphold traditional formulations of Christian belief. As a consequence the exegetes have been led to raise questions and to formulate answers which disregard the efforts of the dogmaticians. Discussion between the two disciplines has largely been broken off, and each goes its separate way. "Exegesis has become visibly aggressive while dogmatics is above all concerned to preserve and protect Church tradition." [6]

Diem frequently calls attention to this opposition, finding it particularly evident in the relation between Barth and Bultmann and their followers. To bring the divergent positions into renewed discussion with each other has been a major concern of his theological labor. His intention is not to chart a mediating path between them, but to discover a way by which the conflicting questions and answers may be so formulated that comparisons may again become possible. In pursuing this purpose he inevitably discloses and develops his own theological standpoint.

The Earthly Jesus and the Christ of Faith

In the debate between dogmatic and biblical theology two questions have emerged: (1) What is the right relationship between dogmatics and exegesis? (2) What is the essential task of dogmatics itself? Diem finds a valuable approach to both questions in the examination of a problem which is important to both Barth and Bultmann—the meaning of the historical Jesus [7] for the preaching and doctrine of the church.

In Diem's view the starting point as well as the historical locus of all Christian theology is the self-proclamation of Jesus in the Gospels. However, this self-proclamation comes to us not as an objective historical report, but as part of the early church's proclamation of Jesus as the Messiah. "The whole history of Gospel proclamation is to be understood as an evangelistic transmission of the preaching of Jesus, to the end that He should be believed in as the Christ." Hence research into the history of the New Testament proclamation must consider the relation between two interpenetrating aspects: the actions and preaching of the earthly Jesus himself and the subsequent proclamation about what he did and preached. In such research our aim cannot be somehow to penetrate behind the text to the supposedly historical facts, but simply to trace the history of the texts

[6] Käsemann, "Probleme der Neutestamentlichen Arbeit in Deutschland," in *Die Freiheit des Evangeliums und die Ordnung der Gesellschaft*, Beiträge zu *Evangelische Theologie*, XIX (1952), 138.
[7] Diem prefers the term *earthly Jesus* to avoid the ambiguity involved in current use of the word *historical*.

themselves. This history is reflected in the formulation of the text, which is "the one historically apprehensible piece of this history of preaching." [8]

Diem is not content with Barth's restriction of exegesis to the canonical Scriptures but insists that we must inquire into their background and genesis. This requires us to adopt the standpoint of the text itself, accepting its understanding of itself as an instrument of proclamation. Our aim must be to allow Jesus Christ to proclaim himself through the rich variety of the textual material. Exegesis must therefore see the text as the consequence of an earlier history of gospel proclamation and expound it with a view to further proclamation. Thus Scripture itself interprets the Scriptures. Diem's own critical method for evaluating the history of the text consists of

investigating whether and in what various ways the individual writings attest the history of the Christ who in His preaching proclaims Himself, what factors have influenced the process by helping or hindering, to what extent the Biblical authors themselves eventually were diverted from their central purpose, and how in this way the single testimonies assumed their present canonical form and are to be understood.[9]

Inquiry into the New Testament proclamation of Jesus Christ raises two questions of truth, historical and theological. The former has to do with the *continuity* of the proclamation-history, a continuity which consists finally in the *identity* of him who proclaims himself in the history, the Jesus Christ who remains throughout as its initiator, object, and active subject. This identity cannot be confirmed by strictly historical methods. However, the person who is the object of faith cannot be separated from his saving work. What he does discloses who he is. The salvation proclaimed is realized by those who believe in him who brings it. Its validity depends on the validity of the authority claimed by the earthly Jesus through whom it comes. Significantly, our oldest tradition puts in the mouth of Jesus the name "Son of Man" as the coming one, while God himself has testified that Jesus is the bringer of salvation by raising him from the dead.[10]

The second truth-question is that of theological truth—whether the Jesus Christ who acts in the proclamation-history, and who therefore meets us in and through it, is identical with the earthly Jesus of Nazareth. Is the

[8] *Dogmatics*, pp. 143, 116-26, 144; cf. pp. 133, 141; *Der irdische Jesus und der Christus des Glaubens* (Tübingen: J. C. B. Mohr [Paul Siebeck], 1957), pp. 10-17.

[9] *Dogmatics*, pp. 146 f., 216 f.

[10] *Der irdische Jesus und der Christus des Glaubens*, pp. 16-20.

preaching of Jesus himself continuous with the post-Easter preaching about him? Diem affirms that it is. In proclaiming the Jesus who declared himself as the Christ the church was transmitting the uniqueness of the preaching of Jesus himself. However, this cannot be scientifically demonstrated. Even a positive answer to the historical question can do no more than leave open the way on which the earthly Jesus may meet us as the proclaimed Christ. This encounter can occur only when the church makes the venture of faith, placing herself on this way by *preaching* the Christ of the Scriptures, in order that he can reveal himself to those who hear and believe as the living and present Christ of God.[11]

Preaching and Doctrine in the New Testament

As we have seen, in Diem's view the Scriptures set forth the history of a proclamation which needs to be further proclaimed. They were composed as a textual basis for Christian preaching, and they continue today to provide this basis. Inevitably the proclamation contained doctrinal elements from the start. Diem opposes Harnack's thesis that dogma, appearing under the influence of Greek thought after the New Testament period, represented an extraneous addition to the purity of the gospel. Instead, "the process of the development of dogma began with the transformation of Jesus' Gospel into the Gospel about Jesus Christ." [12] The preaching of this gospel involved the proclamation of truth which needed to be interpreted. The leaders of the early church therefore included not only apostles, prophets, and evangelists, but also pastors and teachers (I Cor. 12:28; Eph. 4:11). Moreover, teaching implied something to be taught—doctrine. In the liturgical and catechetical life of the church certain definite formulas arose which were accepted and elaborated by the apostles. These were not fundamentals of doctrine to be scholastically explained, but preaching texts interpreted in connection with the proclamation of the gospel.

The claim of the apostles to be reliable bearers of the gospel tradition gradually came to be recognized. Legitimate preaching therefore had to stem from or be in accord with their authority. Following the deaths of the apostles and Paul, who was recognized as their peer, the oral tradition was found to be insufficient to maintain their authority. The weight and influence of the written tradition—brief words from Jesus himself, whole Gospels, and Pauline letters—increased. Such writings, basically sermons

[11] *Dogmatics*, pp. 142 f.; *Der irdische Jesus und der Christus des Glaubens*, pp. 4, 12, 19 f.
[12] *Dogmatics*, p. 170.

which amplified traditional materials used as texts, now came to be regarded in their entirety as texts. Thus the canon of Scripture came into being.[13] If we ask why these particular writings happened to be canonized, we can only reply that they were the ones which authenticated themselves in the event of their proclamation—those which allowed themselves to be preached because they witnessed to the saving act of God in Jesus Christ. Here Diem joins Barth in declaring that certain parts of the oldest written tradition simply established themselves gradually in the estimate of the churches—a fact which formal canonization by later official action could only confirm. "At some time and in some degree . . . just *these* writings in virtue of the fact that they *were* canonical took care that later it was they which were recognized and proclaimed to be canonical." [14]

The self-evidencing authority of the Scriptures implies their basic unity. This is not, however, a unity of doctrine; it consists rather in the fact that amid wide diversity (e.g., Paul and James) they are all witnesses through whom Jesus Christ may be heard proclaiming himself.[15] In the proclamation of these witnesses the church has exclusively heard the Word of God. We, too, can and must hear it there. However, this self-evidence of the New Testament witnesses in preaching varied with different times and circumstances. Likewise, the modern preacher must combine loyalty to the particular texts in which he confronts the proclamation with freedom to present it in such a way that it can be effectively heard in the religious situation of today.

The fulfillment of this task requires the services not only of exegesis, but of systematic theology and dogmatics. Diem insists that the second and third of these disciplines are not the same, and must be carefully distinguished. Each, however, should stand in a cooperative relationship with exegesis.

Systematic Theology and Scriptural Exegesis

According to Diem the essential function of systematic theology is carried out only in relation to scriptural exposition. The exegete is responsible for elucidating not only what particular writings and passages say individually, but also what they say to each other and together to us. For example, we must examine Paul and James within their own unique historical situations and on their own terms instead of judging each from

---

[13] *Ibid.*, p. 193.
[14] *Ibid.*, p. 204; Barth, CD, I/2, 474.
[15] "Die Einheit der Schrift," *Evangelische Theologie*, XIII (1953), 404; *Dogmatics*, pp. 224-39.

the perspective of the other. As Georg Eichholz has shown, James speaks to a different time-situation from that of Paul, and utters a word on the importance of works which is relevant to the new hour, a word not spoken by Paul. Thus James "makes himself responsible *for* Paul in the canon." But in another situation Paul had already clarified the meaning of salvation by grace through faith, thereby standing "surety *for* James in the canon." Thus each as it were *protects* and complements the other.[16] No utterance of a biblical witness is complete in itself. Because of the wide variety of situations and perspectives represented, the canonical witnesses together speak universally to man's condition and proclaim the way of salvation.

It is not enough, therefore, for exegesis to draw attention to the distinctive characteristics of the various witnesses, leaving to the systematic theologian the task of putting Humpty Dumpty together. Such a procedure can only widen the gulf between the two disciplines. Rather, the exegete must do his utmost "to discover whether and in what sense the individual Biblical witnesses become responsible for each other."

Exegesis thus leads directly into the work of systematic theology, the task of which is "to say anew for us today what the manifold witness of the Bible says in common." Initially, it must relate the biblical witnesses to each other. Secondly, it must ask what common message these varied witnesses convey to us in our situation.

More specifically, systematic theology performs both of these tasks as it confronts three basic problems: (1) It examines closely the biblical witnesses to God's self-disclosing action, seeking to discover beyond the conditioning circumstances of each the nature of the revelatory event to which it points. This is the question of historical revelation. (2) It investigates the possibility of contact between the attested event and our present existence as hearers and representatives of the biblical witnesses. This involves the problem of hermeneutics. (3) On the basis of this contact it endeavors to formulate statements which, unconditioned by particular circumstances, can claim general validity and authority, and thus provide a *norm* for further textual exegesis. This is the question of the *regula fidei.*[17]

One or another of these problems may be given special emphasis or attention, but never one-sidedly or in isolation from the others. Each must be seen in its total context. In some detail Diem analyzes the thought of Bultmann, Ebeling, and Gogarten to show that they fail to observe this

---

[16] Georg Eichholz, *Jakobus und Paulus: Ein Beitrag zum Problem des Kanons* (München: Chr. Kaiser Verlag, 1953), pp. 48-50.

[17] *Dogmatics*, pp. 237-42.

requirement. The first two reduce the systematic question to a heremeneutic one, while Gogarten limits himself to hermeneutics and revelation as history. But all of them studiously avoid the third area, refusing to deal with questions or statements which might be termed dogmatic, or to look in Scripture for generally valid truths which might in turn illuminate our interpretation of Scripture. In attempting to correct such one-sidedness Diem inquires into the real meaning of dogmatic thinking.[18]

Dogmatic Theology and Scriptural Exposition

In Diem's view dogma is the formulated confession of the Christian community. It arises as the church's response to and interpretation of the proclamation of the biblical witnesses. "A dogmatic affirmation bears witness to the saving action of God both as regards its actuality and meaning." Dogmatic theology, then, is the connected statement and scientific exposition of dogma. It is the creation of the church, and exists solely to further the church's ongoing proclamation of the message committed to it. Hence it has an authoritative and normative character which distinguishes it from the systematic theology carried on by individuals, and which guards it against the arbitrariness which often marks systematic theology.[19]

Dogmatic statements aim at both completeness and systematic consistency, seeking to declare the whole counsel of the God who acts to save his world. However, they never succeed perfectly, since the divine light is refracted by the human personalities of both the New Testament writers and the formulators of dogma. In the deepest sense dogma is the divine counsel itself, which always eludes our best efforts to capture it in human words. Thus all dogmatic statements are "insecure and debatable." Nevertheless, when the debate is carried on in close relation to careful exegetical study of the biblical testimony, understanding is possible and truth attainable.[20] Dogma may be tested by the biblical witnesses while providing valuable guidance in the interpretation of those witnesses.

Diem points out that the scriptural testimony may be accredited *existentially* as well as *dogmatically*. In the former, the witness appreciates the significance (the *what*) of an event in its sheer actuality (its *that*), and by his acceptance testifies to its truth. In the latter, actuality and significance are fused in the event being attested, and hence must be fused

---

[18] *Ibid.*, pp. 244-81.
[19] "Dogma und Existenz," in Ernst Wolf (ed.), *Unter der Herrschaft Christi* (München: Chr. Kaiser Verlag, 1961), p. 26; *Dogmatics*, pp. 283, 300, 303.
[20] *Dogmatics*, pp. 303 f.

also in the testimony. The former is illustrated by Rom. 8:16, where our sonship to God is founded in our being called to be joint heirs with Christ. The latter is exemplified by the Johannine teaching that Jesus is the Son of God, a truth involved in the historical character of the revelation (John 7:17, 26; 10:38; 14:20; 16:3; 17:7-8; 23:25). This is a truth *sui generis* which because of its authoritative character demands primarily not understanding but acknowledgment.

The two approaches belong together. Rom. 8:16 does not mean that a universally valid truth about humanity is replaced by an occurrence through which God's saving counsel has been realized, but simply that the truth is fulfilled in us, and that we must become personally involved in its actualization. Likewise, the acknowledgment called for by John may lead to understanding, including self-understanding. Yet though the two ways of accreditation do not exclude each other, neither do they condition each other. The dogmatic truth includes the existential, in that God's will attains its goal only through the transforming work of the Holy Spirit in the existence of the believer. But we may not say conversely that the existential possibility includes the dogmatic, so that both the factuality and meaning of what is attested are authenticated simply by the hearer's existential attitude.[21] The reality of God and his saving action always precedes, and objectively underlies, the response which transforms man's existence.

Diem summarizes his conclusions regarding dogma and existence in three theses: (1) Dogma arose in answer to the proclamation of the biblical witnesses, and contains assertions concerning the salvation-decree of God and its realization. (2) Dogmatic statements about this divine action always have to do at the same time with the existence of man, toward whom God's action is directed. (3) Dogmatic statements are to be interpreted not existentially but dogmatically, with primary attention to their own inner content rooted in revelation. Even our own existence is better understood through dogmatically interpreted dogma than through existential interpretation.[22]

What, then, is the relation between dogmatics and exegesis? Since all church doctrine grows out of the proclamation recorded in Scripture, it must constantly be tested by its conformity with that proclamation. Dogma

---

[21] *Dogmatics*, pp. 285-90.

[22] "Dogma und Existenz im theologischen Denken," in *Philosophie und christliche Existenz; Festschrift für Heinrich Barth* (Basel und Stuttgart: Helbing und Lichtenhahn, 1960), pp. 107-17.

is always subject to critical inspection by exegesis, and dogmatic theology is at every point dependent on exegetical inquiry. Conversely, dogma provides the indispensable orientation for exegesis, the necessary perspective for the questioning of the text. Its truths illuminate and resolve problems which could never be solved by textual study alone. As Barth has suggested, dogmatics affords the kind of help which one receives when traveling by rail but lacks when journeying by automobile. He cannot go anywhere he wishes, but must use the available lines and stop only at the station. The restrictions are such only in appearance, since they insure that the traveler will move steadily toward his goal and not lose his way. Diem extends the metaphor by pointing out that the passenger may board the train at any station and travel thence toward his destination. To change the figure, the doctrines wrought out by the church serve to unlock the meaning of the Scriptures.[23]

If we recognize this mutual relationship, our point of departure in dogmatic exegesis will be "that the Biblical testimony can be authenticated as true only by that to which it bears witness: God's eternal plan, in its indissoluble unity of fact and meaning, as a consequence of which the revelation becomes an historical process that both has happened and is happening, as the witnesses attest." [24] This leads to a specific exegetical method which involves a "hermeneutical circle": the witness is to be interpreted only through what is witnessed, but that in turn can be known only through the witness. This is not circular reasoning, but rather two-way support and illumination within one reality. The hermeneutical circle is the mode of hearing and understanding required by the text. It can be opened only from within, by allowing Scripture to interpret itself.[25]

Much more is involved, however, than critical comparisons carried out by a human interpreter. It is God himself who is witnessed to, and he participates in both revelation and interpretation. For this reason the circle might be better expressed by saying that the witness is accredited by the One witnessed to, God in Christ, who in turn is known only through the testimony of his witnesses. The testimony to be interpreted is not an abstract proposition, but a living utterance. It is an *akoé*—a momentous

---

[23] *Der irdische Jesus und der Christus des Glaubens*, pp. 18 f.; *Dogmatics*, pp. 297 f., 310, 313, 340, 347 f., 364 f.
[24] *Dogmatics*, p. 294.
[25] *Was heisst schriftgemäss?* (Neukirchen Kreis Moers: Verlag der Buchhandlung des Erziehungsvereins, 1958), pp. 11-13, 40; *Dogmatics*, pp. 294-97.

declaration which demands to be heard and obeyed in faith, an event in which preaching is joined with responsive hearing.[26] In such an event revelation takes place, and only when the event is somehow relived in exegesis can its meaning be understood. In this occurrence God, as active, bestowing subject, manifests himself anew to man as receiving, obedient subject—a process which the New Testament describes as *summarturein,* or witnessing together. "The word of God . . . is at work in you believers" (I Thess. 2:13). Thus he who is witnessed to confirms the witness who makes him known.

Not only does the living truth contained in Scripture serve to interpret the passages which bear witness to it; the dogmas which were later forged on the anvil of the church's life also illuminate the Scriptures on which they are based and by which they must be tested. Indeed, whether they are in accord with Scripture can be evidenced finally only by their capacity to serve as an aid in sound scriptural interpretation.[27]

Among various illustrations of this process offered by Diem perhaps the clearest is the doctrine of the Trinity. In the subject-minded relation the human hearer realizes his filial status and his partnership in the heritage of Christ through the power of the Spirit. God manifests himself in three distinct modes of being, but in all three he remains the self-identical subject of the process. The church has expressed the nature of this event in the doctrine of the Trinity, which in turn illuminates our study of the biblical texts. It does not tell us what they must say, but from what perspective we should examine them. We should therefore ask whether and how far they speak of the works of God as Trinity. In the joint witnessing of the New Testament writings, do we find that God the Creator makes himself understood by man, whom he has created, whom in Jesus Christ he has redeemed, and to whom he attests himself through the Holy Spirit? Is the result that through Jesus Christ man *may* once more address God as Father, and *can* so address him because his life has been struck by these *opera Trinitatis?* When we carry on our exegesis from this trinitarian standpoint, the meaning of the biblical witness to God's manifold activity is disclosed. The testimony is authenticated by its object, which is however actually the triune divine Subject.[28]

[26] For good scriptural instances of what this means, see Rom. 10:14-17; Gal. 3:2-5; I Thess. 2:13.

[27] *Was heisst schriftgemäss?* p. 40.

[28] *Dogmatics,* pp. 296-302.

The Authority of Dogma

Diem calls particular attention to three dangers against which the theologian must guard as he uses dogma in exegesis. First, concordance *hearing* may easily become concordance *method*. In the former the varying statements of different witnesses are examined on their own terms, yet so related that each may fill gaps left by the other; they "are made comparable through some unifying point of view which is the ultimate end orientating our approach to them." This approach fully recognizes all actual divergences, but presupposes that the various statements *intend* to testify to the same reality. It thus allows Scripture to interpret Scripture. In concordance method, on the contrary, the varied testimonies are reduced to a common denominator derived from a basic principle found in nonbiblical systematic thought, so that their unique historical characteristics are submerged.[29]

Secondly, dogmatics may become a *gnosis* of faith which proceeds independently of the revelatory event. The rule of faith or some other patristic testimony may replace Scripture, or a rational orthodoxy may be set up in the manner of the so-called Athanasian Creed as an authoritative formulation of *fides quae creditur* (the faith which is to be believed). Both Roman Catholicism and scholastic Protestantism have been guilty of this error. Both faith and the confession of faith are called forth and validated by Scripture itself in the living process of the *akoé*, not by the fallible decisions of ecclesiastical bodies.[30]

Thirdly, dogmatics may confuse the systematizing event which is its source with a systematic principle, and thus attempt to deduce the truth of its pronouncements from their interlocking. This can easily occur, since each affirmation does emerge in a sequence of ideas which encourages interconnected inferences, and since it must find expression in specific concepts drawn from some general outlook. The danger is illustrated even in the Apostles' Creed, whose redactors perhaps unwisely began not with Jesus Christ, as did the authors of the confessional formulas of the New Testament, but with statements about God as Creator. Such assertions are not dogmatic, i.e., concerned with the saving work of God, but metaphysical. This beginning encourages "the misconception that one might make affirmations about God quite apart from His self-revelation in Christ." The danger can be avoided only if we recognize that all theologians are speaking

[29] *Ibid.*, pp. 304 f.
[30] *Ibid.*, pp. 348-53, 364 f.

of the plan and action of God, but with humanly conditioned means of expression.[31] Yet this recognition itself is possible only where exegetical and dogmatic discussion are marked by the "freedom in obligation" which arises when all our thinking is focused on the *akoé*—the double event uniting testimony and listening, what is heard and that by which we hear. This living event of gospel proclamation and present hearing is the revelatory point of origin of the exegesis, dogma, and confessions of the church; it is repeated in ever new situations where God's self-disclosure is actualized in believing knowledge.[32]

Exegete and dogmatician alike must avoid arbitrary questioning of the text and inquire only regarding what is attested by the Scriptures, adopting an attitude of listening and responsive faith and heeding also the testimony of other hearers, past and present. Further, they must recall each other to the center, the *akoé*, where "dogma *itself*" saves us from subjective thinking by confronting us afresh as the origin and norm of all our systems. Within this obligation we are free to raise new questions and to reply with new forms of expression. Indeed, only by using this freedom can we advance the purpose of the biblical kerygma. The proclamation continually seeks new enactment, and by it all our theological work must be authenticated.[33]

Thus the question of authority inherent in the formation of dogma can be answered only from the standpoint of the *akoé*. To the degree that this living, revelatory event occurs the circle is closed between the declaration of God's will and man's obedience to it in faith. The truest formulations of Christian belief are those which spring from this event, ever renewed within the community of faith.[34]

Critique

Since Diem offers relatively little systematic exposition of the classic doctrines of Christian faith as such, he makes only a marginal contribution to dogmatic theology in its traditional meaning. However, his primary concern with the heremeneutical questions at issue between dogmatic theology and existentialist exegesis places him in the center of some of the live problems of contemporary theology. Operating from a modified Barthian perspective, he relates his theology of the Word at crucial points to the

[31] *Ibid.*, pp. 309 f., 353 f.
[32] *Ibid.*, pp. 294 f., 308, 340-43, 346-48, 360.
[33] *Ibid.*, pp. 341 f.; *Was heisst schriftgemäss?* p. 36.
[34] *Dogmatics*, p. 343.

theology of existence, thereby providing a valuable concrete example of the kind of conversation for which he pleads.

Values

There is scant foundation for the judgment of Frederick Herzog that Diem's Dogmatics will remain for years "the standard reference work on contemporary Continental Protestant dogmatics." [35] Nevertheless, no other work has delineated so clearly the nature and extent of the chasm which separates exegesis and dogmatics on the Continent today or gone so far to provide a basis for fruitful debate. Nor has any other writer offered more penetrating criticism of so wide a range of contemporary literature in this area. Diem has also made valuable constructive proposals of his own.

1. Diem's critical contributions relate particularly to the theologies of Barth and Bultmann. Though he is in basic agreement with Barth, and though his efforts to heal the rift between dogmatic and exegetical investigations proceed mainly from Barthian premises, he comes to grips with existentialist hermeneutics more directly than Barth does, and develops more clearly than Barth the principle that Scripture must be interpreted by Scripture. He also advances several cogent criticisms of Barth's thought. For example, he points out that Barth's insistence on the unity and authority of the closed canon of Scripture tends to identify the Word revealed with the Word written and proclaimed, to overlook the patent diversity of the biblical writings, and to provide an insufficient guarantee against the deterioration of formal biblicism into material biblicism.[36] Diem also calls attention to Barth's inadequate exegetical use of the historical-critical method which he theoretically accepts; we cannot understand a text without knowledge of the history of its genesis.[37] Diem rejects Barth's "revelation positivism," which on the basis of the Word of God deduces historical positions from theological questions.

Diem's critical powers appear to best advantage, however, in his examination of the theologies of existence, especially the thought of Bultmann. On the positive side, he agrees with the Christian existentialists that man is to be defined not according to determinations of being or essence,

[35] Review in *The Christian Century*, LXXVIII (1961), 114.
[36] *Dogmatics*, pp. 101 f., 106. Formal biblicism here means a biblical *attitude*, the mode of thinking which marks the personal witnessing of prophets and apostles. Material biblicism restricts dogmatics to exegesis of the biblical text and adheres rigidly to a biblical vocabulary. The former seeks agreement with the basic reality attested, the latter with the words and ideas of the testimony.
[37] *Ibid.*, 145 f.

but in terms of a happening or occurring. Doctrinal statements, moreover, concern human existence, toward which God's saving action is directed.[38] The scriptural testimony must therefore be approached existentially as well as dogmatically; the two methods are complementary, not exclusive.[39]

On the other hand, Diem finds Protestant existentialism guilty of not taking seriously the objective truth, both historical and theological, implicit in the New Testament proclamation. Its strictures against "objectification" are possible only because it blames dogmatic theology for a sharper antithesis between subject and object than the facts warrant. Every doctrinal statement means to utter truth regarding some aspect of the action of God in relation to man. The New Testament revelation itself implies the truth which dogma seeks to express. The gospel is good news because the faith it arouses refers to a divine reality whose existence does not depend on its being believed. Hence no purely existential interpretation can suffice, and dogmatics may not be legitimately dissolved into hermeneutics. Doctrinal truth includes and implies the truth of personal encounter, but the converse may not be soundly asserted.

2. Among Diem's constructive proposals, four in particular deserve mention.

a. His central concept of proclamation-history, which stresses the unity of Jesus' self-proclamation, the apostolic preaching of Jesus as the Christ, and the later proclamation of the church in all generations, including the present, represents a creative approach to the hermeneutical problem. The notion of Jesus Christ as at once initiator, object, and continuing subject of the proclamation provides for both the unity and the diversity of the biblical message and relates it closely to the life and thought of the later Christian community.

b. Diem makes illuminating use of the hermeneutical circle, the reciprocity of influence between two associated realities. At least three such circles can be identified in his discussions: that which unites witness (apostolic preaching) and Witnessed (Jesus Christ); that which connects Scripture and church dogma; and that which links the testimony of Scripture to present hearing. In Diem's hands each of these becomes a valuable means of furthering the understanding of both Scripture and contemporary Christian faith, while facilitating a *rapprochement* between exegesis and dogmatics.

[38] "Dogma und Existenz im theologischen Denken," p. 110.
[39] *Dogmatics*, pp. 286-90.

c. He rightly emphasizes the integral relation between proclamation and doctrine, witness and belief. This is intimated in the second of the circles just mentioned, but merits further comment. In contrast to Harnack's view that dogma began mainly in the second century as the Greek spirit sought to make the gospel intelligible, Diem locates the beginning of dogma in the New Testament proclamation itself—at the point where the gospel of Jesus was transformed into the gospel about Jesus Christ. Unquestionably, momentous affirmations regarding God, man, and salvation were involved in the earliest Christian preaching; just as certainly, in all epochs the declaration of truth and the offer of life belong inseparably together in sound evangelism. Diem preserves both the theological content of preaching and the practical relevance of church dogma, guarding the former from shallowness and the latter from abstraction.

d. Diem's understanding of the Christian witness in terms of *akoé* prevents exegesis from being merely an academic activity, making it instead a living process. Rooted in the self-giving action of God, the *akoé* is a dynamic event combining preaching and responsive, obedient hearing. Such a revelatory event is at the heart of all sound exegesis and doctrinal thinking; binding them to a common center, it opens the way to a co-operative relation between them. This conception has the great virtue of placing the scholarly endeavor of Christians in the context of living faith in the God who not only acted historically in Jesus Christ but in every present continues to act as Holy Spirit.

Difficulties

Several areas of difficulty in Diem's theology call for attention.[40]

1. It may be questioned whether he takes with full seriousness the historical-critical method which he in theory supports. We have noted his criticism of Barth for the latter's acceptance of the canon as a closed dogmatic entity which is not subject to historical judgment. However, in the actual process of exegesis Diem himself seems to make relatively little use of critical-historical study. For him an inquiry into the origin of a text has little to do with questions of date, authorship, and the like, but means primarily adopting the text's own understanding of itself as an instrument of proclamation. His idea of proclamation-history aims to provide from the theological side a basis for cooperation with historical criticism, but he

[40] Some of the questions already raised regarding Barth would apply also to Diem, and are therefore not discussed here. See especially the comments on Barth's views concerning natural theology and the role of human reason in revelation, above, pp. 37-39.

is somewhat ambiguous in developing it, and it represents at best a theological construction which the exegete who is committed to historical method can hardly accept.

The same problem appears in Diem's conception that dogma, since it has grown out of Scripture, is the hermeneutical key which unlocks Scripture. He apparently overlooks the possibility that dogma might provide the wrong key, partly because the exegetical methods available to or used by its framers were inadequate. With defective tools of critical research and faulty knowledge of documents, may not church councils and individual theologians on some occasions have drawn false conclusions from the biblical texts? How, then, would the resultant doctrines provide a trustworthy key to textual interpretation? In this connection it may be interesting to inquire what differences might have occurred in the formulation of Christian doctrine if the methods of form criticism had been available before the time of Augustine. However, it must be admitted that Diem provides at least a partial answer to this problem by recognizing that dogma must be continually tested anew by exegesis.

2. Diem's view of the self-authentication of the canonical Scriptures seems unintelligibly to ascribe to the writings themselves a kind of active power to command acceptance. He insists that no investigation of the process of canonization can historically go beyond the conclusion that the canon finally established itself. He agrees with Barth in affirming that precisely *these* writings, through the very fact that they *were* canonical, "took care" that they could later be *recognized* and *proclaimed* as such.[41] God or man may "take care," but not lifeless written documents. Does the language used really mean that God determined the canon? If so, this judgment should be explicitly stated, in which case the question of human freedom thus raised would have to be forthrightly examined. Or does the statement express nothing more than the tautology that the Scriptures were designated as canonical by the church because they were found worthy of canonization? In any case, Diem underrates the importance of concrete historical circumstances in the formation of the canon. Empirical inquiry discloses unmistakably the influence of such factors as belief in the apostolic authorship or authority of the writings chosen, their proven value as channels of the redemptive and life-giving power of God, and the possibility that under other circumstances sound claims might have been made for a somewhat different collection.

[41] See above, p. 47. Barth's German *haben gesorgt,* which in the English version in Diem's *Dogmatics* appears as "took care," is translated in Barth's *Church Dogmatics* as "saw to it."

3. Diem's conception of the theological task threatens to insulate Christian theology from other areas of human life and culture. In his view truth concerning God is found only through the obedient hearing and interpretation of the biblical witness carried on cooperatively by exegetes and dogmaticians. He criticizes the Apostles' Creed for beginning with a metaphysical statement about God instead of with a declaration about God's saving work in Jesus Christ. In his judgment this beginning falsely suggests that assertions about God may rightly be made apart from his self-disclosure in Christ. This implication is not at all clear; in any event, is it not quite possible that the early church did presuppose some knowledge of God as creator in those to whom it proclaimed the gospel? Is it not also likely that the Creed's movement from God's creative action to his redemptive work in Christ provided for Christians a valuable point of contact with non-Christian thought in the Greco-Roman world? The question also arises whether a theology which is limited to an exposition of the biblical testimony can communicate effectively with secular, scientific man in the twentieth century.

In spite of Diem's admission that doctrine must be interpreted existentially as well as dogmatically, he does not relate it adequately to the whole of man's existence. His hermeneutical circle joining exegesis and dogma is in danger of becoming a closed theological circle which not only keeps the natural theologian out but also locks the Christian theologian in, cutting him off from significant communication with other serious-minded seekers after truth.

3. JOSEF L. HROMÁDKA

One convincing indication of the power of the theological movement which centers in the Word of God is the fact that it is not confined to western Europe, but dominates Protestant theology in the land which, except for East Germany, is the most Protestant east of the Iron Curtain—Czechoslovakia. By far its ablest and most influential representative there is Josef L. Hromádka. He is singularly equipped by education and experience to serve as an interpreter between Christians and churches in East and West. He studied theology and philosophy in Vienna, Basel, Heidelberg, Aberdeen, and Prague. After several years in the pastorate he became in 1920 the first professor of systematic theology at the newly founded Hus Protestant Theological School in Prague. When the Nazis occupied Czechoslovakia he came to America, where he taught from 1939 to 1947 at Princeton Theological Seminary. Returning to his native land he resumed his teaching post, and has remained there even though the Communist Party came to power in 1948. He became dean of the theological school when in 1950 it was reconstituted as the Comenius Faculty of Protestant Theology, and retired in 1964.

Among his many writings, most of which are available only in Czech or German, his most definitive full-length book is *Das Evangelium auf dem*

Wege zum Menschen (*The Gospel on the Way to Man*).[1] His most recent book in English is *Theology Between Yesterday and Tomorrow*.[2] He is editor of *Communio Viatorum*, a multilingual theological quarterly, and some of his editorials in this journal afford valuable clues to his thought. His ecumenical and international interests have found expression in his membership on the Central Committee of the World Council of Churches and in his presidency of the Christian Peace Conference, which held international assemblies in Prague in 1961 and 1964.

Theological Heritage and Perspective

Major Influences

Among the influences which have helped to mold Hromádka's theology three are dominant: the theological heritage of the Czech Reformation, which began with John Hus a century before the German Reformation; the new theological movement initiated by the crisis theology; and the revolutionary social events of the past half-century. The third of these will be quite clear in the following discussion; the first two call for brief comment here.

The deep rootage of Hromádka's thought in the Czech Reformation is not generally appreciated by his American critics. Yet the heritage of the reform movements from Hus through the Unity of Brethren[3] to Comenius pervades all of his work and thought, constituting probably the greatest single background influence. The earliest supporters of these movements were largely humble manual workers and farmers who were gripped by the gospel and a deep longing for the rule of Christ in daily life. Many of them shared the view of Wyclif and Hus that the church's life should be marked by Christlike poverty. Their leaders inquired constantly into the meaning of the lordship of Christ for the social and political struggles which confronted them, and related theological concepts to the practical needs of congregational life.

Hromádka notes that his *Gospel on the Way to Man* was written mostly in the year of the five-hundredth anniversary of the Unity of Brethren,

---

[1] (Berlin: Evangelische Verlagsanstalt, 1961).

[2] (Philadelphia: The Westminster Press, 1957).

[3] *Unitas Fratrum*, formed about 1458 by elements drawn from three Hussite groups—Taborites, Utraquists, and Waldenses. It preserved much of the vitality of the Hussite movement, and was the spiritual ancestor of the Moravian Church founded at Herrnhut in Saxony in 1727. Hromádka's high regard for the Unity of Brethren is evidenced by the fact that he has written two books on the movement, *The Meaning of the Reformation of the Unity of Brethren* (1939) and *The Legacy of the Unity of Brethren* (1957).

and gratefully records his debt to the Bohemian Reformers. He lists particularly five contributions: (1) their living obedience to the Word of God; (2) their awareness that faith cannot be limited to individual piety, but must become visible in the fellowship of the congregation and the practical life of the believer; (3) the depth of their understanding of the church as a "community of pilgrims"; (4) their refusal to allow the church to become merely an official religious institution; and (5) their forward look, which directed the hopes of the faithful toward the final victory of Jesus Christ, giving them courage, an open view into the world, and readiness for changes in the social and political realm.[4]

Hromádka calls special attention to the social significance of Comenius' central belief in the kingly power and final victory of Christ. Christ's lordship is unrestricted by time or place, and it is not limited to the church or to any special part of life. His royal authority is confirmed by his resurrection. The believing Christian is therefore in his service, called to reflect in all of life his forgiving mercy, righteousness, and love. Similarly, the church is obligated not only to preach the Word, administer the sacraments, and form a fellowship of prayer, but also to spread in the world the leaven of justice, brotherhood, and the inalienable rights of all who are disinherited, rejected, or enslaved.[5]

In elements like these inherited from the Czech Reformers of different periods Hromádka finds stimulus and strength. He is not content, however, merely to look back. He finds rather that as Christ burst the bonds of the grave, so the living power of our forefathers in the faith refuses to be imprisoned in old orders, dogmas, and customs, but works in our present decisions and strengthens us in the performance of new tasks.[6]

A second major influence on Hromádka's development was the complex movement which rejected liberalism in favor of a theology centering in the authority of revelation. In 1931 he lamented that early twentieth-century theology was inclined to replace the basic themes of biblical thinking with "principles of the modern immanentist and idealistic, pantheistic world view" which identified God with cosmic law and the human mind.[7] Its methods and criteria failed to comprehend the prophetic and apostolic

[4] *Das Evangelium auf dem Wege zum Menschen,* pp. 278 f. Hereafter this book will be cited as *Das Evangelium.*

[5] *Von der Reformation zum Morgen* (Leipzig: Koehler und Amelang, 1959), pp. 304, 189 f. Hereafter this book will be cited as *Reformation zum Morgen.*

[6] *Ibid.,* pp. 297 f.

[7] *Christianity in Thought and Life,* p. 24. Quoted in "From the Works of J. L. Hromádka," *Communio Viatorum,* II (1959), 111.

message or to understand that man's whole existence stands under the judgment of God. Based on human religious experience, liberal thought in Germany prepared the way for the corrupt movement which substituted for divine law the autonomous laws of race and nation.[8] The cure for "relativism and spectatorship" Hromádka found in faith in the biblical God of the crisis theology, whose vertical challenge, uttered with absolute authority in Jesus Christ, cuts across the horizontal line of our human life, demanding here and now a personal, inescapable, life-and-death decision.[9]

Among the "masters of theology" who helped Hromádka to clarify such convictions the foremost was unquestionably Karl Barth. Hromádka's long letter to Barth is the opening essay in *Antwort,* the volume honoring Barth on his seventieth birthday. Here he testifies that he has been upheld in his work by new understandings which Barth achieved of the Word of God as event, the secret and miracle of God in the man Jesus Christ, the sovereignty and the all-embracing covenant of grace, and the unrepeatable, ever-new responsibility of the church of Christ in each particular historical situation.[10] These themes appear repeatedly in Hromádka's writings.

The Nature and Task of Theology

As a result of influences like these, Hromádka has reached convictions on the nature and purpose of theology which color all his views on specific issues.

1. Theology is an activity of the church, the community of those to whom God has made himself known and whom he has called to witness and service. Since it is founded on the redemptive Word of God incarnate in Jesus Christ, not on human ideas, it is the responsibility of the total fellowship of persons whom God has awakened to new life. The church is not an organization of "good and proper" people which stands apart from society. Rather it is in its essence the inner unity of those who share Christ's solidarity with man and amid human suffering and sin show what man can be through the victorious power of God.[11]

2. The task of the theologian is therefore to declare and interpret the ultimate truth committed to the church. His obligation is "to fix his

---

[8] *Doom and Resurrection* (Richmond, Va.: Madrus House, 1945), pp. 102, 90-93.

[9] *Ibid.,* pp. 90-92; Editorial, *Communio Viatorum,* IV (1961), 97.

[10] *Antwort,* ed. Ernst Wolf (Zürich-Zollikon: Evangelischer Verlag, 1956), p. 13.

[11] *Das Evangelium,* p. 266; *Theology Between Yesterday and Tomorrow,* p. 28 (this book will be referred to hereafter as *Theology*); "Aus den Schriften von J. L. Hromádka," *Communio Viatorum,* II (1959), 121; "The Responsibility and Hopes of a Theologian," *Communio Viatorum,* V (1962), 79 f.

gaze on the final and supreme reality, where the Lord of life and death himself inclines to man, and hark intensely and with concentration to the voice of the Word that was embodied in Jesus of Nazareth." [12]

3. In performing this task the theologian must make full use of the most critical and scientific methods of investigating the biblical writings which bear witness to the saving acts of God. He must be willing to sweep away the false conceptions with which traditionalism has covered over the scriptural testimony; for example, the belief in the infallibility of the Bible and inherited notions concerning the authorship and miraculous origin of the biblical books. Likewise, he will not be content simply to stand by the church's historic doctrinal formulations; instead, he will seek to thrust into their glowing center. A truly scientific procedure will free the church and its message from the dead hand of the past, and also guard the church against the negative consequences of scientific research pursued destructively. However, the critical work of the theologian must never be performed in a purely theoretical way, as an end in itself, but always in close contact with the fellowship of believers and as an indispensable aid to the fulfillment of their mission. [13]

4. The theologian pursues his studies not as an indifferent observer, but as one who is personally engaged in his inmost being. He is dealing with questions of life and death and the relation between history and eternity. Hence his scientific efforts must be linked with the personal struggle of faith. He cannot speak the Lord's Word of forgiveness and grace unless he himself is gripped, humbled, and exalted by it and concerned to make it known in all its clarity and creative power. [14]

5. Theology and the church it serves must therefore face with realism and understanding their involvement in the social, economic, and political revolution now taking place. The gospel concerns the objective acts of God in history; hence Christians must be alert to historical changes and their causes, appraise their significance in the light of the gospel, and identify themselves with the struggles of men for a fuller life. "The strength of genuine theology is measured by the courage to take sides." [15]

---

[12] "The Responsibility and Hopes of a Theologian," pp. 80 f.; *Reformation zum Morgen*, pp. 307 f.

[13] *Das Evangelium*, pp. 267 f.; "The Responsibility and Hopes of a Theologian," pp. 81-85.

[14] "The Responsibility and Hopes of a Theologian," p. 83.

[15] "Struggling for Tomorrow," *Christian Peace Conference*, III (March, 1963), 54; "The Responsibility and Hopes of a Theologian," pp. 85 f.; *Theology*, pp. 2-7; Editorial, *Communio Viatorum*, IV (1961), 1-4. These recent utterances echo statements of Hromádka published in an article in 1920 and in his book *Christianity in Thought and Life* (1931), quoted in "From the Works of J. L. Hromádka," *Communio Viatorum*, II (1959), 108, 110 f.

6. A living theology must be a pilgrim theology, an activity of those who are on the way in both life and thought. Dogmatics is not a completed system of unchangeable formulas; it is rather an unceasing search for the clearest and truest knowledge of the Word which confronts man in ever new situations. The truth disclosed in the biblical witness is eternal, but our knowledge is fragmentary, and the conditions we face are constantly changing. Therefore the theologian must always remain open to new insights, combining definiteness with readiness to learn anew and to improve his understanding.[16] Significantly, the theological journal which Hromádka edits is called *Communio Viatorum—Community of Pilgrims*.

Major Theological Emphases

The Knowledge of God

Hromádka asserts repeatedly the inability of man by his own efforts to gain any true knowledge of God. The biblical message is to be radically distinguished from all philosophical attempts to penetrate the riddles of human life. It speaks of one who is above and beyond everything we know, and therefore incomprehensible to even our best capacities.[17] The God of Christian faith is not a world idea or a moral law. No contemplation of the starry heavens, no meditation in the depths of the human soul, no artistic endeavor, and no works of mercy can bring him near.[18]

The God of the Gospel is with respect to man and the world incommensurable. The highest religious or philosophical thoughts do not touch even the edges of his being. He is something wholly other than all human and cosmic being together. He is inaccessible and uncontrollable intellectually as well as cultically or "religiously." [19]

Man's only way to the knowledge of God is that which God himself has opened. From above comes the voice of the Lord of glory and grace, who breaks through our history to manifest himself amid the ruins of our ideas and ideals. He addresses us and gives himself to us, calling for our total surrender in trust and obedience. Our only reliable testimony to his revela-

---

[16] *Das Evangelium*, pp. 265 f., 273 f.
[17] *Ibid.*, pp. 73 f.
[18] From an article published in a Czech evangelical weekly in October, 1924. "Aus den Schriften von J. L. Hromádka," *Communio Viatorum*, II (1959), 117.
[19] *Das Evangelium*, p. 75; cf. *Reformation zum Morgen*, p. 387; *Theology*, pp. 22-24.

tion is the biblical writings, which though subject to human imperfections are the vehicle of the superhuman, living Word.[20]

God's self-disclosure elicits a faith which by its very nature is cognitive, since it brings man into firsthand encounter with God. In this concrete act of knowledge the believing community plays an essential role. It is in the living congregation, through the witness of its members, that faith arises. Likewise it is the church alone that transmits the Scriptures which confront us with the testimony of prophets and apostles. Thus both subjectively and objectively the fellowship of the faithful is indispensable for the birth and growth of our knowledge of God.[21]

Moreover, the knowledge peculiar to faith is much more than rational awareness of theological truth. Such knowledge comes by an act of our whole existence—an act of obedience and of the imitation of Christ. "We can know God . . . only by *walking* the way which he himself has *walked* . . . , by participating in his work, by being committed with our whole human being to the service of man, for whom God himself became man and suffered death." [22] Therefore theologians dare not be content with speaking *about* God or redemption; they must be personally involved. Empowered by the Crucified One they must join with their fellow Christians in living their faith amid the struggles of men in the world.[23]

From the perspective of the gospel we can understand and respect the philosophical attempts of man to discover the meaning of human life. Such endeavors are "in the hands and under the guidance of the gracious providence of God." Each human being is obligated to join other men in seeking truth, justice, and beauty. The ultimate truth, the Word which was made flesh in Jesus, is on another plane than terrestrial truth; it comes as a gift of grace by God's intervention from above. However, it is at the same time an appeal to man to devote himself to the service of his neighbor with his philosophy and his science, his technology and every other ability. The gospel does not negate but illuminates man's search for truth. It

in no sense treats the question of truth as trifling; on the contrary, it leads man also in the search for earthly truth to deeper responsibility, more steadfast honesty, and greater courage. If you are a philosopher, be a serious philosopher! If you are a scientist, be a fearless and conscientious scientist.[24]

---

[20] "Natural Religion" (1929), in "Aus den Schriften von J. L. Hromádka," *Communio Viatorum*, II (1959), 115; *Theology*, pp. 15, 24 f., 33, 35 f.; *Das Evangelium*, pp. 34 f.

[21] *Das Evangelium*, pp. 34 f.

[22] *Ibid.*, p. 87.

[23] *Reformation zum Morgen*, p. 387.

[24] *Das Evangelium*, pp. 236 f.

Nevertheless, it is only in the faith called forth by the gospel that we can see the natural order as the creation of God or discern in its laws indications of his wisdom and power. In an early essay Hromádka goes so far as to say that "natural knowledge" of God is the "outer court" of the temple. Yet he quickly adds that "only the true temple of theology imparts to this knowledge the character of the temple's outer court." [25]

The Lordship of Christ

Since for Hromádka saving knowledge of God comes only through God's revelatory action culminating in Jesus Christ, Christology is the center of theology.[26] The main theme of the Bible from Genesis to Revelation is the gospel—the announcement that the holy and gracious God has entered redemptively into the depths of human existence. The message of the creation of the world and man is part of this message of joy. The history of Abraham, Isaac, and Jacob, of the deliverance from Egypt, and of Israel's wandering through the wilderness to the promised land is the gospel of the marvelous deeds of God amid human guilt, weakness, unbelief, and death. This good news reaches its climax in the coming of Christ, where God becomes man, takes on himself man's suffering, sin, and finitude, and opens the way to his salvation. "Our God is the God as we know him through the Incarnation, the Cross and the victory of Jesus of Nazareth." [27]

Hromádka rejects all adoptionist or purely symbolic interpretations of the incarnation. "Jesus Christ," he declares, "is not only the Son of God but God the Son." [28] Demythologization is needed, but it must not reduce the gospel to an occurrence in man's self-consciousness. The biblical witness demands personal decision, but it involves far more than an inward act of belief. It is the answer to the objective action of God in history. The incarnation, crucifixion, descent into hell, and resurrection of Jesus Christ are nonmaterial realities discernible only to faith, but they are objectively real, nonetheless.[29]

[25] "Natural Religion," *Yearbook* of the Hus Faculty of Theology, 1929, p. 198.

[26] Editorial, *Communio Viatorum,* V (1962), 1-4; *Das Evangelium,* pp. 73, 123, 276 f.; *Kirche und Theologie im Umbruch der Gegenwart* (Hamburg-Bergstedt: Herbert Reich Evangelischer Verlag, 1961), p. 88. The last mentioned work will be cited hereafter as *Kirche und Theologie.*

[27] *Das Evangelium,* pp. 6 f., 76, 97; Editorial, *Communio Viatorum,* IV (1961), 99.

[28] Interview with Donald Grey Barnhouse, *Eternity,* September, 1954, p. 6.

[29] "Was heisst Herrschaft Christi heute?" *Unter der Herrschaft Christi,* ed. Ernst Wolf (München: Chr. Kaiser Verlag, 1961), p. 58. This work will be cited hereafter as *Herrschaft Christi.*

Moreover, the events which center in the incarnation are a demonstration of the lordship of Christ, the deepest dimension of which can be grasped only in a cosmic perspective (John 1:1, 10 f.; Col. 1:16-20; Heb. 1:1-3). The whole world is created by and grounded in him, and man himself can be understood only in the light of his rule. "The lordship of Christ, which means the same as the power of holy love and self-sacrificing grace, is the primary datum of human existence." It is not limited to those who believe in him, and it is not connected with any religious, ideological, cultural, or social-political system. The gospel itself recognizes the widespread rejection of his authority even while asserting it: "The whole world was made through him, yet the world knew him not. He came to his own home, and his own people received him not" (John 1:10, 11). Until his return his reign is manifest mainly on the level of sinful humanity, which stands under judgment. Nevertheless, no ignorance or denial overthrows it. He is present in his kingly rule both among his followers and in the world at large, whether or not he is acknowledged or accepted.[30]

In Hromádka's view the primary significance of Jesus Christ is found in his redemptive work. He therefore says relatively little about the person of Christ, but much regarding his atoning death and victorious resurrection. In fact, with Melanchthon he declares that the secret of Christ's person lies in his work. Jesus Christ is above all else Reconciler, who through his life, suffering, and death canceled the prescriptive law and tore down the wall of hostility which separated God and man. He "breaks through all that has come between God and man, man and man, in order to bring men again to the place where God in his holy love wills to live in fellowship with them." He descends into the guilt and transitoriness of human life in order to perform there the work of deliverance and renewal and open the way to life eternal.[31]

Here, too, Hromádka insists that Christian faith is concerned with objective reality. The proclamation of the cross and the resurrection is not myth, legend, or symbol. Rather it has to do with the reality of the love of God, who seeks men out even in their weakness and despair, and who conquers death by enduring its curse himself. The entire world is the realm of his redemptive action.[32]

---

[30] *Ibid.*, pp. 60 f.; *Das Evangelium*, p. 92.

[31] *Das Evangelium*, p. 127, 168; *Theology*, p. 39.

[32] *Das Evangelium*, pp. 34, 53, 75, 176; Editorial, *Communio Viatorum*, V (1962), 2.

Man and Society

Hromádka's christocentric approach to theology provides the clue to his views concerning man and society. Only in the light of Jesus of Nazareth can we rightly understand the nature and destiny of man. The incarnation is God's coming to man; when God speaks he speaks to man. Therefore, when we speak of the Word of God we are speaking simultaneously of man. Pilate's ironic words "Ecce homo" were spoken of Jesus himself; at the same time they express effectively the apostolic understanding of man. In the gospel of one who was both truly God and truly man we perceive the dignity and final destiny of man as well as his misery and corruption.[33]

The incarnation is also our ultimate basis of concern for society. The Word made flesh is the point of intersection "where the Lord of Glory broke (and continually breaks) through the horizontal line of human life." Hence no believer in Jesus Christ may pursue the spiritual life in separation from the world. Earthly society is the sphere of the creative and redemptive activity of God himself. To come to God is therefore to find ourselves instantly in the presence of men, and we cannot rightly love him unless we love those to whom he has given himself in infinite love. "Every man is of our concern, and every man, believer and unbeliever, decent or living in degradation, healthy or leper, righteous or unrighteous, church-goer or prodigal is to us equally dear." [34]

Moreover, love for those whom God loves leads to concrete action for a better social order. Every aspect of human life is related to the purpose of the God who in Christ became man. Hence there is no basis for separating the "orders of creation" in which law is presumably operative from a higher realm where the gospel holds sway. The gospel is not law, and it should not become the blueprint for a program of social action. However, Christ is Lord over all our life on earth, and his lordship both commands and releases us to act in repentant obedience and love to free man both inwardly and outwardly, even in those difficult areas which seem far removed from Christ and the essence of the church.[35]

The gospel declares not only the boundless love of God made flesh, but also his purpose to found in this world the kingdom of God as an enduring

---

[33] Editorial, *Communio Viatorum*, V (1962), 3; *Reformation zum Morgen*, 369; *Das Evangelium*, pp. 120-26.

[34] *Theology*, pp. 92 f.; *Das Evangelium*, p. 249; *Reformation zum Morgen*, pp. 364 f.; Editorial, *Communio Viatorum*, IV (1961), 99.

[35] Editorial, *Communio Viatorum*, V (1962), 3 f.; *Reformation zum Morgen*, pp. 376-78; *Herrschaft Christi*, p. 58.

covenant-fellowship between God and man. Therefore, the more vigorous our faith in Christ, the more responsible we become in our attitude toward the "profane" world, and the more we are called upon to adjust our individual and social life to what we ought to be and do "in the light of the prophetic and apostolic Word." [36]

The Church

A direct result of the incarnation is the church, "a fellowship of men who have been called out of the world by the sovereign Word of God, who have been made sons and servants of the Lord, who together in prayer, singing, and listening to the Word . . . continually renew, in the presence of the Crucified and Risen, their pledges of obedience and loyalty." [37]

The church's mission is the proclamation of the gospel through witness (*kerygma*), fellowship (*koinonia*), and service (*diakonia*). It is entrusted with a *message* of forgiveness and commandment which it is responsible for transmitting undiluted by the preferences of men. It demonstrates the divine entrance into human life in a *community* which transcends all differences of race, sex, nationality, class, culture, and ability. As a company of *servants* it follows its Lord in identifying itself self-forgetfully with sinful men. More traditionally, the functions of the church correspond to the prophetic, priestly, and kingly offices of Christ. It preaches the Word which, prefigured in the prophets of the Old Testament, is consummated in Jesus Christ; it points to the cross of Christ by losing itself in behalf of sinners; and it proclaims joyfully the victory and the kingship of Christ in all of human life and in the whole of reality.[38]

In Hromádka's view, if the church is to be true to its mission in our day it must meet several quite specific conditions.

1. It must rise above all divisions of class, race, nationality, and political power blocs. By its proclamation of forgiveness and deliverance and its witness of unconditioned serving love, the church opens the way of reconciliation between man and man. It must accept a full share of "responsibility for the just ordering of human society—for law and justice, for the overcoming of differences between white and black, rich and poor, the powerful and the suppressed, the well-to-do and the multitudes who are still dying in misery, ignorance, and humiliation." However, it pursues these ends on a profounder level than any other group. While supporting the

[36] *Das Evangelium*, p .171; *Theology*, pp. 94 f.
[37] *Theology*, p. 39.
[38] *Theology*, pp. 30-32; *Reformation zum Morgen*, pp. 303, 357, 371-74.

struggles of men for justice and beauty, it seeks to awaken in them a longing for the deeper justice and beauty without which a genuinely good
society is impossible. Even in the most perfect social order it will still be
necessary to strive for the soul of man—for the purity of his conscience
and for true love.[39]

The responsibility of the church to transcend all boundaries is especially
urgent in today's international situation, when much of mankind is divided
into two hostile camps. The saving work of Christ was performed for the
reconciliation of all men. Hence a truly ecumenical church—the whole
household of God in the whole world—should seek the reconciliation of
opposing blocs, not the defeat of one by the other. It should oppose both
the position which makes the individual subservient to the state, and the
policy which allows to individualism complete license and fails to check
the evil dimensions of human egoism. Its path of renewal is that of
obedience to Christ in solidarity with weak and sinful men, in East and
West alike.[40] "What really matters is that we help one another. . . . Our
present struggle and mission goes beyond any curtain, be it iron, bamboo,
or golden, and beyond any secular or religious ideology."[41]

2. The church must also reach out continually beyond its own organized
life to proclaim the gospel of reconciliation and righteousness *in the world*.
The mission of Jesus extended far beyond the confines of the temple and
institutional religion; so must that of the church which truly proclaims
him.[42] Its message cannot be restricted to "religious" gatherings, but directly concerns all of the ordinary relations of men—in state, school,
science, industry, agriculture, and elsewhere. The lives of the members
are closely intermeshed with those of other men. Hence it teaches and
strengthens them to perform at their places of daily work the service to
which Christ has called them.

When Christians seek new paths and structures for men's social life they
do so within the kingdom of their Lord. That kingdom knows no limits.
The Christian community therefore has the whole world as its parish, and
it must vigorously bear its witness in "worldly" affairs as well as in the
literal preaching of the gospel, seeking to arouse the consciences of men

[39] *Das Evangelium*, pp. 236-39; *Kirche und Theologie*, p. 28.
[40] *Kirche und Theologie, passim; Sprung über die Mauer* (Berlin: Käthe Vogt Verlag, 1961), pp.
131, 140 f. This book will be cited hereafter as *Sprung*.
[41] *Theology*, p. 61.
[42] Editorial, *Communio Viatorum*, V (1962), 2.

and to guide all human endeavors toward worthy goals.[43] This very effort, however, makes us painfully aware that we cannot pass judgment on the world without first passing judgment on ourselves. "The world is within us, inseparable from our life." We cannot speak a prophetic message to the world unless we take its sins and failures on ourselves.[44]

3. The church is a congregation of pilgrims; it is always on the way, and as it moves forward the scenery is constantly changing. At all stages it must proclaim the same gospel and witness to the same Lord, but in ever new situations which impose new demands. It must therefore free itself from inherited customs, prejudices, and petrified forms in order to understand the *living* Word of God and to offer fresh food and drink to men who are living, struggling, and dying *today*. Such a church is nowhere at home. It can never settle down comfortably in any social, political, or ecclesiastical status quo. It is always preliminary, pointing beyond itself to its Lord. Yet when it yields unlimited obedience to him rather than seeking to absolutize itself, it is everywhere at home. Even in dangerous revolutionary circumstances, when long-familiar institutions are cast aside and nothing seems secure, it knows that its sovereign Lord continually creates new opportunities, and it therefore faces present and future with open eyes and does its work in faith and joy.[45]

Eschatology

Hromádka's commitment to the struggle for justice on earth is matched by the vigor of his eschatological hope. In his view the Christian, while seriously concerned about the affairs of this world, always sees them in a transhistorical perspective. "Christian civilization" is an illusion, and efforts in its name to combat so-called unchristian social and political ideals are for the church a dangerous self-deception. The new heaven and earth expected by Christian faith will be wrought not by men, but by the mercy and righteousness of God. Our hope is in the final victory of Christ. However, this hope does not lead to acceptance of the status quo and a passive waiting for the end, but provides strength for our struggles here and now. Sustained by it the soldiers of Christ march forward, knowing that tomorrow is in the hands of the Suffering Servant who is not only crucified but risen. They are sustained by one who constantly acts in "judgment and

[43] *Theology*, pp. 40-44; *Reformation zum Morgen*, pp. 325 f., 377; *Das Evangelium*, pp. 28, 180; *Kirche und Theologie*, pp. 68, 80; and a 1933 article quoted in *Communio Viatorum*, II (1959), 121.
[44] *Theology*, pp. 42 f.
[45] *Kirche und Theologie*, p. 30; *Theology*, pp. 44 f., 64 f.; *Reformation zum Morgen*, p. 305; Editorial, *Communio Viatorum*, IV (1961), 2 f.; *Das Evangelium*, p. 68.

grace, authority and freedom, wrath and inexpressible love," and whose triumph will be complete at the end of history. "He is our Companion in doom. He is the Lord of the resurrection. With him we can leap over all walls." [46]

Christianity and Communism

Repeatedly Hromádka points out the tragic failure of the church to be true to its nature and mission. Marked by a self-righteous middle-class mentality, the majority of its members have failed to sympathize with the desperate need of working people and their aspiration for economic justice. They have comprehended neither the depth of the convulsion which has taken place in recent decades nor the degree of their own guilt and responsibility. Large numbers of Christians, having absorbed the spirit of anticommunism so prevalent in western society, identify Christianity with liberal democratic philosophy and politics, and thereby block the reconciling work of Christ. Moreover, they are blinding themselves to the most dangerous enemy of the gospel today—the materialistic humanism which dominates West as well as East.[47]

The events of the past half-century have produced a radically changed political situation. Two developments are especially important. First, the nominally Christian liberal democracies of the West no longer exercise undisputed international leadership. After World War I they failed to utilize their opportunity to organize the world on sound social foundations. As a result, socialist and communist countries, and more recently new African and Asian nations, are playing decisive roles, and a vastly different social order is in the making which the West cannot control.[48] Secondly, the long centuries of "Constantinian Christianity" have come to an end. In many lands, both eastern and western, the churches can no longer rely on the friendly protection of the state, but confront instead either hostility or indifference in the political order. We cannot speak today of "Christian peoples"; even the nations where Christianity is strongest are themselves mission fields. Political and economic leadership is often in the hands of persons who, if not openly atheistic, are beyond the effective influence of the churches.[49]

[46] *Theology*, pp. 31 f., 58, 105 f.; *Kirche und Theologie*, p. 76; *Sprung*, p. 141.

[47] *Sprung*, pp. 136 f.; *Theology*, p. 51; *Reformation zum Morgen*, pp. 314-27; *Kirche und Theologie*, pp. 13-14, 78, and *passim*.

[48] *Reformation zum Morgen*, pp. 311-23; Editorial, *Communio Viatorum*, IV (1961), 3; "Struggling for Tomorrow," *Christian Peace Conference*, III (March, 1963), 55.

[49] *Reformation zum Morgen*, pp. 323-25; *Theology*, pp. 88 f.; *Sprung*, p. 138; *Das Evangelium*, p. 279.

Since Marxian communism is the most powerful competitor of traditional democracy, Hromádka believes that Christians must bend every effort to understand it and its relation to Christian faith. He calls attention to four features of communist ideology which deserve commendation. (1) The fundamental goals of Marxism are the elimination of human exploitation, special privilege, and class differences; the conquest of poverty, hunger, and misery; and the attainment of a classless society in which men can live in justice, freedom, and dignity. Such ends are in basic accord with the biblical message. Unfortunately they have often been sought by violent means, which can be justified *only* on the ground that they are necessary in given historical circumstances to remove the old quickly so that the new which they serve may not be annihilated in its beginnings. (2) At heart the atheism of dialectical materialism is a positive assertion of the worth of man's life on earth, as against belief in a god falsely conceived as having no interest in social righteousness. Such atheism actually has much in common with the prophetic strain in Hebrew-Christian faith. Christian churches themselves are partly responsible for the misunderstanding which character-izes it. (3) Marxist social philosophy recognizes the organic community of men, instead of isolating the individual from society, as does liberal democracy. (4) It rightly perceives that merely political freedom without material safeguards and social equality may only deepen the disparity be-tween rich and poor and fail to provide the prerequisites of true dignity and freedom.[50]

Hromádka also offers some incisive negative criticisms of communism. (1) In its efforts to free men from oppression, it has frequently resorted to extreme and brutal measures. (2) Its radical historicism treats man merely as the product of a continuous process of natural and historical de-velopment. This fails to do justice to the true nature of man as a responsible, moral, creative being, able to affect his environment and influence the course of history. (3) Its atheism is shallow, sterile, and outmoded, not having advanced beyond Feuerbach and the nineteenth-century free-thinkers. It has failed to plumb the spiritual depth of human life or to understand the dynamic faith of the Hebrew prophets and the gospel. (4) Communism fails to probe beneath social and economic conditions to the real root of human misery in the radical sinfulness of man himself. In contrast, the biblical witness realistically recognizes the depths of man's responsibility without denying the urgency of his struggle for social change.

[50] *Reformation zum Morgen*, pp. 369 f.; *Theology*, pp. 74-84; *Sprung*, p. 136.

(5) There is in a "classless society" no redeeming power capable of solving all moral and social problems. Such a society will still be made up of selfish, sinful, corruptible men, and will desperately need the Christian message of the forgiving grace and reconciling love of God.[51]

How, then, should Christians proceed in their practical confrontation with communism? Hromádka's writings offer several guidelines.

1. We must not consider Christian theology to be in the same frame of reference as, and therefore in competition with, Marxist ideology. It functions on a different level from all human ideologies and political systems, and therefore does not identify itself with any. Originating in the Word of God, it seeks to understand human life and history in the light of God's living Word and action. Our mission, therefore, is not to oppose a Christian ideology to a communist ideology, but to arouse faith and obedience to the living God. This does not require us to accept the communist revolution without reserve or criticism, or to adjust our faith and thought to the ideology under which a new social structure is arising. It does demand that in all situations we proclaim the gospel of Christ as the only answer to man's deepest needs. Inevitably this will sometimes involve struggle with communism and its claims. However, if there is genuine mutual understanding the controversy can be creative.[52]

2. Christians must therefore endeavor to understand Communists and to help them toward the attainment of worthy goals. While rejecting the Marxist interpretation of human life as a by-product of nature and history, we must take seriously the *man* behind the ideology and recognize the genuineness and validity of his concern for justice. In some circumstances a state led by atheists may seek ends which are closer to the righteous purposes of the real God than are the reactionary social attitudes and the self-righteous indifference to justice which typify many traditional churches. Christians living under a Communist government must therefore bear a positive and critical witness marked by loving understanding of those who are responsible for the rebuilding of society. Sometimes it may even be necessary for them in the name of Christ to support atheists in preference to formally "Christian" political leaders.[53]

[51] *Theology*, pp. 74 f., 78-87; *Kirche und Theologie*, pp. 85-87; *Das Evangelium*, p. 238.
[52] *Kirche und Theologie*, p. 17; *Theology*, pp. 67, 80, 83 f.; *Reformation zum Morgen*, p. 311; cf. pp. 318, 351, 367-71.
[53] *Kirche und Theologie*, 19, 84; *Reformation zum Morgen*, p. 367; *Theology*, pp. 68 f., 83 f.; *Evangelium für Atheisten* (*Unterwegs*, eine evangelische Zeitbuchreihe, 6. Berlin: Käthe Vogt Verlag, 1960), pp. 46 f.; "Comenius Faculty—Task and Aims," *Communio Viatorum*, III (1960), 208.

3. The church must in its witness transcend the divisions between East and West and minister to people on both sides. Christians must refuse to allow their activities to be determined by political, economic, and ideological antagonisms. The only real dividing line runs not between Communists and non-Communists, but between the Lord of history and human sinners. The task of the church in East and West alike is therefore to proclaim the gospel of Christ to sinful men. The methods of proclamation permitted in communist lands may be very limited, but by every means at their disposal Christians must witness in love to the truth of Christ, minister in his name to the material and spiritual needs of their fellow men, and demonstrate in life the meaning of their faith, which is something quite other than that which Marxists picture as religious.[54] Only so can they fill men's deepest hunger and thirst and save them from the dangers to which merely external change would lead. At the same time, Christians in the West must strive to understand the efforts of their brethren in communist lands to relate themselves constructively to the societies in which they live. Both groups must work to advance ecumenical Christian fellowship.[55]

4. Christians must refuse to support the anticommunism so rampant in our time. This movement has furthered a false, negative, and sterile view of the new society being constructed; it has blinded Christians to the real meaning of the gospel, deepened their self-conceit, and barred the way to self-knowledge and repentance; and it has prevented the ecumenical Christian community from comprehending its spiritual task, from understanding the aspirations of multitudes of people, and from helping millions of Communists to perceive the depth and majesty of the gospel. Instead of entertaining vain hopes for a reversal of history, Christians should take a positive though critical attitude toward the new developments.[56]

Critique

Critical attention might profitably be devoted to Hromádka's Christocentrism, his belief in both the providential guidance of the philosophical quest and the complete inaccessibility of God to human thought, his in-

---

[54] In an interview during the Evanston Assembly of the World Council of Churches, Hromádka declared, "Christ demands of me that I live among Communists. . . . I love them as individuals, and I want to represent Christ to them." Donald Grey Barnhouse, "Hromádka . . . Red Stooge," *Eternity*, September, 1954, p. 7.

[55] "The Crisis of Ecumenical Fellowship," *Christian Advocate*, January 7, 1960, p. 12; *Theology*, pp. 86 f.; *Evangelium für Atheisten*, pp. 42-49.

[56] *Theology*, pp. 66-70; *Kirche und Theologie*, pp. 14, 21.

carnational anthropology, his maintenance of the objective reality of God's redemptive action, his conception of the church, and his pilgrim theology. However, issues similar to most of these have already been discussed in connection with the views of Barth and Diem, and will be considered again in later chapters. It therefore seems wise to concentrate now on the problems raised with peculiar urgency by Hromádka—those concerning the relation between Christianity and communism.

At the outset it is important to note that Hromádka's attitude toward communism and his conception of his role as a Christian in a communist country, though influenced strongly by social factors, grow directly out of his incarnational theology. We have noticed, for example, his central stress on the present lordship of Christ—the power of God's holy love and self-sacrificing grace—and the promise of his final victory; his conviction that God is working creatively and redemptively in earthly society; and his view of the church as a pilgrim community with a reconciling mission, finding new opportunities in every new historical situation. These and related beliefs find expression in Hromádka's conception of the function of the Christian and the church in a communist society.

Several important aspects of his analysis deserve the unqualified approval of socially sensitive Christians. Such features include: (1) his insistence that a large share of responsibility for communistic revolutions must be borne by otherworldly churches which have been indifferent to the sufferings of exploited people; (2) his conviction that revolutionary events in history for the most part exhibit the judgment and the grace of God; (3) his awareness that some of the basic social ends of Marxism are cherished also by prophetic Hebrew-Christian faith; (4) his clear recognition of the dominance of materialistic humanism in *both* East and West, with Christian standards openly opposed in one case and verbally honored while subtly rejected or ignored in the other; (5) his appeal to Christians to transcend political and ideological discussions in a genuine ecumenical fellowship; and (6) his demand for the withdrawal of Christian support for anticommunist crusades.

At several other points Hromádka's position arouses a mixed response. 1. The incommensurability between Christian theology and Marxist and other "ideologies" is hardly so great as he insists. It is true that the gospel of the saving act of God in Jesus Christ places theology on a very different foundation from that of Marxism. It is equally true that the Christian view of man and society is not identifiable with any political or economic system, but relevant to man's situation in all systems. Yet in two respects Christianity and Marxism do operate in the same universe of discourse. First, both make claims regarding the ultimate character of reality, and Christian theology cannot avoid the task of exposing the falsity of dialectical materialism and its corollary, historical-economic determinism. Secondly, in affirming its own social responsibility faith is confronted with some of the same ethical and social questions as those dealt with by Marxist thought, and its answers inevitably bring it into relations of agreement or opposition with the Communists.

Hromádka nowhere deals fundamentally with these areas of confrontation. He does agree in principle that the positive proclamation and interpretation of the gospel lead inevitably to conflict with some communist claims. He also points out some of the serious errors or inadequacies in communist thought, such as its view of man as a product of natural and historical development, its failure to recognize man's radical sinfulness, its atheism, and its lack of truly redemptive power. However, he does not undertake any thorough critique, from the standpoint of Christian theology, of either the metaphysics or the social and ethical theory of Marxism. The omission is regrettable. Such an appraisal by a theologian as competent as Hromádka from within a communist society would be peculiarly valuable to Christians in both East and West.

The absence in Hromádka of a thorough theological critique of communist theory may be due in part to his belief that the two levels of operation of theology and communist ideology render such analysis unnecessary. It may also be attributable partly to the inhibitions to free criticism which are inherent in any totalitarian order. Still more important is Hromádka's belief in the responsibility of the Christian theologian to identify himself with the struggles of men for a better life. This includes "the courage to take sides." The Christian is required to witness and work in the place where he lives and on the side closest to his deepest commitments, challenging his society not wholesale and indiscriminately, but discriminatingly from within. To oppose communism *in toto* would mean to flee the responsibility of witness; on the contrary, to accept the socialist revolution as accomplished fact and the post-Constantinian status of the church as both a fact and a value entails working for modification rather than overthrow. The conscientious theologian may understandably feel that thought and action so directed represent for him a wiser use of time and energy than major attention to comprehensive theoretical criticism.

2. Further problems are raised by Hromádka's views on the freedom of the church in Communist countries. Western churches, he notes, ask

whether the churches in the East are permitted to maintain worship, to educate their youth, and to exercise a prophetic ministry by criticizing the state or the social order. In his view, though such questions may be relatively legitimate, they concern chiefly the external preservation of the existing church, they reflect a certain self-satisfaction and traditional stereotypes in those who ask them, and they miss the real danger confronting today's churches. That danger is within, in the attitudes of Christians themselves. Though the church has done much good, it has failed to see behind the so-called atheism of our time the deep longing of men for a justice and a freedom exceeding anything attained under earlier social-political forms. It has failed to minister to the whole man, in his spiritual and material hunger, his inner and outer needs. But if it is moved by its awareness of the fullness of the gospel to carry on such a ministry, it need not fear for its own future. Its real strength lies in its solidarity with humanity, not in its freedom to preach the gospel in words.

Certainly the church which seeks only its own perpetuation is unworthy of its Lord, and doomed to failure. But Hromádka's contrast between the inward and the outward, between witness in word and demonstration in act, is overdrawn. How can the church minister most effectively to the whole man if it is not free to evangelize, instruct the young, and deal forthrightly with the ills of society? How can it carry out its mission most fully if its members, present or prospective, are threatened with the denial of university admission or job opportunities and promotions? The freedom which Hromádka dismisses as outward is important for both the proclamation of the gospel and the interpretation of its meaning for social life, including those situations where injustice is perpetrated in the name of justice.

3. Hromádka has said relatively little in criticism of communist demands for total allegiance, stifling of dissent, police methods, and brutal suppression of opposition. Though he has on occasion decried the resort to violent measures, such utterances occur only rarely. The question readily arises: How can these limited public expressions be reconciled with acceptance of the lordship of Christ over all of life? Objectively such reconciliation seems impossible. However, a fair-minded weighing of the issues requires recognition of the difference between the circumstances confronting Christians in totalitarian lands and those obtaining in the western democracies. In America any Christian or church agency is officially free to criticize openly any governmental policy. In a communist-controlled society, on the contrary, verbal criticism publicly expressed may be futile,

and it may be interpreted by those in power as politically rather than religiously motivated. Much direct criticism would probably produce even more drastic restrictions on church activity than those already prevailing. In this situation Hromádka has sought other ways of registering his convictions. For example, he has access to men in important government posts, and frequently goes personally to individual officials in behalf of specific persons or concerns—a method which in Czechoslovakia is doubtless more effective, if less dramatic, than public attack. Indeed, Hromádka would jeopardize this relationship if he publicized his use of it or substituted public criticism.

Hromádka is first and foremost a Christian committed to bearing his witness in his homeland and to serving his people in the name of Christ. He may be acting on the recognition, conscious or unconscious, that the careful exercise of restraint in public utterance is the price of his being free to preach and teach at all. Christians in the West may disagree with his choice, but they can hardly fail to acknowledge that he is facing with active faith the reality of history as it confronts him.

Section II: Theologies of Existence

4. RUDOLF BULTMANN

About the end of World War I, in company with other dialectical theologians,[1] Rudolf Bultmann rejected the tendency of his liberal heritage to treat Christian faith mainly as a phenomenon of the history of religion. Instead, he and his colleagues interpreted faith as man's answer to the Word of the transcendent God encountered in Jesus Christ. However, he was never satisfied with a simple condemnation of liberalism, and in all his exegetical labors he has sought vigorously to carry forward the tradition of historical-critical research. This appears alike in his important early contributions to form criticism and in his later insistence on demythologizing the New Testament writings.

Increasingly, however, Bultmann came under the influence of existentialist philosophy, especially through his discussions in the mid-twenties with Martin Heidegger, and this orientation became for him decisive, providing the "conceptuality" which makes it possible to speak adequately of the existence of the believer. During the years when Barth was casting off ex-

[1] Notably Karl Barth, Emil Brunner, Friedrich Gogarten, and Eduard Thurneysen.

istentialist influence, Bultmann was seeking a closer connection between the gospel and man's existence today. The resulting opposition highlights one of the major divergences in Continental theology today.

The Gospel and Human Existence

Impressed by the early Heidegger's portrayal of man as "thrown" into the anxiety, finitude, and mortality which constitute the predicament of his existence, Bultmann makes the questions thus raised his avenue of approach in interpreting the Scriptures, and finds in the New Testament message the decisive answers. In his view, however, the response of Christian faith can be discovered and validated only when the New Testament proclamation is "demythologized," that is, when it is divested of the pre-scientific first-century imagery in which it is cast—in particular the dualistic conceptions of Jewish apocalyptic and the gnostic myth of redemption. Concepts such as the three-story universe; miracles; angels and demons; the preexistence, virgin birth, resurrection, ascension, and substitutionary sacrifice of Jesus; original sin as inherited corruption; and the end of world history through the return of Christ must be reinterpreted if their real meaning is to become clear.

Previous efforts to do this, such as allegorical interpretation and the early liberal search for essential religious and ethical foundations or eternal and universally valid truths, have failed. They remove from the New Testament its kerygma-character, and fail to recognize that these writings have to do with a decisive action of God which is proclaimed as bringing salvation to men. We must therefore go behind the objectifying and externalizing representations of the New Testament mythologies and interpret them existentially, in terms of the understanding of existence which they reflect. When we do this we discover the declaration that in the event of Jesus Christ God has spoken his forgiving Word, which discloses to men the meaning of authentic existence and challenges them to decision. So presented, the New Testament proclamation confronts also the man of today, who thinks not mythologically but scientifically, with the possibility of self-understanding and a demand for the personal decision which may transform his life.[2]

Rightly interpreted the New Testament is not primarily *Historie*, an objective, impersonal, factual account of past events. Rather it is concerned

---

[2] "New Testament and Mythology," *Kerygma and Myth, a Theological Debate,* ed. Hans Werner Bartsch, tr. Reginald H. Fuller (New York: Harper & Brothers, 1961), pp. 9-16.

centrally with history in the sense of *Geschichte,* the meaning, significance, or intentionality of events for the persons who encounter them. In speaking of the incarnation, Christian faith presupposes certain objectively historical (*historisch*) occurrences, but overwhelmingly it focuses attention on the personally or existentially historical (*geschichtlich*) event in which the human individual is addressed by God and confronted with the demand to turn from unauthentic to authentic existence.

Like modern abstract art Bultmann is interested in the personal meanings involved in human statements about reality, not in objects or facts "out there." Truly seen, existence in his view is always the existence of someone for whom it is "my existence." Moreover, I cannot really speak *about* my existence, but only *from* it, or on the basis of it.[3] Truth must always be truth *pro me,* for me.

According to Bultmann's analysis of the structure of human existence, man exists in and through his decisions. "Existence is at any time *event* in the decisions of the moment. It is nothing abiding but that which happens again and again." [4] The "nature" of man is realized in his life acts, in the intentionality of the decisions which he makes ever anew, expressing his whole being. What we call personality

is not a substance behind the decisions, a substance in relation to which the concrete historical decisions are only accidents. My self-understanding as personality depends on my decisions, which may for the most part be unconscious, made without reflection. . . . The I is an ever-growing, ever-becoming, ever-increasing entity.[5]

Involved in a man's concrete decisions, both resulting from them and contributing to them, is his understanding of himself in the light of the possibilities of his life. The self-understanding is not a subjective conception of himself which arises through reflection on his existence; it is rather part and parcel of the act of existing. It is prephilosophical, concrete, ontic reality. Such self-understanding or existential understanding Bultmann calls *das Existentielle,* in distinction from the existentialist understanding of philosophical analysis which he labels *das Existentiale.*[6]

According as man understands himself one way or another, he exists either authentically or unauthentically. Unauthentic existence is the search

---

[3] *Glauben und Verstehen,* III (Tübingen: J. C. B. Mohr [Paul Siebeck], 1960), 120.
[4] *Ibid.,* p. 117.
[5] *History and Eschatology* (Edinburgh: The University Press, 1957), p. 146.
[6] *Jesus Christ and Mythology* (New York: Charles Scribner's Sons, 1958), p. 74.

for satisfaction and security in the realm of visible, tangible, measurable reality; trust in one's own achievements; bondage to the past. In contrast, authentic existence is the life based on unseen and intangible realities, the renunciation of all self-centered security, being in faith, free and responsible openness to the future.[7]

How does one reach the self-understanding which makes possible authentic existence? "Natural" man cannot accomplish this himself, either by "metaphysical inquiry or by moral effort." It comes only as he makes the free response of faith to God's gifts of grace proclaimed in the Christian kerygma. He finds his life by losing it. However, this statement is more than a general truth. Man "cannot say this word to himself, it must be said to him—always individually to you and to me." [8] The Christian message does not assert the idea of the grace of God, but addresses the individual and calls on him to receive the grace which frees him from himself.

Man's existential need prepares the way for this event, but cannot produce it. When men apart from revelation reach out toward God, the knowledge involved in their inquiry is initially knowledge concerning themselves and their finitude. Thus the concept of God as omnipotent reflects their awareness of their own powerlessness; their idea of God as a holy and demanding judge signifies their consciousness that they are not what they ought to be; and their talk of God's eternity and transcendence bespeaks a recognition of their own transitoriness. *"God is reckoned to be the power which breaks through this finitude of man and thereby raises him up to his real nature."* [9]

Christian belief confirms this knowledge; it too means by the term "God" the power which frees man from finitude. However, it asserts that this liberation occurs only through the revelatory action of God. Solely on this basis is man given a knowledge which is not merely about man, involving simply a *concept* of God, but about God himself. Our relation to nature and history makes us aware of our creaturely limitations and our inability to deliver ourselves, thus undermining our self-assurance and providing no answer, but pointing us toward the attitude of faith which is our only way of receiving the revelation of God's forgiving grace in Christ. This disclosure illuminates and transforms our whole existence.[10]

[7] *Kerygma and Myth,* pp. 17-20.

[8] *History and Eschatology,* p. 151.

[9] *Essays Philosophical and Theological,* tr. James C. G. Grieg (New York: The Macmillan Company, 1955), pp. 94-98 (italics Bultmann's). This book will be cited hereafter as *Essays.*

[10] *Ibid.,* pp. 98-118.

For Bultmann, therefore, demythologizing the gospel message is really a radical application of the doctrine of justification by faith to the sphere of knowledge and thought. True faith abandons the longing for security based on objectifying knowledge along with the desire for security founded on good works. It is faith "nevertheless" or "in spite of," as in Ps. 73:23. God encountered as acting is the transcendent and hidden God, not an object at man's disposal. We can believe in him "only in spite of experience, just as we can accept justification only in spite of conscience." But when we surrender all merely human security, we overcome the despair which the quest for it engenders, and are freed to become our true selves before God.[11]

The Christian preaching of the New Testament declares that God addresses men in the event of Jesus Christ, revealing his grace and calling them to decision. An affirmative response has three aspects: man embraces a new understanding of himself as free from himself and endowed with a new self by divine grace; he accepts the new life which is founded on the grace of God; and he decides on a new understanding of his responsible acting which sees it as born of love.[12]

Specifically, the salvation-event proclaimed by the New Testament is the cross of Christ. By the cross, however, Bultmann does not mean the objective (*historisch*) fact of the crucifixion of Jesus of Nazareth, but the personally historical (*geschichtlich*) faith-event which the primitive church related to the crucifixion. In its abiding meaning the cross is God's liberating judgment on man. In this sense Christ is crucified "for us." The cross has thus created a new situation in history. "The preaching of the cross as the event of redemption challenges all who hear it to appropriate this significance for themselves, to be willing to be crucified with Christ." To believe in the cross of Christ, therefore, does not mean to declare that God's offended honor has been satisfied or that the penalty he demands has been paid through some externally observable occurrence outside of us. Rather it means "to make the cross of Christ our own, to undergo crucifixion with him." [13] The cross is not simply an event of the past which can be contemplated from afar. In its meaning for faith it is an ever present, ever repeatable reality—for example in the sacraments and in the daily life of the Christian.

---

[11] *Jesus Christ and Mythology*, pp. 40, 83-85; cf. pp. 65 f., 72 f.; *Glauben und Verstehen*, III, 191 f.
[12] *History and Eschatology*, p. 152.
[13] *Kerygma and Myth*, pp. 36 f.

Inseparable from the cross is the resurrection, which is a further proclamation of the meaning of the cross rather than a miraculous external proof
that Jesus was the Son of God. It makes plain that Jesus' death is the
judgment and salvation of men, taking away the power of death. "Cross
and resurrection form a single indivisible cosmic event which brings judgment to the world and opens up for men the possibility of authentic life."
The resurrection is "the eschatological event *par excellence*," signifying the
newness of life now realized by those who in faith accept God's grace.
Like the cross, it is an occurrence of faith; indeed, *"faith in the resurrection
is really the same thing as faith in the saving efficacy of the cross."* We do
not base our belief in the cross on a prior belief in Christ; rather, belief
in Christ is equivalent to belief in the cross as the cross of Christ. "The
saving efficacy of the cross is not derived from the fact that it is the cross of
Christ; it is the cross of Christ because it has this saving efficacy." [14]

How, then, do we come to such faith? Through the proclamation of
the cross and the resurrection as the salvation-event. The word of Christian
preaching is not a *what,* but an event in which we meet Christ as crucified
and risen. Decisive for the concept *word* is not its content or its eternal
truth, but simply its being spoken.[15] In this word—and nowhere else—
Christ is manifested to us as both crucified and resurrected.

The real Easter faith is faith in the word of preaching which brings illumination. If the event of Easter Day is in any sense an historical event additional to
the event of the cross, it is nothing else than the rise of faith in the risen Lord,
since it was this faith which led to the apostolic preaching. . . . The historical event
of the rise of the Easter faith means for us what it meant for the first disciples—
namely, the self-manifestation of the risen Lord, the act of God in which the redemptive event of the cross is completed.

The preached word makes the cross and the resurrection repeatedly present
for all who hear. The twofold message calls men to faith and confronts
them with "the question whether they are willing to understand themselves
as men who are crucified and risen with Christ." [16]

So understood, Jesus Christ is the "eschatological event." For Bultmann,
however, this event is not the catastrophic end of cosmic history; it is instead the end of the old world of the believer. His "old man," torn by

[14] *Ibid.,* pp. 39-41.
[15] "Der Begriff des Wortes Gottes im Neuen Testament," *Glauben und Verstehen,* I (Tübingen:
J. C. B. Mohr [Paul Siebeck], 1954), 269.
[16] *Kerygma and Myth,* p. 42. Cf. II Cor. 6:2; Rom. 10:17; John 5:24-25.

anxiety, sin, and strife, has come to an end, renewed and transformed through his response to the action of God proclaimed in Christian preaching. He is now "a new man," a free man, a new creation, belonging to the world beyond this one. Beginning with the appearance of Jesus Christ, the eschatological event occurs again and again when preaching is answered by faith.[17]

"The Christian existence is eschatological. . . . It exists only in so far as it constantly presses beyond its limits." Eschatological existence is nonworldly existence within the world. Here *world* must be understood dialectically—personally and inwardly as well as cosmically. The old world is man himself under the power of his rebellion against God. The new world is that of the man portrayed in I Cor. 7:29-31, who lives in this present world with the attitude of *hos me* (as not)—as though he were not in it and had no dealings with it—and from this perspective is freed and obligated to serve to the world in love. It is the life of those who live no longer for themselves but for the Lord. Having renounced all claims of self and the security of things they are open to God's future.[18]

What it means to live eschatologically is simply and vividly described in the sermon on Luke 14:16-24 which Bultmann preached in the University Church in Marburg on June 22, 1941:

To be ready for God's call means just this—to be prepared to live in the conviction that our life of earthly work with its cares and projects, its sorrows and joys, is not the ultimate reality. What then is the essence of God's invitation? It is surely the call to a higher life, to a future life, to a life that lies beyond this world. It is the call to free ourselves from this world and to become centered in God's world.[19]

The Repudiation of Objectivity

Bultmann's existentialist interpretation of Jesus Christ inevitably raises two related questions having to do respectively with the issues of historical and metaphysical objectivity. First, what is the relation between Jesus Christ as the eschatological event and the actual earthly life of Jesus?

---

[17] *History and Eschatology*, pp. 151 f.; *Glauben und Verstehen*, III, 202-12.

[18] *Glauben und Verstehen*, III, 88, 165. Bultmann often cites the passage from I Corinthians. He also points out illuminatingly the parallelism between Gal. 6:15 ("For neither circumcision counts for anything, nor uncircumcision, but a new creation") and Gal. 5:6 ("For in Christ Jesus neither circumcision nor uncircumcision is of any avail, but faith working through love").

[19] *This World and the Beyond; Marburg Sermons*, tr. Harold Knight (London: Lutterworth Press, 1960), p. 152.

Secondly, to what degree does the faith-encounter produced by the kerygma shed light on the real nature of God?

According to Bultmann the fact of the earthly life of Jesus is a presupposition of the kerygma. Also there is a point of contact between Jesus' preaching and that of the primitive church. Bultmann's early work on Jesus (1926) portrays Jesus himself as proclaiming the word through which God's forgiveness becomes actualized in those addressed.[20] Thus both messages are existentially interpreted. However, Bultmann makes plain that the early church did not simply continue Jesus' preaching, but preached Jesus himself. In its proclamation the original proclaimer became the one proclaimed as God's decisive act for men.[21] Moreover, the preaching of the church leaves us in the dark regarding the kind of person Jesus was and what he taught. Exegesis can disclose to us the heart of the church's message, but it cannot and need not go further. The earliest kerygma included nothing of Jesus' own message. It proclaimed the *that*, but not the *what*, of Jesus. Even in the Synoptic Gospels, which are less reliable guides to the kerygma than John or Paul, the *what* is secondary.[22]

The coming of Jesus is actually misunderstood if it is treated as "an objectifiable historical phenomenon," [23] a past occurrence which can be studied by ordinary historical investigation. The data which might be gained by such research would at best fall far short of disclosing the real significance of the events examined.

This is the real paradox. Jesus is a human, historical person from Nazareth in Galilee. His work and destiny happened within world-history and as such come under the scrutiny of the historian who can understand them as part of the nexus of history. Nevertheless, such detached historical inquiry cannot become aware of what God has wrought in Christ, that is, of the eschatological event.[24]

Bultmann quotes with complete approval the statement of Erich Frank that "to the Christian the advent of Christ was not an event in that temporal process which we mean by history today," but "an event in the history of salvation," an eschatological moment in which profane history "came to its end." For Bultmann, therefore, Jesus Christ *comes* when he

---

[20] *Jesus* (Tübingen: J. C. B. Mohr [Paul Siebeck], [1926] 1951), p. 178.

[21] *Theology of the New Testament*, I, tr. Kendrick Grobel (New York: Charles Scribner's Sons, 1951), 33; cf. 34-53.

[22] *Ibid.*, pp. 3, 43, 300-306; *Das Verhältnis der urchristlichen Christusbotschaft zum historichen Jesus* (Heidelberg: Carl Winter-Universitätsverlag, 1960), p. 95.

[23] *Essays*, p. 288.

[24] *Jesus Christ and Mythology*, p. 80.

is encountered "in the Word of preaching at any given time." [25] This encounter can occur without knowledge of Jesus' earthly life, and no amount of information concerning that life can of itself bring it to pass. There is therefore no point in asking how the Christian kerygma arose historically. To do so would imply that information of this kind could establish its validity, and it would make faith in God's Word dependent on the outcome of historical research. In the word of preaching we are confronted with the Word of God. We have no occasion to question its credentials. Instead, we ourselves are questioned—asked whether we will believe or reject the word which offers us the self-understanding that saves us.

This brings us to the second question posed by the existentialist Christology. To interpret the event of Jesus Christ in terms of objective metaphysical reality is for Bultmann equally as impossible and misleading as to locate it merely in the past. The distinction between *Geschichte* and *Historie* has ontic as well as noetic implications. Just as we cannot characterize the continuing "nature" of the human personality which exists in its successive decisions and actions, so "we cannot speak of what God is in Himself but only of what He is doing to us and with us." I can speak of God only as he meets me in his Word. On this basis I can speak of him in fear and quaking, gratitude and trust. I can know his goodness not objectively but only in self-surrender, in the decision of faith. Even to speak of God as acting involves the events of our personal existence, not events which we perceive without ourselves being involved as acted upon. To say that God acts means that "we are confronted by God, addressed, asked, judged, or blessed by God.[26]

This view, Bultmann feels, finds emphatic support in the New Testament. The God affirmed by Jesus is not an order in nature, a cosmic power, or any kind of metaphysical reality; rather he is the God who as holy Will qualifies my concrete existence.[27] According to the New Testament writers "God's Word is directed not to the intellect but to the will; it is not understood but heard; it is perceived not by scientific investigation but by obedience." [28] To believe in God, therefore, is to submit reverently to the power which calls me into existence and makes me finite, and to will to implement this submission in every moment. Belief in God is not acceptance of an idea or the intellectual affirmation of the reality of a being

[25] *Essays*, p. 288.
[26] *Jesus Christ and Mythology*, pp. 68, 73; cf. p. 43; *Glauben und Verstehen*, III, 120.
[27] *Jesus*, pp. 128, 133.
[28] *Glauben und Verstehen*, I (Tübingen: J. C. B. Mohr [Paul Siebeck], 1954), 272 f.

who is at our disposal; on the contrary, "it always implies a decision to be taken." To believe is to heed the demands of the "thou" which confronts me.[29]

Therefore Christian theology cannot make dogmatic pronouncements concerning the nature or attributes of God, or indeed regarding the objective content of any Christian belief. There is no justification for statements purporting to express metaphysical truth with respect to the person or work of Jesus Christ. Declarations about Jesus' divinity deal with his significance *pro me*. He does not help me because he is God's Son; rather he is the Son of God because he helps me. Thus the declaration, "We believe and are sure that thou art the Christ, the Son of the living God" (John 6:69), is not a doctrinal pronouncement, but a confession of significance for the persons making it at the "moment" in which it was uttered. "Christ's lordship, his deity, is always only an event at any given time." [30]

Hermeneutics

It is thus by way of exegesis rather than dogmatics that theological truth is attained. But exegesis implies hermeneutics—the science of interpretation or the methodological principles which guide exposition. For Bultmann hermeneutics involves not only linguistic and grammatical analysis and historical research but one's whole understanding of existence; it implies both an ontology and an anthropology.

In any exegetical effort our own relation to the subject matter is basic; it prompts the questions we bring to the text and evokes the answers we obtain from it.[31] Hence the fundamental presupposition for the understanding of any biblical or other writing is "the connection of text and interpreter, which is founded on the life relationship of the interpreter—on his previous relation to the subject, which is passed on by the text." A further presupposition is "a prior understanding of the subject." [32]

At first sight it may seem that this cannot apply to the Scriptures, the subject of which is the action of God. We cannot have prior understanding of God, which comes to us rather through the revelatory action of God of which the Bible speaks. Nevertheless, I can interpret records about events as the action of God if—though only if—I have some advance understanding of what may in my case be regarded as God's action, some conception

---

[29] *Essays*, pp. 14 f., 19.
[30] *Ibid.*, pp. 280, 286.
[31] *Jesus Christ and Mythology*, p. 51.
[32] *Essays*, p. 256; cf. pp. 241 f.

of the kinds of events which for me indicate the divine activity. The very inquiry concerning God implies some prior relation to God and some awareness as to who he is. If this quest were not the underlying motive of my existence, as it was in Augustine's "Thou hast made us for Thyself, and our heart is restless until it rests in Thee," I would not recognize God even in the most authentic manifestation of him. When I inquire about happiness, or salvation, or the meaning of human life and history, or the real nature of my own "being," I already have an existential (*existentiell*) knowledge of God.[33] The preunderstanding which prompts such questions provides a basis for understanding the kerygma when it speaks to me of God.

Man has a knowledge of God in advance, though not of the revelation of God, that is, of His action in Christ. He has a relation to God in his search for God, conscious or unconscious. Man's life is moved by the search for God because it is always moved, consciously or unconsciously, by the question about his own personal existence. The question of God and the question of myself are identical.[34]

Here is the hermeneutical principle which enables us adequately to understand what the Scriptures have to say to present-day man. The key question is, *"How is man's existence understood in the Bible?"* [35] Scientific interpretation of the biblical writings is inquiry about God and his manifestation; this means in fact inquiry into the reality of human existence. In examining each document we need to ask primarily what understanding of human existence finds expression therein. Hence we must concern ourselves reflectively with "the relevant concepts in which human existence may be spoken of," "the abstract facets of the existential understanding of existence." These are found in the living relationship of the interpreter to the subject which is directly or indirectly expressed in Scripture, and is an advance understanding of the subject. Only with such a prior understanding and the concepts arising from it can we really understand a word of the New Testament as the Word of God.[36]

Ethical and Social Responsibility

Important in Bultmann's view of Christian existence is his understanding of the bearing of faith on ethical and social responsibility. As we have seen,

[33] *Ibid.*, p. 257.
[34] *Jesus Christ and Mythology*, pp. 52 f.
[35] *Ibid.*, p. 53.
[36] *Essays*, pp. 258 f.

when man responds trustfully to God's gracious address to him in the event of Jesus Christ, he becomes a new man who is enabled to live authentically in openness to the future. In short, he receives the gift of freedom. The forgiveness of sins means more than remission of punishment; it is freedom from sin, which in turn involves freedom for obedience. Beside the indicative stands the imperative. The loving act of God frees man from himself to himself by freeing him to a life of devotion to others in faith and love. This is the meaning of Paul's declaration that "love is the fulfilling of the law" (Rom. 13:10; Gal. 5:14).[37]

Ethical living is therefore a definite obligation of the Christian.[38] In a wartime sermon Bultmann declares that Jesus himself calls us when the distress of our brother demands our compassionate help. He also laments the frequent failure of professing but self-centered Christians to be sensitive to industrial problems, housing shortages, and similar social needs, as well as to the spiritual and intellectual struggles of men.[39]

However, faith offers neither ethical prescriptions nor principles. "To the question 'What am I to do?' . . . Christian belief has but a single answer: 'Thou shalt love the Lord thy God . . . and . . . thy neighbor as thyself.'" This command is

not a programme, nor an ethical theory, nor a principle, from which isolated moral demands can be evolved in such a way as to be generally applicable. . . . Such an undertaking would only confuse the issue. The Christian command to love keeps telling me in my particular "moment" what I have to do, so that in this moment, as one who loves, I hear the claims of the 'Thou' which confronts me, and discover what I have to do in that capacity.[40]

Indeed, with regard to specific moral choices Christian faith offers no distinctive guidance other than that they should be rooted in and ordered by love. The Christian cannot derive from his faith any peculiar ethical wisdom, but draws on the same moral insights which are open to all men. Bultmann points out that when Paul enjoined the Philippian Christians to think about the things which are honorable, just, pure, lovely, and gracious

---

[37] "New Testament and Mythology," *Kergyma and Myth*, p. 32.

[38] In a conversation in Marburg on July 5, 1960, Bultmann commented critically on the failure of Heidegger to deal adequately with the ethical question.

[39] *This World and the Beyond*, pp. 147 f. The sermon, based on Luke 14:16-24, was preached in the University Church in Marburg on June 22, 1941. This passage is almost the only one with a clearly social reference in this book of sermons preached from 1936 to 1950.

[40] *Essays*, p. 20.

(Phil. 4:8), the apostle was advocating virtues generally recognized by the best ethical thought of his day.

In practical life, including politics, the Christian should act as a Christian. This means simply that he should be aware of his responsibility for political life and act accordingly. This he can do only when he uses his best reason in every situation to master the facts, to understand the political possibilities and the consequences of various actions, to engage in critical discussion with others, and to form independent judgments and make his own decisions. Theology and church must clarify and emphasize this duty, but they should not set up binding rules and thus deprive the individual Christian of responsibility. Indeed, the church must vigorously reject all demands that it provide answers to political questions, such as those having to do with elections, the use of atomic energy, or the rearmament of Germany. The church is composed of individual members, and they can offer only their personal judgment. It can and should impress on all men their responsibility to prevent war, but how to do this is a political question which theology and church cannot judge or decide.

In fact, Bultmann goes so far as to say that the church is not *permitted* to deal with such questions. "She is called to proclaim the Word of God, not to hand down political judgments." A judgment expressed in a concrete political situation is not the Word of God. Theology must therefore strenuously avoid "politicization," guarding carefully against any mixing of Christian faith with a political program, since this would in effect brand as unchristian men of other political persuasions.[41]

It is clear that for Bultmann the attainment of authentic existence by the individual is so all-important that he is relatively little concerned about social relationships. Our life together, he writes, should be that of "a community of free and isolated persons." We must not allow the clamor of voices around us to deceive us about "our solitariness." Yet each of us "exists in the world and in time, in the community and as a responsible being." [42] Christian faith affords no security within the world; however, as faith in God's manifest grace it gives us freedom to face darkness and mystery in confidence, and to accept responsibility for action in the loneliness of our own decision.[43]

[41] *Glauben und Verstehen*, III, 195 f.; cf. "Theology for Freedom and Responsibility," *Christian Century*, LXXV (1958), 967-69.

[42] *Essays*, pp. 7, 9.

[43] *Glauben und Verstehen*, III, 196.

Critique

Like the kerygma, Bultmann's theology itself calls for decision. By its very nature it arouses debate, personally involving those who seek to understand it and summoning them to form judgments for or against. It raises issues which are crucial for Christian thought and life alike, and we must accept responsibility for examining them critically. When we do, both positive and negative considerations quickly appear.

Values

1. By his use of the existentialist analysis of the early Heidegger, Bultmann has brought theology and philosophy into renewed contact with each other. He has no use for the metaphysical inquiries of either Greek philosophy or German idealism, but his hermeneutical use of existentialist emphases has opened the way for constructive collaboration between critical New Testament research and a major movement in contemporary philosophy. Bultmann is not himself an existentialist philosopher, but essentially a Christian theologian who seeks to interpret the gospel to modern man. However, the course he follows demonstrates at least in a limited way that friendly conversation may be mutually beneficial to philosophers and theologians as they carry on their investigations.

2. Bultmann has made irrefutably clear the need for interpreting the New Testament message in terms which speak intelligibly to the questions which contemporary men are asking. Whether or not the process is called demythologizing, and whether or not it proceeds along Bultmannian lines, it must somehow enable the Word of the Bible to be heard by those to whom it is addressed, as it was when first proclaimed. It will not really be heard unless it is concretely related to the search for identity, the loneliness, the personal guilt, the awareness of mortality, the depersonalization of business and industry, the secularization of culture, the realities of injustice, war, and violence, and the threat of nuclear destruction which characterize men's daily existence. Only a gospel so related can move to decision and become truly the word of salvation.

3. Bultmann eloquently upholds the authentic *nevertheless* of Christian faith. He rightly sees that faith cannot be extrinsically validated by supposedly objective "proofs" or undermined by the absence of such evidence. In centering the Christian message in trust in God rather than in reliance on human knowledge or deeds, and in stressing the primacy of gospel over law, he is true to the biblical view of salvation.

4. Bultmann is profoundly right in insisting that faith must be an

existential event. The gospel concerns man's existence. From beginning to end the Scriptures proclaim what God has done and is doing in relation to men. The God of the Bible is the God of Abraham, Isaac, and Jacob, who in love creates and in forgiving mercy visits and redeems his people. Moreover, the evangel is addressed to the whole person, not to the intellect alone, and the response called for is the trustful commitment of one's total existence, not merely the theoretical acceptance of true ideas. If God is to make any real difference in my life, he must be far more than an object believed in; he must be personally encountered—real for me. The true believer is not a detached observer, he is a participant. On the one hand, he knows the meaning of finitude, suffering, and guilt through direct involvement; on the other, he can speak with assurance of the divine gift of newness of life because he has himself experienced it.

Difficulties

If Bultmann's existentialist orientation went no further than the emphases just noted, our judgment on his total theology might be overwhelmingly positive. However, these insights are interwoven with other aspects of his analysis of human existence, and this analysis as a whole, providing the framework for his interpretation of the New Testament, leads to conclusions which must be seriously questioned. As we have seen, for Bultmann personality has no abiding nature, but exists wholly in the decisions and actions of each moment. These involve for each individual a self-understanding, the direction of which determines whether he exists authentically or unauthentically. The Christian kerygma calls him to receive in trust the gift of grace which frees him from unauthentic existence to become his true self.

The question which inevitably arises is whether this use of the existentialist understanding of human existence as the decisive clue to the meaning of the New Testament clarifies or distorts the gospel message. Does the adoption of existentialist presuppositions permit the New Testament to speak to us on its own terms, or does it change the character of the biblical message by recasting it in a foreign mold? There is weighty evidence that the latter is the case. When the knowledge of God is approached by way of human self-understanding, when God's being can be spoken of only in terms of his being for man, when history is dissolved into historicity or the historical quality of existence, when being and meaning, fact and significance are separated in reality as well as in human knowing, the New Testament affirmation that God acted in Jesus Christ on the plane of history to reconcile men to himself is radically modified if not discarded in deference to existential presuppositions. In a sense, all of the criticisms now to be offered are specifications of this basic difficulty.

1. Bultmann gives inadequate recognition to the claim of the New Testament writings to describe realities and events which transcend the existence of the believing man. In his sound aversion to making God merely an object at man's disposal, he forgets that according to the biblical witness the revelatory and redemptive acts of God were prior to and independent of the awakening of faith and the proclamation of the church. They were in fact the source of both faith and proclamation. Christian existence with its new self-understanding was not *sui generis*, but evoked by the previous action of God in Jesus Christ.

Christian faith must indeed be an existential event; the salvation of which it speaks must be *pro me*. Yet this recognition must never be allowed to obscure the fact that it is the God disclosed in Christ who is *pro me*. When Paul declares, "It is no longer I who live, but Christ who lives in me," he is not only describing his own new existence, but referring to its origin and object—"the Son of God, who loved me and gave himself for me" (Gal. 2:20). Prior to faith is the reality of the God who calls it forth.

2. Bultmann breaks the essential continuity between the earthly Jesus and the Christ believed and proclaimed by the primitive church, thereby raising grave doubts regarding the rootage of the kerygma in historic events. He acknowledges that the kerygma presupposes the fact *that* Jesus lived and was crucified, but denies that we can know—or need to know —anything concerning the *what* of Jesus' teaching or character. The *that* roots the kerygma in history, preventing it from being a mere myth. However, the historical *what* is irrelevant, so it does not matter that it cannot be recovered. All that really matters is the significance of Jesus Christ for faith, the sole ground and content of which is the kerygma which proclaims him as God's eschatological act opening a new life to man.

Actually, however, the New Testament itself neither makes nor justifies this separation. On the contrary, in its call to faith it claims to communicate a content which is derived from what has happened in history. Primitive Christian preaching identifies the Christ it proclaims as Lord and Savior with Jesus of Nazareth, who as a real man lived, taught, suffered, and died in utter devotion and obedience to God, renunciation of physical security, and self-giving love. In his life it sees revealed the redeeming love of God himself. When Paul preaches the forgiveness of sins through faith in Christ, he apparently assumes that God really acted in the earthly Jesus to disclose his reconciling love, and it is this love which makes us new creatures. The historical personality of Jesus is thus the indispensable ground of his meaning for Christian faith. Apart from this historical and ontological reference the claims of the kerygma become purely subjective.

The same conclusion may be reached if we consider the possibility of a basic incongruity between the kerygma and the earthly Jesus. If it should be discovered that the early church read into Jesus' life and death a meaning unsupported by historical actuality, the truth of the kerygma, at the very least, would be called in serious question. Would it then be any more than the private and probably mistaken claim of the primitive Christian community? Would men be likely to respond in faith to this kind of proclamation?

The *what* of the kergyma is explicable only on the basis of the *what* of Jesus' life. Even the kerygmatic *that* presupposes a special quality in the one designated. It is this particular life which is interpreted and proclaimed as the salvation-event for us. The kerygmatic Christ is identified with the Jesus of the Synoptic tradition. For example, events recorded in the Synoptic accounts are reflected in and decisive for the preaching of Peter as reported in Acts 10:36-43. Apart from such rootage the proclamation would be lacking in concrete content, hence in genuine meaning for human existence.

Bultmann is right in insisting that the kerygma expresses the meaning of Jesus for the early Christian community. He is wrong in holding that this meaning is in its substance independent of the historical events interpreted. In the paintings of Picasso and Léger, the objects which provide the original stimuli have disappeared completely in the abstract forms which alone are visible. Bultmann's view of Christian faith is a theological counterpart of such abstract art. On his canvas the original Jesus of flesh and blood, who lived and died in suffering love and in loyalty to his God-given mission, becomes an unknown X, and the faith aroused by him is dissolved into abstraction and subjectivity.

3. In excluding from theology all statements regarding the divine nature, Bultmann unjustifiably narrows the meaning of historic Christian faith and ignores weighty considerations which support the possibility of true knowledge of God. For Bultmann God is so transcendent that he can be known only as the event of his acting—in specific individuals at particular mo-

ments. We can assume that he exists apart from man,[44] but we can speak of his being or attributes only through speaking of the human being who encounters him. The affirmation that God is the Creator of the world can be only a personal confession, in thankfulness and commitment, that "I understand myself to be a creature which owes its existence to God." [45] I can speak even of his goodness or grace only in the obedience and self-surrender of the personal faith aroused by his address to me.

There are several serious objections to this view.

a. On Bultmann's own premises, there is no warrant for regarding knowledge of God's reality as more accessible to man than knowledge of his nature. Bultmann argues that since our knowledge of God is limited to the event of his acting in man, we cannot make statements about his abiding character—who or what he is. But does not the same limitation with equal cogency exclude statements concerning God's *existence* independently of man? In this respect can I say any more than that I understand myself to be a finite creature who has encountered the Infinite? Obversely, if the event of God's acting in specific individuals justifies the assertion of his existence, why does it not provide equal warrant for statements about the kind of being encountered? Whether knowledge of God or the lack of it is affirmed, both kinds of declaration make judgments about a reality beyond man on the basis of an event in man. Is not one as dependent on man's experience as the other?

b. Though the New Testament does deal centrally, as Bultmann maintains, with God's action on behalf of man, its writers assume that God really *is* what his redemptive acts manifest him to be. Not only in the Scriptures but throughout later history the believing and worshiping community makes affirmations which purport to refer truly to the abiding nature of God no less than to God as encountered. He is Creator of heaven and earth, Judge of all men, and Father of our Lord Jesus Christ whether or not he is acknowledged as such, and whether or not he is God for me. Infinite mercy is structural in his being before it is disclosed to men in Jesus Christ and responded to in repentance and faith—or disbelief. Moreover, the answer of faith is to praise God himself no less than the event of his acting.

---

[44] Bultmann admits that when man is understood as having his reality in concrete situations and decisions, "faith, speaking of God as acting, cannot defend itself against the charge of being an illusion." On the other hand, "faith does not mean a psychologically subjective event." *Jesus Christ and Mythology*, p. 71.

[45] *Ibid.*, pp. 69 f.

The historic affirmations imply that he is encountered as righteousness and love because he eternally is righteousness and love.

c. A faith which refers only to God *pro me* is exposed to the danger of serious distortion. If the knowledge of God open to each individual is determined by his own needs and his particular life-situation, he is likely to worship not the Most High, but a god created in his own image. Is there enough content in the kerygma as portrayed by Bultmann to guard against this practical polytheism? Even if complete individualism is avoided, existential relevance may easily mean that the gospel, instead of being spoken to a specific age and situation, is spoken simply "in accordance with it, being fashioned by its concerns and needs and aspirations." [46] Paradoxically, although Bultmann's insistence that we can speak of God only in relation to our own existence springs partly from his belief in God's transcendence and hiddenness, one result is a faith imperiled by subjectivistic immanence. A God who is chiefly *pro me* is even more likely to be treated as an object at man's disposal, subject to human manipulation, than is the God who is regarded as objective to man because his existence and character are independent of man.

d. Belief in the attainability of truth concerning the real nature of God is supported by at least two considerations which are nowhere sufficiently recognized by Bultmann. First, the God of Christian faith is encountered not by individuals in isolation, but by members of a community whose religious experiences can be compared and found to point to an Other who discloses himself to all. He is not only *pro me*, but *pro nobis*. In conversation with Bultmann several years ago I asked, "Assuming that each person may confront God in the decisions of his own existence, do we not find many common elements as well as peculiarities in the events we report to each other? We may speak existentially of God for me, God for you, God for her, God for him, and so on, but do we not assume that we are talking about one God rather than many private deities, that we have all met the same God, and that we are speaking of him as he really is when we describe how he has acted?" Bultmann's reply was, "My insistence is that all meaningful statements I make about God arise from my experience of him, and are statements about *my* God." This is true as far as it goes, but it leaves the specific question unanswered.

Am I so confined to my own private existence that I can learn nothing of God from the decisions and confrontations of others, nor form any

---

[46] Karl Barth, CD IV/3, 823.

judgment whatever concerning what God is for all men? True, in my
encounter with God I find some aspects of the divine activity particularly
significant for me, but this need not mean that they can have such significance for me alone. I must experience God's forgiveness and renewing
power myself, but other men have similar experiences, and in mutual witness we inevitably refer them to a single source. The God who loves us
one by one is himself one, not many. *My* Father is also *our* Father.

Secondly, God's actions in relation to us afford dependable clues to his
real being. He must be much more than he is disclosed to be in human life.
This more we cannot know, but at least partially true conclusions as to
his nature may be drawn from his deeds in our world. Even the encounter
of faith implies behind the kerygma a reality which accomplishes the salvation that man trustfully accepts, and the total experience affords a firm
basis for affirmations concerning the character of that reality. The thought
involved in such assertions need not be, as Bultmann assumes, a work of
the law seeking security in human reason rather than God. Instead, it may
be a joyous, grateful acknowledgment of truth which God has given.

4. Concentrating as he does on the Christian existence of the individual,
Bultmann deals insufficiently with the bearing of faith on men's group
relations, in either the church or society as a whole. He assumes the need
of the church as the proclaimer of the kerygma, both at the beginning of
the Christian movement and today, but he fails to do justice to its reality
as the people of God, to its social responsibility, or to its agency in the
coming of God's kingdom. He recognizes that human beings exist in communities, but he underrates the individual's need of the community, its
power for good or ill over his existence, and the positive values of its in-
terdependent life. For Bultmann church and world remain largely periph-
eral to the personal salvation of the individual.

Such a view is hardly in accord with the message of the Bible which
Bultmann is concerned to interpret. Both major divisions have to do centrally with covenants between God and his people. The Old Testament is
pervaded by his concern for Israel, and the New Testament announces the
coming of Christ because "God so loved the world." In the New Testament
true *agape* is not only a relation between two individuals, but a *koinonia*
love, involving the profound fellowship of those who "in Christ" share his
"unsearchable riches" (cf. John 17; I Cor. 12; 13; Eph. 4:1-16; I John).
Such love binds persons together in a community of interlocking relationships rooted in the activity of the Holy Spirit.

Those who are truly members one of another in such a fellowship, and who are aware of their mission, can hardly evade their corporate responsibility for the total life of the world in which they themselves participate. They are called to introduce others to the life they know in Christ, but this they cannot do if they ignore the conditions which dehumanize persons and alienate them from one another and from God.

To regard political action for the control of atomic energy, the reduction of armaments, and racial justice as unrelated to the proclamation of the Word of God is to misunderstand the Word. The God whose Word we are to preach was in Christ, reconciling the world to himself, and he has given to us the ministry of reconciliation. The new existence to which he calls us all is existence-in-community. Obviously the church is not as such equipped to originate technical programs, but if it refuses to support or oppose any specific social proposals and is silent regarding social structures it is confessing its irrelevance to much of human life and forfeiting its claim to point the way to salvation.

This difficulty in Bultmann grows partly out of his ambiguity regarding the objective nature of God. Christian concern for the welfare of others is based ultimately on men's common relation to God as he is disclosed in Jesus Christ. If we can know nothing about the divine character, or if our "encounter" with God remains an internal human experience, the major ground of Christian social responsibility is weakened or removed.

5. Bultmann's existentialist eschatology eliminates the future dimension which characterizes biblical and most later expressions of the Christian hope. In portraying the eschatological event as the end of the old world of the individual believer and his entrance into a new and transformed life brought about by the decision of faith, Bultmann offers an illuminating interpretation. In so doing, however, he changes futurity into an essentially nontemporal category. The "future life," the life "beyond this world," seems to be viewed in purely symbolic fashion as the life of utter trust in God here and now. This is no doubt a fundamental quality of Christian experience, but it need not be cut off from the expectation of a future consummation of the divine purposes. Bultmann's repudiation of all objectivity bars him from making any assertions about the fulfillment of God's will and rule at the end of human history. However, the biblical writings deal repeatedly with the eschatological hope in this sense, and questions regarding the end of human existence on this planet cannot be repressed. A view which ignores this dimension can hardly claim to conserve the full meaning of historic Christian faith.

5. FRIEDRICH GOGARTEN

Although Friedrich Gogarten first became known in theological circles as one of the pioneers of dialectical theology, his collaboration with Karl Barth lasted little more than a decade. In the later twenties Barth protested vigorously against what he termed the anthropologizing tendencies of Emil Brunner, Bultmann, and Gogarten. Gogarten in turn objected that Barth's system was in danger of becoming "a timeless, self-sufficient theology." [1] His decisive break with Barth occurred in 1933.

During the twenties Gogarten published a number of works dealing with central issues in systematic theology. In the thirties his interest shifted somewhat to questions of political ethics and the ideological controversies aroused by the Nazi regime.[2] However, after World War II he again won attention as a creative theologian through a series of important works beginning with *The Preaching of Jesus Christ*.[3] This volume deals with the synoptic proclamation of Jesus and its implications for his person,

---

[1] *Gericht oder Skepsis. Eine Streitschrift gegen Karl Barth* (Jena: Eugen Diederichs, 1937), p. 8.

[2] Typical publications were *Faith and Revelation* (*Von Glauben und Offenbarung*, 1923), *The Religious Decision* (*Die religiöse Entscheidung*, 1924), *I Believe in the Triune God* (*Ich glaube an den dreieinigen Gott*, 1926), and *Political Ethics* (*Politische Ethik*, 1932).

[3] *Die Verkündigung Jesu Christi* (Heidelberg: Verlag Lambert Schneider, 1948).

Paul's proclamation of Christ, and Luther's conception of the Pauline understanding of faith in Christ. Like the closing section of this work, Gogarten's later writings are to a considerable degree new interpretations of Luther. However, except for *The Preaching of Jesus Christ* and his next book, *Man between God and World*,[4] they present Christian faith, the relation between law and gospel, man and salvation, and related questions from an avowedly existentialist standpoint sometimes called theological personalism.

As a systematic theologian Gogarten has been concerned with many of the same problems which have occupied Bultmann in his New Testament interpretation, and he has strongly supported Bultmann's insistence on demythologizing. Nevertheless, he is an independent thinker, with distinctive and important contributions of his own. The major features of his thought may be set forth under four headings: the falsity of subjectivism, Christian faith as the answer, the understanding of history, and secularization.

The Falsity of Subjectivism

A major target of Gogarten's critical thought is the view which conceives the relation of historical man to the world according to the subject-object scheme adopted in the world view of Descartes. Such "subjectivistic" thinking, Gogarten believes, separates the presumably self-contained human subject from the being of the world which is his object. Subjectivism is "man's independence toward the world when that independence is understood as a kind of world view." [5] Modern thought, having given up belief in the createdness of both man and world, grounds the independence of man in human preeminence, the unconditionedness of the human subject. The world has become *his object*, which he can control according to *his* measure and the guiding principles which *he* determines.[6] Reacting against this enthronement of man, modern science has gone to the opposite extreme, asserting the complete objectivity of the world to man and adopting a world view which is basically identical with subjectivism. In either case thought isolates man from his world, destroys the real historicity of both,

---

[4] *Der Mensch zwischen Gott und Welt* (Stuttgart: Friedrich Vorwerk Verlag, 1952). This book will be cited hereafter as *Der Mensch*.

[5] *The Reality of Faith* (Philadelphia: The Westminster Press, 1959), p. 95. This is a translation by Carl Michalson and others of *Die Wirklichkeit des Glaubens; zum Problem des Subjektivismus in der Theologie* (Stuttgart: Friedrich Vorwerk Verlag, 1957).

[6] *Ibid.*, pp. 103 f. Here Gogarten is expounding with approval the view of Martin Heidegger in *Holzwege* (Frankfurt am Main: V. Klostermann, [1950] 1952), pp. 81-98.

and disrupts the original historical relation between them. According to that relation the world is not a final reality containing man, but a creation of God for which man, likewise a creature of God, has been given responsibility.[7]

In theology subjectivism appears, on the one hand, in the view which concentrates everything on the subjective faith of the individual believer, seen in separation from the object of his faith; and on the other, in the very attempt to avoid subjectivism by an assertion of the "objectivity" of the ground of faith or the historical "reality" of the so-called facts of salvation. "It is the nature of this thinking to objectify the being it thinks." However, the reality with which Christian faith has to do is the reality of the Word of God which man encounters in faith, and never that which is called "objective" or "factual" reality. "To objectify God and his Word is to deny him."[8]

In the life of man the net effect of this subject-object antithesis is a double bondage. First, man attempts to exist on his own terms and in his own strength, and inevitably he fails. Denying his creatureliness and trusting his own reason instead of his Creator, he forfeits his sonship and loses his freedom. Secondly, he seeks to manipulate the world as his object and falls victim to its power. No longer seeing the world as God's creation, an inheritance granted to man as God's son, he is enslaved by its law and forfeits his inheritance. In both respects man sins, worshiping the creature rather than the Creator, and ends in captivity.[9]

The Existential Answer of Christian Faith

In Gogarten's view the errors of subjectivism arose from a false interpretation of faith which separated its subject from its object. Hence theology today must above all regain an understanding of what faith really is in its concretely historical reality. Such faith is witnessed to in the New Testament, and it is called forth by the proclamation of the Word of the cross. In Paul and Luther the proper task of faith is "to safeguard the freedom for God as it is newly regained for man through the death and resurrection of Jesus Christ, to deliver the world and its law from every kind of religious worship, and so enable man's independence toward the world and

[7] *Demythologizing and History*, tr. Neville Horton Smith (New York: Charles Scribner's Sons, 1955), p. 50. The German title is *Entmythologisierung und Kirche* (Stuttgart: Friedrich Vorwerk Verlag, 1953). This work will be cited hereafter as *Demythologizing*.

[8] *The Reality of Faith*, p. 95; *Demythologizing*, pp. 84 f., 87.

[9] *The Reality of Faith*, pp. 61, 186.

its law." Through faith in the crucified and risen Christ man's double bond-age is replaced by a double freedom: "the freedom of the son for God and the freedom of the heir toward the world." [10]

Man now learns of a new quality of existence, existence as he can live it from God and in freedom for God, an existence given him solely by the power of the one who "makes the dead live and calls the nonexistent into being." In faith he now sees both himself and the world as rooted in the creatorhood of God.[11] Hence the world no longer stands over against man as a final reality, or as an eternally valid order which incloses him and to which he is responsible. Rather it is the creation of God *for* which he is under God responsible, and *in* which he is called to live as God's mature son. In it, therefore, he is not subect to the demands of an external law, dependent on his own works for salvation, but free for the service of God. This is true "independence toward the world."

The being of man and the world as they are purposed by God and his eternal power and deity is the being of the son who is free for God and the being of the world as the creation of God, entrusted to man in his filial maturity as an in-heritance from God. That being is the reality that concerns faith. Man's task, which can be fulfilled only by him, is to safeguard this reality by being aware of it in the only way one is able to—by faith.[12]

Gogarten's existential understanding of faith emerges with special clar-ity in his exposition of Luther's view, which he obviously embraces. Genuine faith does not consist in holding either historical facts or theological be-liefs to be objectively true. The event in which Christian faith believes is not one of which man is first a neutral spectator, but one in which he is " 'intended' from the outset and into which he is taken up." Jesus Christ is called Christ not because his nature is human and divine, but because of the work he has undertaken for us. Everything hinges on these words, "for us," and only when we insert them in thought after each assertion about Christ in the Apostles' Creed—"conceived for us, born for us, suffered for us, . . . ascended for us,"—do we really apprehend in faith the event called "Christ." The pronouns *our, we,* and *us* should be written in gold letters, since they disclose not merely the fact but the purpose of Christ's history.[13]

---

[10] *Ibid.,* pp. 98, 167. Cf. *Was ist Christentum?* (Göttingen: Vandenhoeck und Ruprecht, 1956), pp. 87 f.
[11] *The Reality of Faith,* pp. 116-18, 167, 103.
[12] *Ibid.,* p. 111.
[13] *Ibid.,* pp. 130 f.

Genuine faith is focused not on the *what* of the event, but on its *use* or its *why*, the *word* in which the meaning of the event is expressed. The knowledge that makes for true faith is the personal knowledge of Christ as the One who justifies. It can never be confirmed by an "objective" event; such proof in effect neutralizes the event, placing it in a realm where it could be known without faith.

The same is true regarding faith in God. Luther is so bold as to assert that faith is "the creator of deity," though to avoid misunderstanding he adds that God is thus created "not in his person but in us. Outside faith God loses his righteousness, honor, power, etc., and where there is no faith nothing remains of his glory and deity." In Luther's view the faith called forth by the Word of God uttered in Christ has to do immediately with being—both the being of God and the being of man. The believer, therefore, "stands" before God, responding to God's "eternal power and deity" in which God gives being to that which was not. The nonbeliever, on the contrary, denies to God his deity by denying himself to God's deity. In this sense faith "creates" the deity "in us" by letting him be God "for us," "our God." [14]

For Gogarten, too, "God is God only to the believing person." Conversely, the reality we encounter in faith, as we encounter it, is not objective. Indeed, we could speak of objectivity with respect to God only if we could conceive his reality without its concerning us. Actually, however, it *always* concerns us, because it concerns us originally in our very being as wrath and mercy.[15]

At this point it becomes evident why the theology of existence is sometimes described as theological personalism.[16] According to Luther the Christ-event to which Christian faith responds is a word-event, one which happens in and through the word. But "rather than refer to it as verbal, we could speak of it as personal. That is, . . . it is an event that in a real sense occurs between persons, hence through and in persons." By understanding the relation between God and man in this personal manner, Luther recaptured the biblical meaning of the relation and restored to faith its central meaning.[17]

[14] *Ibid.,* pp. 135-38.

[15] *Ibid.,* pp. 153, 137.

[16] Gerhard Gloege, "Der theologische Personalismus als dogmatisches Problem," *Kerygma und Dogma,* I (1955), 23-41.

[17] *The Reality of Faith,* pp. 138 f. The theological personalism of Gogarten should not be confused with the philosophical personalism which stems especially from the thought of Borden Parker Bowne in America.

Elsewhere Gogarten points out that in the New Testament salvation is presented in exclusively personal terms. The conceptions typically employed are drawn from relations between persons. Salvation occurs through a Person, Jesus Christ. The new life proclaimed in the gospel is the life of sonship with God, and God himself in Person—not what he gives—is the salvation offered. He promises and gives himself, neither more nor less.[18] In this relation, entered through the hearing of the Word in faith, man becomes truly personal.[19]

Closely related to Gogarten's view of faith as personal encounter is his insistence that man's relations with God have to do with *being*, and not only with *doing*. As understood by the New Testament, terms like sin and righteousness are to be interpreted existentially rather than morally. Sin, for example, designates the being of the man whose world is subjected to nothingness. Righteousness is being in, from, and to Christ, through whom man and his world are freed from sin and the power of death. Responsibility, too, must be understood in terms of the being of man. In its original meaning the word signifies not an attitude arbitrarily adopted without basis, but a response called forth by a proclaimed word and given only with one's own being. It is the answer one makes with his whole self when he is addressed.[20]

The Understanding of History

Gogarten's rejection of the subject-object antithesis, previously noted in his view of the relation between man and his world and that between man and God, appears also in his conception of history. It is false, he insists, to objectify history, treating man as the subject who stands over against history as an object external to him. Actually, man himself is historical; in history he has his origin and existence, and he cannot remove himself from it by making it his object. If he attempts to do this he misses the meaning of both himself and history.[21]

Christian faith must be understood historically, not metaphysically. It originated in historical events recounted in the New Testament, above all in the history which occurred in the birth, life, proclamation, crucifixion, and resurrection of Jesus Christ. However, there are two very different

---

[18] *Verhängnis und Hoffnung der Neuzeit; Die Säkularisierung als theologisches Problem* (*The Doom and Hope of the Modern Age; Secularization as a Theological Problem* [Stuttgart: Friedrich Vorwerk Verlag, 1953]), pp. 154-58. Hereafter this book will be cited as *Verhängnis und Hoffnung*.

[19] *Die Kirche in der Welt* (Heidelberg: Verlag Lambert Schneider, 1948), p. 105.

[20] *Demythologizing*, pp. 49 f., 53.

[21] *Ibid.*, pp. 57, 80.

ways of construing these events. One conception regards history as that which has "objectively" taken place in the past. It is concerned primarily with "factuality" in order to conserve the "trans-subjective" reality of faith. The task of historical science therefore becomes that of reconstructing the past on the basis of documents which have been handed down.

The other view, which is Gogarten's own, maintains that

the genuine history and . . . historical quality of the events which are witnessed to in the New Testament is to be sought not in their "objective" occurrence [Geschehensein] which can be historically established, but in the "kerygma," the witnessing proclamation of the gracious coming of God to men and their world which occurs in this history. If we separate the history of Jesus Christ from the proclamation which is the only way in which it comes to us, then we lose . . . precisely the history on which everything depends, since without it there is no genuine, justifying faith.

According to this view history is present as well as past, and historical science has much more to do than to ascertain "objective facts" through investigation of the past. Wherever we have to do with history we are concerned with the historical quality (Geschichtlichkeit) or event-character of human existence, since this is the presupposition of the very possibility of history. Man's life consists of significant occurrences, the meanings which he ascribes to events. In all historical inquiry this inner historical quality of human life plays an important role. Hence the goal of such inquiry is reached only when we go beyond the reconstruction of past facts to understand them in the light of the human existence which gives them meaning.[22]

Man's existence, moreover, is not to be thought of in general terms; most authentically it means that of the person most directly concerned. This appears clearly in Gogarten's discussion of hermeneutics, which he regards as the decisive problem of history. History cannot be understood from the outside, but only from within,

on the basis of the historical quality of human existence, and indeed of my historical quality [Geschichtlichkeit]. It is therefore the essence of historical understanding that in it man understands himself or, otherwise stated, that in it each understands himself according to the possibilities of human existence.[23]

[22] Ibid., pp. 37 f.
[23] Ibid., pp. 57 f.

Secularization

Gogarten's rejection of subjectivism in his understanding of man's relation to the historical and natural world reaches its climax in his positive advocacy of "secularization." In some respects his insistence on the "worldliness" of the world, as seen from the perspective of Christian faith, is his most characteristic emphasis.

Fundamental in Gogarten's view is the Lutheran doctrine of salvation by grace through faith rather than by the works of the law. By denying to works any saving significance, faith preserves their earthly meaning; that is, it secularizes them, allowing them to become an affair of the *saeculum* or world. As such, they are under the administration of human reason.[24] "Secularization means that a mental activity, which originally became possible through faith, frees itself from faith and now can be accomplished by man with the capacities at his disposal."[25] This new relationship applies to every aspect of man's life in the world.

Apart from justifying faith, man sees himself as subject to the "many 'gods' and many 'lords'" of which Paul wrote (I Cor. 8:5), and seeks to serve them and win his salvation by appropriate deeds. Through Christian faith, however, he is delivered from this subjection; his works are "secularized"—divested of all "religious" meaning as duties which he must perform to be saved. As a consequence, in "the freedom of the son for the father," he may now claim not only freedom from the world but lordship over it. All the powers which comprise the natural and historical world operate according to definite laws; when man by rational investigation attains understanding of those laws he can rule the world. For the man of faith "all things are lawful" (I Cor. 6:12; 10:23). The world is surrendered "to man and his reason as a possession that man has to administer independently."[26]

This new freedom involves demands, but these the believer understands in the light of the gift of freedom which he has received; thus he becomes "free for God"—free for the life of faith before Him. This means that he regards both himself and the world whose lord he is as created by God and belonging to God. He accepts and discharges his responsibilities in the world as a divine trust, persuaded that nothing whatever can separate him from the love of God which is in Christ (Rom. 8:38, 39).[27]

---

[24] *Verhängnis und Hoffnung*, pp. 98 f., 150.
[25] *Der Mensch*, p. 186; cf. *The Reality of Faith*, pp. 168-78.
[26] *Verhängnis und Hoffnung*, pp. 99, 101; *The Reality of Faith*, p. 170.
[27] *Der Mensch*, pp. 198 f., 283, 161.

Such secularization or historization of the believer's relation to the world belongs to the essence of Christian faith, so that without it faith would not be justifying faith at all.[28] However, it may easily degenerate into another and very different form, which Gogarten in accord with general usage calls secularism. Cutting loose from Christian faith, man may imagine that in his freedom he belongs wholly to himself, and that he is the absolutely autonomous lord over himself and his world. Instead of seeing himself as God's creature he elevates himself to the place of God. In so doing he is not "free for God," but becomes wrapped up in himself against God.[29]

Secularization in the true sense is possible only because the God-relation disclosed in Christian faith is realized in man's personality and concerns him as a person. "To be a person is to belong to another who is a person." To this degree I *am* a person through and before the other. Idealistic philosophy understood this in the most profound way, but at the same time it provided an imposing example of false secularization, or secularism, "because it did not allow personalism to remain secular but understood it religiously." [30]

Man easily but mistakenly ascribes "religious" meaning to the activities which through faith have become the responsibility of his reason. Instead of recognizing the God-given limitations which confine the sway of reason to this world, man presumes to use his reason to answer questions concerning the whole of reality. Entrusted with control over this world of time and space, he goes on to construct a world view after the analogy of his own powers. In short, his relations with this world do not remain secular, but are absolutized and given an ethical-religious, metaphysical flavor. Seen in the context of Christian faith this means that man forgets or denies the distinction between law and gospel, since he now relies on his own achievements for salvation. However, when "Christianity" transforms justifying faith into faith regarded as a true world view, it actually surrenders Christian faith. Such Christianity is powerless to save men or to "participate" in history with real meaning, that is, with openness to the future.[31]

It is therefore necessary to preserve the distinction between the realm of faith (gospel) and that of the truly secular (law). However, faith

[28] *Verhängnis und Hoffnung*, pp. 102, 106, 141.
[29] *Der Mensch*, pp. 161, 198 f., 107.
[30] *Ibid.*, pp. 186 f.
[31] *Verhängnis und Hoffnung*, pp. 138, 217 f.; *Der Mensch*, p. 283.

and true secularization are in no sense opposed to each other, competing over their proper areas of responsibility. If secularization claims authority over the sphere of faith it becomes secularism. If faith denies to secularization its rightful role it ceases to be faith. The function of faith is to help secularization to remain in secularity, thus preserving man's freedom for God and removing religious power from the world and its law. Faith cannot fulfill this task unless it remains faith as distinct from work, clearly distinguishing the divine reality of salvation from the earthly-worldly meaning of all human action.[32] With such faith man is truly "open to the future"—exposed to uncertainty and unable to anticipate what is to come, yet in trust making decisions one by one in each new situation.

The meaning of Gogarten's conception of secularization will become clearer if we examine briefly its implications in two areas—the interpretation of history and the status of ethics.

1. No Christian "philosophy of history" is possible. The world and its history have been secularized by Christian faith; therefore we cannot with the help of faith answer the question of the meaning of history. The attempt to do so could succeed only if it were possible to reverse the secularization of history produced by Christian faith. A presumably Christian faith concerning history in effect transforms faith into a world view. Thus it abolishes the distinction between law and gospel and falsifies the Word of God, which includes and preserves the distinctive reality of both. Such a "faith" turns the gospel into law, and on the basis of this law attempts to understand both salvation-history and all other history. Actually, the gospel is concerned only with calling men to the trust through which they are saved.[33]

Through the secularization wrought by faith the world has become historical and man secular. Thus world and man are exposed to a futurity which cannot be anticipated. Secularized man confronts darkness and uncertainty; these, as the "unformed," threaten every previously attained form of existence with dissolution and annihilation. But over against this, man perceives the demand of wholeness and unity. Historical man can never escape this tension between his secularized activities and the demands perceived in them. His life must be lived in a questioning uncertainty which defies all efforts to comprehend it within a neatly ordered scheme.

Man is tempted to regard as "Christian" the demands which arise in

[32] *Verhängnis und Hoffnung*, p. 139.
[33] *Der Mensch*, pp. 425 f.

secular life, and to identify them with the demand of God which has been revealed in the proclamation of Jesus Christ and the apostles. When he does so, he assumes that in the former demands he has the answer to the question of the meaning of human existence and history. Thus he falls into the most fateful of all utopianizations. Secularized Christianity becomes "Christian" secularism, which seeks to Christianize the world and thereby to achieve salvation. In this process true faith—in the reality of salvation accomplished by God in the death and resurrection of Jesus Christ—is obscured and lost. Justifying faith has been changed into objectifying faith whose task is to hold as true the factuality of the events of salvation. Thus the demands of God are no longer seen as revealed, and the strength to fulfill them is ascribed to man rather than God.

Actually God's commands can be fulfilled only within the reality of the salvation wrought by him—the reality of him who calls us out of non-being into being, from prison into freedom, from conflict into peace, from death into life. This reality is guarded by faith. Such faith alone, from its God-given strength, preserves the appropriate earthly-human meaning of the works which man does.[34]

2. True secularization also has far-reaching implications for Christian ethics. Since the ethical element is widely regarded as that which is distinctive in Christianity, it would be easy to conclude that to secularize the good life would mean surrendering the Christian faith. However, this view betrays a moralistic misunderstanding of faith. Faith is really surrendered if it is changed into knowledge of ethical truths grounded in ultimate reality, hence robbed of its questioning uncertainty and its unconditional openness to the future. Such "faith" claims to know too much, and substitutes for salvation ideas which imitate salvation. On this basis man, claiming knowledge of the whole of reality which he does not in fact possess, seeks to become in himself whole and well. This path leads to secular utopianism, not Christian morality.

The situation is utterly different with truly Christian faith, which does not try to anticipate the future as though it were a timeless, transhistorical idea. Genuine faith faces the uncertainty and threat of the future trusting in the salvation accomplished by God, and in the light of this reality it makes its decisions as each new situation arises.[35] It turns over to the reason of man the care for the whole of his earthly life insofar as it is knowable

[34] *Verhängnis und Hoffnung,* pp. 203-6.
[35] *Ibid.,* pp. 217, 203.

and at his disposal. Both that whole life and the secularized reason which deals with it are threatened with dark calamity (*Unheil*). Of course this calamity appears differently to the reason and the faith of the Christian. To his reason the predicament is seen only as a threat, since rationally he perceives the demands of the whole but not their fulfillment by God. To faith, on the other hand, God's salvation is revealed in the very midst of man's lostness and darkness, and thus he faces these realities "faithfully," unconditionally, passionately.

When Christian ethics accepts the secularization of life, it retains a legitimate place for the demand for unity and wholeness in existence. But instead of claiming knowledge concerning the whole and human ability to fulfill its demands, it exposes itself in faith to the uncertainty of man's future. In so doing it need not surrender knowledge, but keeps it as a knowledge of concrete ethical phenomena which is given its rightful and important place by secularizing Christian faith. In such knowledge the historical destiny of man is guarded, since this has to do with thinking and the decisions consigned to it. Only in this way can faith keep possession of the realm which is peculiarly its own.[36]

Critique

Values

1. Gogarten's theology is an original and astute attempt to interpret the whole of Christian doctrine from the perspective of justifying faith. Though his understanding of the law-gospel relation is rooted in both the New Testament and Luther, it is given a new slant by his keen awareness of man's present situation. He makes unmistakably plain that salvation comes not through meritorious human deeds, but through the trustful acceptance of the forgiving action of God. His rejection of the subject-object schematization is a counterpart of his acceptance of the Reformation principle of *sola fides*; all objectification, whether historical or metaphysical, is for him a form of righteousness through works, since it seeks security in human constructions. His insistence on the "worldliness" of the world, which is to be administered by human reason independently of faith, is yet another way of guarding faith by denying the saving significance of obedience to the civil and moral law. In ways like these his reinterpretation of faith becomes the foundation of his entire theology.

2. Like Bultmann, Gogarten exposes the inadequacy for salvation of a

[36] *Ibid.*, pp. 218-20.

merely intellectual acceptance of historical facts or metaphysical truths, and shows convincingly the need of personal involvement in the faith-event. However, he succeeds to a considerable degree in avoiding Bultmann's individualism by replacing the *pro me* of faith with *pro nobis*. We have noted his insistence that "for us" is implied after each assertion of the Apostles' Creed, his agreement with Luther that in a sense faith "creates" deity "in us" by regarding God as "our God," and his recognition, also Lutheran, that the Christ-event occurs between, through, and in persons. Such views are true to the historic faith of the Christian community.

3. Gogarten contributes significantly to the Christian understanding of history by focusing attention on the personal meanings which men find in events. He does not take full account of the importance of accurate information regarding past events in the formation of our judgments concerning their meaning. Nevertheless, he argues persuasively against false objectification in interpretation. History, he makes abundantly clear, is lived by people, and is not an object external to the human subjects who participate in it or think about it. Hence historical investigation can never be content with the discovery of alleged "objective facts." It is at every point concerned with present as well as past significance, and it is inevitably affected by the perspective of the historian and his judgment as to what is important. With respect to Christian faith, no knowledge of past events having to do with Jesus Christ will make much difference unless the new life made possible by him is somehow reenacted in us.

4. Gogarten's strong advocacy of secularization, as distinguished from secularism, manifests a positive appreciation of life in the world and a clear recognition of the Christian's responsibility in society. Man enters a saving relation to God solely through his faith in Christ. His actions in ordinary life therefore cannot win his salvation. But precisely for this reason the man of faith is released for the free exercise of his human capacities in responsible secular action. As we shall see, there are problems involved in this conception of the connection between faith and responsibility for earthly affairs. However, it enables Gogarten to derive a "secular" ethic from the gospel itself, to preserve an affirmative relation between church and world, and to present the life of the Christian in the world as a trust from God.

Difficulties

A number of the problems which appear in connection with Gogarten's thought are strikingly similar to some of those discussed in the chapter on

Bultmann. For example, his stress on history as personal meaning leads him to minimize the importance for faith of accurate knowledge of the events related to the earthly Jesus. Yet the significance of the Christian proclamation for both the New Testament witnesses and ourselves is inseparably linked with the historical personality of Jesus and the quality of his relations with other persons. Would not the meaning of the gospel for us be radically changed if serious error should be discovered in the assumptions of the primitive church regarding the life, character, teaching, and death of the one whom it proclaimed as Christ? This question has already been examined with reference to Bultmann's view of the historical Jesus, and need not be further discussed here.[37] There are, however, several other difficulties involved in Gogarten's characteristic emphases. We turn now to an examination of three of these.

1. A serious problem arises in connection with Gogarten's complete repudiation of any subject-object terminology to characterize the relationship between man and God. He raises valid objections to the "subjectivistic" thinking which makes both God and the world objects at the disposal of man for his ends and according to his norms. We can also learn from Gogarten the importance of distinguishing carefully between the otherness of God and that of the material world. Though the world is the object of man's theoretical knowledge, God for Christian thought is primarily the Source and Sustainer of man's life and the Author of his salvation. Man is summoned to respond to him in trust and commitment. However, the God who is thus encountered in trust and served in gratitude and love is other than man. Is he not in that sense objective to man? To think of him in this manner need not "de-divinize" him or reduce him to the status of a thing. Nor is the man who recognizes God's independent reality thereby necessarily denying his own creatureliness or trusting his own reason instead of God.

For historic Christian faith God is of course the Subject, not an it. But he is also the Object of man's adoration and devotion, and therefore necessarily in some degree also the object of man's thought. Moreover, the fact that he is worshiped does not prevent his being regarded as Creator of the world. On the contrary, he may be the Object of worship partly because creation is ascribed to his action. On this basis even the material order, far from being manipulated for man's selfish ends, is seen as the Lord's and husbanded by the worshiper as God's steward.

[37] See above, pp. *96* f.

2. Under the spell of his "personalistic" ontology, Gogarten unjustifiably denies any abiding nature or essence in either man or God. In his
view Christian faith knows only God and man in relation. The salvation-
event is a personal relation of man to God which can best be described as a
new life of sonship. To conceive of man as subject and God as object destroys this relation, which alone is concretely given. We cannot probe behind it to say what either God or man is in himself. Since God is God only to
the believing person, we can speak of him not in terms of his supposed
metaphysical nature, but only of his reality as it concerns us. Similarly,
we know nothing of a presumed essence of human personality, but only
of persons who respond to an encounter in faith or unbelief.

Actually, the relation which for Gogarten is ultimate can be nothing
more than an abstraction unless there are two real existences which are
related. What is given in the empirical faith-encounter is not an empty
relation, but one between two realities regarded as Creator and creature,
Redeemer and redeemed, Forgiver and forgiven, Giver of grace and ac-
cepter in faith. Without such a duality the relationship would vanish.

Gogarten's unwillingness to speak of either God or man except in relation to each other raises questions regarding God to which Gogarten
offers no satisfactory answer. Apart from the existence of men who see
themselves related to him, in what would the existence of God consist?
Before the appearance of man in the world, was there no God? If not, how
could man be his creature? Does man first emerge in the evolutionary
process and then by his faith bring God into existence? Questions like
these suggest that Gogarten's rejection of the subject-object distinction
points in precisely the opposite direction from that intended. Instead of
conserving the creatorship of God and the creaturehood of man, it tends
to make God the creation of man. Even the supposed relation is above all
else an aspect of human existence. The net result is not to curb human
self-centeredness but to confirm it.

Gogarten's denial of any continuing character in finite persons is also
questionable. In his view man cannot be said to have a nature, but becomes
what he is to be through his decisions. Gogarten is true to the realities of
personal existence in stressing its dynamic, volitional quality. However,
it is not clear why *personal* and *having-a-nature* must be treated as mutually exclusive alternatives. Decisions are inseparable from the persons who
make them; they do not float in midair like the smile of Alice in Wonder-
land's Cheshire cat. A man has to *be* something before he makes a choice;
he must exist as the kind of being who is capable of decision-making—

as distinguished from those forms of life which lack this potentiality. It is true that he changes and grows as he chooses one alternative to another, but in all his actions there persists a personal identity which binds them together and distinguishes him from other persons with different identities. Recognition of this persistence-in-change does not require a substantialistic view of the self, and it is quite consistent with the voluntarism which Gogarten is rightly concerned to uphold.

3. Gogarten's plea for secularization threatens to consign faith and worldly action to two separate regions which have no genuine relevance to each other. He specifically states that to secularize works is to deprive them of all "religious" meaning. This means, it is true, that man's actions in the world must not be regarded as ways of earning salvation. In Gogarten's view such secularization guards justifying faith and is demanded by it. He also insists that though faith and secular activities represent different areas of responsibility, they are not antithetical; the former concerns the divine reality of salvation; the latter, the earthly meaning of human action. He likewise maintains that the Christian, freed for the life of faith before God, fulfills his worldly responsibilities as a divine trust. Nevertheless, the impression left by his interpretation of secularization is that it erects an artificial wall of separation between the realm of faith and man's ordinary life in the world. This impression is reinforced by his rejection of all attempts to find in faith clues to the meaning of history or guiding principles for ethical decisions. His view really amounts to a Christian existentialist version of the Lutheran doctrine of the two realms, the heavenly and the earthly kingdoms.

Three objections may be made to the sharp division involved in Gogarten's conception of secularization. First, he assigns to human reason a sovereign authority which is difficult to reconcile with his view that man discharges his worldly responsibilities as a trust from God. According to Gogarten reason is not only freed through faith but frees itself from faith. As the possessor of this freedom man has responsibility for the world and power to act independently in administering it. Through rational understanding of the laws of the secular order he attains and exercises lordship over it. It is hard to escape the conclusion that this conception creates between faith and conduct, salvation and daily action a gulf too broad to be bridged by the reminder that man's responsibility is ultimately a divine trust. Reason operating in trusteeship to God would function not independently, but in a constant reliance on God's active presence, an acknowledgment of his lordship rather than man's, and a concern to find and do his will.

Secondly, Gogarten seems to blur the relation between faith and works, as well as that between justification and the growth in grace traditionally called sanctification. In his concern to deny to ethical action all saving efficacy he overlooks the fact that it nevertheless plays an indispensable role in the maturing life of the man of faith. Practical action does not earn the divine favor, but it is profoundly significant for our relation to God. We are not forgiven because of our meritorious works, but we *must* work, and the absence of deeds of righteousness demonstrates that our faith is not real. Even the apostle Paul nowhere treats works as unrelated to salvation. In the very letters which assert most emphatically that we are justified by grace through faith he insists on the necessary connection between faith and works. God, he declares, "will render to every man according to his works. . . . It is not the hearers of the law who are righteous before God, but the doers of the law who will be justified" (Rom. 2:6, 13). The essence of the Christian life is "faith working through love" (Gal. 5:6). Those who in faith have answered God's call to freedom are called upon to serve one another in love and thereby to fulfill the law (Gal. 5:13-14). Such service is for Paul not divorced from faith; it is rather the inevitable outgrowth of faith. The works of love do not earn our salvation, but they spring from it and are necessary to complete it. This Pauline view, which Gogarten would certainly support, offers scant support for his consignment of faith and secular activity to different areas—his separation of man's earthly responsibilities from the salvation wrought by God.

The conscientious effort of the Christian to order the life of society according to justice and concern for persons is not an attempt to prove his worthiness or to achieve salvation through noble deeds, but a grateful expression of his faith in God to whose grace he owes all. Christian faith arises initially as a joyous, thankful response to the redemptive action of God in Jesus Christ and the maturing life in Christ which results in the believer's continuing answer in trust, love, and obedience to God's manifold activity—as Creator, Redeemer, and Life-giver. Both responses occur in persons who are inextricably involved in the lives of other persons in the world. The initial commitment of faith through which the believer becomes a new creature touches all aspects of his existence. Likewise, the growth in grace which should be a lifelong reality is not a thing apart; it occurs in the midst of and in close relation to the decisions and actions which compose secular life.

Finally, the disjunction between faith and secular existence involved in Gogarten's view leaves the Christian without clear ethical guidance from the gospel. The man of faith is freed to act in the world according to the laws which his reason discovers there—in a realm which is apparently outside the jurisdiction of faith. Though he is motivated by the love of God encountered in faith, he derives from the revelation in Jesus Christ no norms which would guide his concrete decisions. Though the gospel provides him with a formal basis for the performance of his duty in the world, it gives him no standards for discriminating between actions which are in accord and those which are not in accord with God's will for society.

It is true that the gospel prescribes no code of ethics. However, it does summon Christians to think and act in ways which represent a fitting response to the forgiving, self-giving, reconciling love of God disclosed in Christ. The members of the Christian community are called upon to let the Spirit of Christ rule in their lives, and hence to accept in love the responsibility for one another which binds them together in deep mutual concern. In all their relations they are to acknowledge the reign of God, to see in all men persons who are the objects of his creative and redemptive love, and hence to devote themselves in self-forgetful love to the welfare of their fellow beings. Such guidelines are admittedly general, needing to be related specifically to each new situation, but they do expect and enable the Christian to live in the world by and from his faith.

6. GERHARD EBELING

It would be inaccurate to describe Gerhard Ebeling simply as a Christian existentialist—a label which he vigorously rejects because it obscures specific meanings and suggests a much closer connection with existentialist philosophy than he acknowledges. He is more critical of Bultmann than is Gogarten, and he is also seeking to transcend the opposition between Bultmann and Barth. Acknowledging great indebtedness to Luther, he identifies two main roots of his thought: the Protestant heritage as found in Luther, Schleiermacher, and Wilhelm Herrmann; and the historical-critical methodology which emerged in the seventeenth and eighteenth centuries.[1]

Nevertheless, the theological tree which for Ebeling has sprung from these roots has been powerfully affected by the soil and air of contemporary theologies of existence, and the fruit has in part an existentialist flavor. To speak of Christian faith is to speak of man. Questions concerning faith involve *me*. I not only ask such questions; I am asked and challenged to answer, with responsibility for the answer given.[2] Moreover, to speak of

[1] In conversation May 7, 1960. See *Word and Faith*, tr. James W. Leitch (Philadelphia: Fortress Press, 1963), pp. 17-61, especially pp. 52-55. This volume is a collection of 18 essays published between 1949 and 1960. The German edition is *Wort und Glaube* (Tübingen: J. C. B. Mohr [Paul Siebeck], 1960).

[2] *The Nature of Faith*, tr. Ronald Gregor Smith (Philadelphia: Muhlenberg Press, 1961), p. 11. The German edition is *Das Wesen des christlichen Glaubens* (Tübingen: J. C. B. Mohr [Paul Siebeck], 1959).

man is inevitably to speak of God, and vice versa. Ebeling is also emphatic in rejecting the subject-object antithesis. God must not be viewed as an object at man's disposal; likewise the attempt to isolate man in terms of externally ascertainable facts obscures and falsifies the distinctively human. " 'God and man' are not two themes, but one." They are known only in their mutual relation. Indeed, all of man's relations are a part of him. "They are not additional to his life, but they constitute it." In faith God, world, and man must be spoken of as a single, connected reality. In our approach to reality the decisive difference is not the epistemic or metaphysical one between transcendent and immanent, or supernatural and natural, but the difference between a relation to reality in faith and such a relation in unfaith.[3]

A corollary of this is that we cannot know God as he is in himself; such knowledge, which keeps God at a distance, is a self-contradition. "True knowledge of God is of God who is for us and with us." In the Old Testament, for example, the righteousness of God does not mean a divine attribute, but an action of God in accordance with his covenant, an act which sets things right and brings salvation to his people. Similarly, when Paul declares that the righteousness of God is revealed, he points to the saving action of God in Jesus Christ. God is known only in terms of what he does in relation to man. Conversely, true knowledge of man has to do not with what man is in himself, but as he is in relation to God, the reality which concerns him.[4]

In the preface to *Word and Faith* Ebeling asserts that his fundamental concern has been to state responsibly in present-day terms the meaning of the Reformation concentration on word and faith as theological principles. Later he declares that in essence systematic theology elucidates the word-event which in the name of Jesus, by calling forth the response of faith, brings God and hence also the world to understanding.[5] We shall therefore consider in order Ebeling's views regarding the word, or word-event, and the nature of faith.

The Proclamation and Interpretation of the Word

Ebeling's theology, almost as appropriately as Barth's, might be termed a theology of the Word of God. In his view all theological thinking, whether it concerns revelation, proclamation, or faith, is the "coming to ex-

---

[3] *Word and Faith,* p. 200; *The Nature of Faith,* pp. 123, 108.
[4] *The Nature of Faith,* p. 108.
[5] *Word and Faith,* pp. 15, 431 f.

pression" of the Word. Its subject matter is the word-event which occurs only in the Word of the coming of the justifying God to sinful man.[6] Hence Ebeling bends every effort to clarify the meaning of *word* in general and of God's Word in particular. Inevitably he has become deeply involved in the hermeneutical problem.

What is needed, he makes plain, is understanding not merely of individual words or even of connected passages but of the word itself. The effective proclamation of Christian faith requires not a new means of speech, but a new coming to speech. Basically, the word is oral, self-expressing, happening content, or still better, the communication of a person; it is his existence, the man himself, not merely information about him. When, for example, one man seriously makes a promise to another, he pledges himself and his future for the future of the other; when he gives the other his word, he gives a share of himself.[7]

The Word of God, then, is God's self-communication, God's address to man. Through it the world, as the whole of the reality that concerns us, "enters language anew." God's Word is a light which shines not *on* him, but *from* him on man's existence, imparting new meaning to it. The entire sphere of man's life has now a new look; it is seen as God's call and question to us. Therefore human words are at their deepest level answers.

Man speaks because he is addressed. Language is the manifold echo to the question of God. So the event of the Word of God is necessarily bound up with the entire life of language. For if the Word of God brings the whole of our reality into language anew, then the reality which is already in language is addressed anew.[8]

The Word of God must always be a present reality. "God's Word is expressed anew only when it is heard anew, with tense attention to how the traditional Word manages to make itself understood in the real circumstances to which our lives are exposed." For each hearer it must be a new word-event. For dogmatics, however, this poses a difficult question. The Word which it seeks to clarify claims to be the absolute Word uttered in history in Jesus Christ for man's salvation, yet it is one which must happen again and again in those it addresses. How then can the Word re-

---

[6] *Ibid.*, p. 433; *Theologie und Verkündigung; Ein Gespräch mit Rudolf Bultmann* (Tübingen: J. C. B. Mohr [Paul Siebeck], 1962), p. 16. Hereafter this book will be referred to as *Theologie.*
[7] *The Nature of Faith*, pp. 16, 109 f., 164 f., 185-87, 190.
[8] *Ibid.*, p. 190.

main identical with itself, retaining both absolute validity and present reality?[9]

To answer this question we must undertake a hermeneutical task, in which systematic theology joins with biblical and historical theology. Each biblical text must be painstakingly studied as the word-event which it was when written. But the explanation of the text carried out in exegesis must become explanation *through* the text. The text exists not for its own sake, but for the sake of the word-event which is both the origin and the future of the text. The main function of systematic theology is thus to bring the word-event to living reality. "It . . . brings God's Word to speech. It is the language school of proclamation," or of faith. In its work of interpretation it uses two interrelated methods: It traces the language-history of the Word of God; and it keeps itself open to new encounters in which the Word comes again to expression.[10]

For Ebeling hermeneutics is not primarily, as in the customary view, the theory of exposition as distinguished from exegesis, the process of exposition itself. It is rather the investigation of how the Word of God comes to understanding. In general hermeneutics the word itself possesses hermeneutical character. "The primary phenomenon in the realm of understanding is not understanding *of* language, but understanding *through* language." The word is not a problem for understanding; instead, it opens up and mediates understanding. The same is true of the Word of God. It "does not suspend understanding, but opens the way to understanding." Therefore, as general hermeneutics is at heart the doctrine of the word, *"theological hermeneutics is the theory or doctrine of the Word of God."* The divine Word is not a special supernatural word, but a true, authentic, ultimately valid word. However, it is the ground of the language-character of all reality, and is therefore "the ultimate ground of understanding." [11]

Ebeling maintains that theology must clarify the meaning of reality and undertake the ontological task. Instead of assuming the opposition of personal and ontological thinking it must make "the intention of personalism fruitful for fundamental ontology." It must attain a conception of reality which is oriented toward historical encounter rather than objectification, toward the language-character of reality rather than disposability, toward

---

[9] *Ibid.*, p. 191; *Word and Faith*, pp. 37 f.; *Theologie*, p. 18.

[10] *Theologie*, pp. 15, 18; *Word and Faith*, p. 433. Ebeling makes telling use of the common rootage of the German words *Sache* and *sagen* when he writes that the concern of theology is to utter or say (*sagen*), and that its subject is matter or content (*Sache*).

[11] *Word and Faith*, pp. 314 f., 318, 322-24; *Wort Gottes und Tradition* (Göttingen: Vandenhoeck und Ruprecht, 1964), p. 158.

openness and futurity rather than present factuality. Though such an ontology will be theologically productive, it will also be valid for general
discussion. In it various views of reality, such as that of the natural sciences,
will have their place. In this ontological perspective language by its very
nature mediates understanding, and the divine utterance personally encountered becomes the basic hermeneutical principle.[12]

Ebeling opposes both the separation of God from other reality and the
disjunction between the Word of God and the word uttered by men. "God
cannot be spoken of in theology without the world thereby coming to expression as event, and the world cannot be spoken of in theology without
God thereby likewise coming to expression as event." By the same token,
in the Bible the Word of God means unqualifiedly word as word, in the
same sense as the normal, natural, oral word which occurs between man
and man. The declaration that "the Word became flesh" means that here
"word" has happened in so full a sense that the being of the word and the
being of man have become one. There is no contradiction between God
and word any more than between man and word; rather it is the word
which binds God and man together.[13]

In the biblical meaning word is to be understood historically rather
than timelessly. It *occurs* as an event in which something is exposed to view.
Its content appears in what it effects. Hence it involves at least two persons;
its basic structure is not assertion, but communication or participation.

Here the basic need for the word becomes clear: it enables man to
express or manifest himself. It is that in which he who speaks is exhibited
as man, and is thus enabled to fulfill his destiny.

For his destiny is to exist as response. He is asked what he has to say. . . . His
existence is, rightly understood, a word-event which has its origin in the Word
of God and, in response to that Word, makes openings by a right and salutary use
of words. Therein man is the image of God.[14]

Here becomes apparent man's need for the saving word. He fails to utter
to men the word he owes to them—and thereby also to God. Hence he
stands in need of the true, healing, justifying word which, because it is in
keeping with his destiny, corresponds to God. Through such a word "one
man can speak God to another so that God comes to man and man to

[12] *Ibid.*, pp. 199 f.
[13] *Ibid.*, pp. 324 f.
[14] *Ibid.*, p. 327.

God." Thus salvation comes from God alone and also from the word alone, so that it is both wholly from God and wholly from man.[15]

In the word-event which occurs in the Christian gospel the speaker promises and imparts himself to his hearer, thereby arousing faith in the other and opening to him a future. The word-event is fulfilled when between the men of God's promise room is given to the divine Word. God, word, faith, and future comprise in unity the requirements for man's redemption, bringing him to full manhood. "God's Word makes man human by making him a believer, i.e., one who confesses God as his future and therefore does not keep from his fellow men the word that is absolutely necessary and salutary, that is to say true." [16] This word of salvation is the responsibility of every man to utter.

What, then, is the relation between Scripture and proclamation? The biblical text becomes the text of the sermon because they are both a coming-to-expression of the word-event; the text is intended to serve the proclamation. There is a movement from text to oral word in which the proclamation that *has* occurred becomes *occurring* proclamation. In the sermon the text becomes God's Word again. Preaching aims to fulfill the intention of the text by making present the reality with which the text has to do.

The task of exegesis, therefore, is to interpret the text as real word, living utterance. Basically the sermon is the execution rather than the exposition of the text. *"Thus the text by means of the sermon becomes a hermeneutical aid in the understanding of present experience.* Where that happens radically, there true word is uttered, and that in fact means God's Word." This is existentialist interpretation. Recognizing that "existence is existence through word and in word," it interprets the text with a view to a new occurrence of the word-event. In this sense the word-event itself is the hermeneutical principle.[17]

Ebeling uses this approach to resolve the tension between systematic theology and preaching, and to bridge the gap between theology and the faith of the ordinary congregation. Both theology and preaching are more concerned with understanding through the text than with understanding of the text. Both have to do less with historical correctness than with the truth which opens up the future—truth with which the speaker identifies

[15] *Ibid.*
[16] *The Nature of Faith*, p. 190; *Word and Faith*, pp. 327 f.
[17] *Word and Faith*, pp. 330-32, 431 f., 455.

himself and with which he charges the one addressed. Both use the text to make available the freedom and power of the word.[18]

The Nature of Faith

Since the goal of the proclamation of the Word is the response of faith, Ebeling deals extensively with the meaning of faith, thereby bringing out the dogmatic implications of his hermeneutic standpoint. In the spirit of Schleiermacher, Herrmann, and Harnack he reinterprets Christianity from the standpoint of faith.[19] However, in the process he replaces old terms with words and meanings centering in personal existence. For example, Father, Son, and Holy Spirit become respectively the truth, the communication, and the courage of faith. Justification is the reality of faith, and the church is the summons to faith.

The Meaning of Faith

Ebeling insists that the faith which is the essence of Christianity is not a special kind of faith but simply faith. The term does not occur universally in religion, but originates in the Old Testament and reaches its full significance in the New Testament. In fact, faith is to be sharply distinguished from "religion," which involves "care about oneself, self-assertion before God, the desire to give God something, instead of simply receiving everything from him." To turn faith into religion, as has widely occurred in Christianity, including Protestantism, is to pervert it. But when the essence of faith is truly understood it *is* Christian faith, and the addition of the adjective is not necessary.[20]

Ebeling's view of faith may be characterized under four headings.

1. It is faith—and faith alone—that justifies. Properly understood this is not one doctrine among others, but "the whole of Christian faith." Only through faith can man receive his true freedom which is a gift. Since man does not create himself, he cannot free himself from himself; he receives his authentic self from beyond. "It is the mystery of human personal being that it is summoned from elsewhere, that it exists in response and as response, and that man is therefore wholly himself when he is not caught up in himself, but has the real ground of his life outside himself." [21] This relationship is realized through faith.

Justification by faith alone is not a partial emphasis which needs to be

---

[18] *Ibid.*, p. 431; *Theologie*, pp. 5-9, 14.
[19] *The Nature of Faith*, pp. 20, 119.
[20] *Ibid.*, pp. 144 f., 18, 21, 28; cf. *Word and Faith*, pp. 207-14.
[21] *The Nature of Faith*, pp. 115, 150, 125; *Word and Faith*, pp. 212 f.

completed by sanctification. It is in itself complete. This does not mean that good works are excluded altogether; they are ruled out only in the sense that we may not depend on them before God for salvation. Sanctification is not irrelevant but itself depends on faith. It is faith which provides the saving, healing power; it alone enables human existence to become whole and holy. This it does because it relates man to the ground of his existence.[22]

2. Faith involves the whole person. Faith concerns not some partial or secondary level of human personality, but rather the very depths of man's being, determining actually who he is. Its question is the most radical which can be addressed to man: "Adam, where art thou?" It answers that man's real place is not in himself but in Christ. In the New Testament faith is the basic decision as to "where man is, where he lives and is at home." This decision in the being of man precedes, underlies, and determines all his actions. Such faith is "being in Christ"; it is not something added to what a man does, suffers, or hopes, but a reality which functions in all of these. It brings wholeness and healing because it relates the whole man to the ground of his being—to God in his wholeness.[23]

Faith is therefore not a specialized matter, of interest only to those who happen to be gifted in religion. It aims to bring man to his true humanity as the creature and child of God. Hence it is the affair of every man, having to do with what concerns him ultimately—his salvation. It alone opens the way to genuine existence. In fact only faith is existence which is sure of its ground, and is therefore enduring existence.[24]

3. Faith is an event. Faith is something lived rather than thought, an event rather than an idea. "It is movement and happening, it is life, fulfilled life." "Believing" is primarily not a noun but a verb. This means that faith is personal. Its subject is not *it* but *I*: *I* believe. Real faith is always the response of a person to the communication of faith. It happens when one is so affected that the event witnessed to takes place anew. Justifying faith produces a total transformation, yet it "never becomes a possession but remains an event"—the continuing, lifelong justification of the sinner. It is always coming into being in new acts of repentance, new decisions, throughout the life of the believer.[25]

Such faith is not, however, simply an inward event; rather, it occurs in

[22] *The Nature of Faith*, p. 34; *Word and Faith*, p. 245.
[23] *The Nature of Faith*, pp. 115 f.; *Word and Faith*, p. 214.
[24] *The Nature of Faith*, p. 116; *Word and Faith*, pp. 211-14, 239 f.
[25] *The Nature of Faith*, pp. 21, 109 f., 127, 152, 167 f.

the "relation between the existing person and that which is outside himself, namely, God." It "takes place between man and the whole of reality which concerns him." Thus its sphere is the realm of time and space. As in the parable of the sower, "the field is the world" (Matt. 13:38), the real world which constantly confronts us with the need for decision. "Faith lives not in the abstract, the general, and the timeless, but in the concrete, the particular, and the historical."[26]

4. Faith is historical. Christianity came into being because of a unique historical occurrence regarded as revelatory. Moreover, faith always results from the witness of faith, and it is nourished by the constant renewal of that witness. "It comes to us out of history, and it takes us into its history." It holds fast to its origin in time and place. It is proclaimed by a succession of believers who have lived, acted, suffered, and rejoiced together in a concrete community of believers. Thus faith and history belong together. In faith-full obedience to a command from above, Abraham in expectation and hope left his home on a journey into the unknown. His existence in faith was simply "the acceptance of truly historical existence." So must it be for us who are joined to Abraham by the decisive event of Jesus Christ.[27] "The God of Israel is the God of history."[28]

This means also that faith, like the Word, is related to God's promise for the future. Here the connection of faith with historicalness appears most clearly. For the man of faith the present is not an isolated point without memory or expectation, but the transition from yesterday into tomorrow. His existence is that of a pilgrim or a nomad for whom time is directed toward a goal. Human existence is essentially movement toward the future, whether hopeful, anxious, or resigned. Faith, being oriented toward God and his Word, enables man to face forward with hope. The future belongs to God. Hence faith in him unlocks the very possibility of belief in a future—futurity itself.[29]

Jesus Christ

The history with which faith is connected centers in the event of Jesus Christ. According to the New Testament faith is occasioned only by an encounter with him. The doctrine of justification by faith alone corresponds to the doctrine that salvation is only through Christ. To understand faith,

---

[26] *Ibid.*, pp. 164 f., 152.
[27] *Word and Faith*, pp. 28 f., 37; *The Nature of Faith*, pp. 25-27.
[28] *Word and Faith*, p. 215.
[29] *Ibid.*, pp. 214 f., 240 f.

therefore, we must become involved in Christology. However, the question of Jesus' identity cannot be separated from the meaning of "faith in Jesus," which for Ebeling is the basic question of systematic theology.[30]

1. Jesus as Witness and Ground of Faith. Ebeling makes plain that faith must have a ground other than "certain objects of consciousness." Yet he refuses to call this the "object" of faith, since such language would suggest that certain articles of faith must be mastered. Strictly speaking not even Jesus is the object of faith. Rather he is the witness and the basis of faith, confronting men with the reality of God. Jesus testifies to what it means for man to encounter God, in death as well as in life. But he becomes also the basis of faith, bringing men to realize that in relation to him they have to do with God.[31]

Jesus uses the word *amen* in a most unusual manner. By placing it before his own words, he does much more than declare that they are true. Rather he implies that they are essentially God's own words, that his certainty is based on the reality of God on which his own existence is totally grounded, and that therefore he has become for others the source and ground of faith. Only in this sense is Jesus the object of faith.[32]

2. Faith and the Historical Jesus. The problem of the relation between faith and history, already briefly treated, arises primarily in Christology. As a result of historical criticism this question has become largely that of the relation of the historical Jesus to the Christ preached in the kerygma of the primitive church. According to Bultmann the kerygma deals only with the *that* and not the *what* of the historical Jesus, telling us that a man named Jesus lived and died, but shedding no light on the kind of person he was or what he taught. Against this view Ebeling offers three criticisms which bring out clearly his own position.

a. The kerygma itself speaks of a historical person; hence the theological interpreter must take seriously the historical reality to which the kerygma refers. Why is it Jesus rather than another who is proclaimed as the Word of God? Bultmann gives scant attention to the Synoptic Gospels, yet the very fact that they were written shows that the early church connected the Jesus portrayed in them with the one proclaimed as the way of salvation. The one common, constant element in the varying New Testament proclamations is that all call on the name of Jesus. It is therefore artificial

[30] *Ibid.*, pp. 201-6, 243 f.; cf. *Theologie*, p. 44.
[31] *The Nature of Faith*, pp. 158, 75, 47.
[32] *Word and Faith*, pp. 236-38.

and false to separate the *that* of his existence from the *what* of his person and character.[33]

b. In Bultmann the kerygma about Christ takes the place of the historical Jesus. In effect, however, this means that the church itself replaces Jesus. This in turn arouses the suspicion that, in spite of the claim of the real presence of Christ in the kerygma, the replacement actually means the proclamation of an absent entity.[34]

c. Even Bultmann's *that* is not completely empty. He regards it as fundamental that we know that the Jesus who was crucified was a preacher and that his preaching was kerygmatic. He also asserts that Jesus' appearance and preaching imply a Christology, since Jesus demands a decision as to his being the bearer of the Word of God. This means that the historical Jesus and the Christian kerygma are related as implicit and explicit Christology. The implicit christological proclamation—the person of Jesus himself—is the basis for the explicit Christology of the church's preaching. To take the latter without the former is to ignore the reality explicated, hence to proclaim an unreal and powerless word which cannot lead to faith.[35]

Hence the question of the historical Jesus is integrally relevant to our understanding of the kerygma. We must seek the ground of the kerygma in order to understand it as the Word of God. The historical Jesus must not be lost in the kerygma. They must be distinguished, yet also positively connected, so that Jesus is seen as a truly human figure. If he never lived, or if he contributed nothing to our understanding of the kerygma, or if faith in him were a misconception of what he historically was, then the ground would be swept from under Christian faith. Faith in Jesus must be based on Jesus himself.[36] "The historical Jesus is the Jesus of faith. . . . Faith is the coming to its goal of what came to expression in Jesus. The man who believes is with the historical Jesus." [37]

Ebeling nevertheless recognizes fully the powerful formative influence of the early tradition. The New Testament writers inevitably saw the life of Jesus in the light of their faith in him. Their "aim was not to communicate who Jesus had been, and how he had once been regarded, but who Jesus is and how he may now be understood in faith." They were not

---

[33] *Theologie*, pp. 19-21, 59-64, 67-69, 72 f.
[34] *Ibid.*, pp. 78 f.
[35] *Ibid.*, 69 f., 73-75, 79-81.
[36] *Ibid.*, pp. 63, 77 f., 22 f., 51, 207 f.; *The Nature of Faith*, p. 46.
[37] *Word and Faith*, p. 298.

interested in passing on a biography of Jesus or a psychological explanation of his actions. From their accounts "we do gain a historically reliable general impression" of him.[38] Yet we miss the decisive import of their message if the faith they proclaim does not become ours.

3. The Resurrection. The primary ground of faith is the resurrection of Jesus, though not as an objectified fact. The resurrection appearances occurred only to those who were ready to become believers, not to neutral observers. He who had been known before as the witness of faith was now recognized by those who accepted his witness in faith. The resurrection of Jesus was therefore closely identified with the coming to faith of those who "were approached and overwhelmed and claimed" by him. The appearances, moreover, had the nature of a call: Those who encountered Jesus were awakened to faith and summoned to become themselves witnesses of faith. For us, too, "faith in Jesus" means entering his way. To believe in him is "to believe in that which is promised to faith, namely, the omnipotence of God. . . . It means to confess the power of God who raises from the dead." However, to say that Jesus rose from the dead "does not mean that he returned to this earthly life as one who has death ahead of him once again." It means rather that he "has death (not just dying, but death) finally behind him, and is finally with God." For this reason he is present in this earthly life. Therefore resurrection can be truly understood only when we grasp what God means.[39]

God

God meets us as the Word of faith is made flesh in Jesus Christ and communicated in the gospel. We can speak of him appropriately only in personal commitment, not in objectifying statements, as we might of some superbeing whose existence could be verified apart from faith. The speaker himself is involved in speech about God; hence the truth he utters is of such a kind that he "must commit himself, in his own reality, for the reality of God; he must engage his own existence for the existence of God." Any talk about God in truth both arises from faith and arouses faith.

The term "god" points initially to the "radical questionableness" of every man's existence, or his experience of passivity. We are as it were "thrown" (cf. Heidegger) into existence without choice as to time, place, or circumstances. From birth to death man is "as one who is approached, summoned, commanded, questioned." In effect, he is asked, "Adam, where

[38] *The Nature of Faith*, p. 52.
[39] *Ibid.*, pp. 69-71.

art thou?" and challenged to reply responsibly. In part, "the word 'God' is
this radical question about where man is, the question which concerns him
unconditionally." However, to faith, "God" is also the answer called forth
by his Word. His "righteousness" is his act of salvation.[40]

Yet this does not mean that the way of faith is easy; like Bultmann,
Ebeling stresses its "nevertheless." In the face of the stark reality of sin
and death, which declare that in the end we have no future, faith has the
courage to affirm that God *is*—that we do have a future. In the concrete
situations which make up human existence faith finds both its material and
its opposition. To "believe" in God often means holding out in face of, or
taking a stand against, all that contradicts faith. The God whom faith trusts,
precisely because he is believed or trusted, cannot be an object of experience. In this sense faith and experience exclude each other. "Faith not
only believes more than it experiences, but it also believes in face of all
experience." However, in the affirmations it makes in spite of the hard
realities it encounters, faith finds both its material and experiences which it
alone can know.[41]

The man of faith faces existence in neither fear nor resignation, but as
a participant in the omnipotence of God. Faith is not a resigned submission
to reality but a winning of power over it. "The certainty of faith is . . .
taking sure steps although no way can be seen, hoping although the outlook
is hopeless, refusing to despair although all is desperate, being firmly
grounded although stepping into a bottomless pit." [42]

Salvation

To recognize the victorious power of faith is to discern both the nature
of salvation and its source. When the unbeliever believes, when the man
who is powerless shares in the divine omnipotence, when the sinner is freed
from himself, salvation becomes real. This is rebirth, forgiveness, reconciliation; it is also freedom for the future, release from bondage to the past
to the open-endedness of expectancy and newness. This comes to pass and
continues through the miracle of divine grace, which cannot be comprehended, confirmed, or critically examined, but only received.

When the miracle of faith occurs, man's relation to God, the world, and
himself is changed. He now knows that he is loved, and thus he is liberated

---

[40] *Ibid.*, pp. 81-83; "Die Evidenz des Ethischen in der Theologie," *Zeitschrift für Theologie
und Kirche*, LVII (1960), 343, 348 f., 351.

[41] *Ibid.*, pp. 159, 169 f.

[42] *Word and Faith*, pp. 240-43 (translation mine).

from self-love. "He who is loved by God no longer needs to love himself.
. . . He is therefore free to love his neighbour." However, these freedoms
are the consequences of faith, not the cause. Here Ebeling quotes Luther
approvingly: "Faith is the doer, and love the deed." [43]

Church and Society

When men are claimed by the word of faith, they are gathered into a
community, a movement which plays a vital role in the nurture and spread
of faith, and hence in God's saving work. Men today receive the call only
because the church was there before they were, and those who compose it
are themselves responsible for passing on the summons to others. Thus the
church is centrally the summons of faith.[44] So understood, it carries forward
the word-event begun in Jesus. Indeed, it is the *happening* of its ground,
the historic presence of the Resurrected One, the body set free through his
death. Its constitutive mark is its responsible participation in this word-
event, which unites Jew and Gentile by making God present to faith as
freedom for love. Thus the church explicates the ecclesiology which is
already implicit in the coming of Jesus. Though he is not literally its
founder, as God's authoritative Word, the gospel in person, he is its foundation, its *raison d'être*.[45]

The church exists to serve. Its whole life is worship, *Gottesdienst*, the
service of God, and therefore service to man. Worship per se seeks not the
upbuilding of a closed fellowship, but the service of God through the
proclamation of his presence in the world and devotion to that presence.
All churchly ministries are but different manifestations of the one word-
event summoning men to faith and freedom. Therefore when Christians
receive the benediction they "do not leave as those who are dismissed, but
as those who have a summons and a sending." Clergy and laity alike are
called to "service in the summons of faith." Everything the church does
must be judged by this "revolutionary criterion," the application of which
would radically transform and renew its life.[46]

There are definite social implications in Ebeling's view of the church.
As authoritative word-event it carries on its work "to the glory of God
among men through men for the sake of men." It is concerned with man
as *fellow* man. "The freedom of sonship is freedom for brotherhood, . . .

---

[43] *The Nature of Faith*, pp. 136 f., 124; cf. "Die Evidenz des Ethischen . . . ," pp. 348, 356.
[44] *Ibid.*, pp. 146-48.
[45] *Theologie*, pp. 93-101.
[46] *Theologie*, pp. 102 f.; *The Nature of Faith*, pp. 147 f.

the united freedom of the free for universal liberating love as the breaking in of the new humanity, the body of Christ." [47] Both theology and preaching demand love for our fellow men, without which no action can be right. Concretely, Ebeling asks whether the church is "even remotely challenging men to a decision," whether in the east-west conflict it has shown the liberating authority which might help to break the vicious circle of threat and fear, and whether it is really concerned to help the so-called underdeveloped nations.[48]

It is apparent, however, that he is not calling on the church to change social structures. He states that questions like those just raised are fruitful only if we go beyond symptoms to causes: the church must fulfill its responsibility as the summons to faith. Sin as understood in the Bible is not basically a moral matter; it is rather unbelief—violation of the first commandment—though unbelief does weaken man's capacity for disinterested love.[49] Hence the remedy for sin is faith. The chief social significance of the church's task is that those who respond to her call to faith are freed from self-love to love for God and neighbor.

Faith is significant for society in another respect. Ebeling will not assert that Christianity has made mankind better, but he does declare that faith has made the world different. The change may have intensified the possibilities of both good and evil, but even this demonstrates that the consequences of faith are public and social as well as inward and private. "Man since Christ is in a fundamentally different situation from man before Christ." Christian faith has produced irreversible consequences in politics, culture, art, morals, the general awareness of truth, scientific thinking, and philosophy. In particular, the revolution which heralded the modern age shows "how faith, instead of being a turning away from history, opens up true freedom for history," which is the sphere of faith. Like Gogarten, Ebeling calls attention to the role of faith "in the rise of historical thinking and the de-divinization of the world." [50]

Similarly, in the spirit of Bonhoeffer he calls for "worldly talk of God." [51] In fact, in his view we cannot rightly speak of God without the world's being present, since God's own speech is directed to the world, and God himself absolutely has to do with the world. Truly understood, worldly

[47] *Theologie*, pp. 100 f.; cf. "Die Evidenz des Ethischen . . . ," pp. 348, 353, 356 f.
[48] *Word and Faith*, p. 432; *The Nature of Faith*, p. 146.
[49] *The Nature of Faith*, pp. 146, 117, 135.
[50] *Ibid.*, pp. 30, 121-23.
[51] The title of an essay in *Word and Faith*, pp. 354-62.

talk about God is identical with "spiritual" talk. True worldliness, far from being an addition to speech about God, is that which occurs whenever we speak of God concretely and clearly.

To talk of God in worldly fashion is therefore to speak effectively. "It is 'word' which brings God and the world together," and "this word is no abstract statement, but a concrete word-event, address, call, by which God is proclaimed in the world." In this speech-event God becomes wholly divine because he loves the world, and the world becomes wholly worldly because it belongs to God and is his creation.[52]

Critique

Ebeling's interpretation of Christian theology according to the complementary categories of word and faith is fresh and original. In stimulating fashion it combines emphases derived particularly from Luther and Schleiermacher with insights drawn from contemporary thought concerning human existence.

Values

Five elements of strength deserve particular mention.

1. Ebeling stresses the dynamic nature of the relation between God and man. His conception of the language-character of being speaks eloquently of a reality which is ultimately alive and active, and of a God who is constantly seeking to speak to man, especially to communicate himself. Even a seemingly inanimate text on an ancient parchment has something to say to man today, because it resulted originally from the action of God in a human mind, and because the living God uses it to disclose himself to our present understanding.

2. The assertion that biblical exegesis seeks a new occurrence of the word-event points up a related emphasis of importance in Ebeling's account of faith—his insistence on firsthand personal encounter. There is no place in his interpretation for belief as merely intellectual assent to general propositions guaranteed by allegedly factual evidence. God's Word is rather a letter personally addressed to each recipient, to whom it becomes a present reality, and from whom it calls forth a response which he alone can make.

3. Ebeling soundly asserts the unity and wholeness of man's life when it is lived in faith. God, man, and world belong together, constituting one connected reality. The language-character of this reality makes possible

[52] *Ibid.*, p. 361; "Die Evidenz des Ethischen . . . ," pp. 320-24, 328, 355.

general as well as theological understanding. There is no disjunction between the word and the Word of God; the former is rooted in the divine activity, while the latter is a truly human word, an event in our experience. This stress on relatedness is a valuable corrective to the separation represented by Barth's failure to acknowledge that any Word of God to man must utilize language and forms of thought which are fully human, hence subject to human misinterpretation.

4. Ebeling upholds effectively the importance of the historical Jesus for Christian faith, offering cogent arguments against Bultmann's view that we can and need to know only the *that* of Jesus' life. He admits that the purely factual details available to us regarding the earthly Jesus are very sparse, that our knowledge of Jesus comes to us through a tradition that was determined by faith, and that in our own lives knowledge of historical data can never replace personal faith. However, he takes with due seriousness the connection made by the early church between the Christ it proclaimed as the way of salvation and the historical, truly human life which called forth the proclamation. For him the kerygma did not spring from the faith of the first Christians alone; rather it was integrally related to and materially shaped by what Jesus actually was and taught. The soundness of this judgment is evidenced by the simple fact that the Christian community judged it desirable to produce and circulate the Gospels, and later included them in its canonical Scriptures.

5. Ebeling understands well both the shortcomings and the importance of the church and the nature of its mission. He is realistic in criticizing the traditionalism, the suppression of truth and free inquiry, the confessional strife, the love of power, and the remoteness from reality which so often have marked its history. However, he does not fall into Bultmann's error of largely overlooking the role of the community in calling men to decision and nourishing and interpreting faith. In eloquent manner he writes of the "togetherness" and unity of men who have been claimed by faith and are themselves commissioned to summon others to believe. He rightly regards this as a "revolutionary criterion" in today's situation, though it is clearly assumed in the believing fellowship portrayed in the New Testament.[53]

In hermeneutics, too, Ebeling recognizes the significant function performed by the community. The individual's understanding must be verified by "joint understanding." Furthermore, the existence which is il-

[53] *The Nature of Faith*, pp. 146-48.

lumined when word or the Word of God "happens rightly" always means "existence in association with others." [54] The narrow individualism of much Christian existentialist thought is absent in Ebeling.

Difficulties

Among the questions raised by Ebeling's theology four call for at least brief consideration.

1. His very stress on the unity and relatedness of existence, combined with his vigorous repudiation of the subject-object antithesis, runs the risk of obscuring real distinctions. The truth involved in thinking of God, the world, and man as one connected reality cannot change the fact that in important respects they are different. The effort to think clearly about the differences need not involve making God merely an object at our disposal, but may further the understanding to which Ebeling himself is committed.

He speaks of the Holy Spirit and faith as "one and the same" in man. Man is the subject of faith and God the subject of the Spirit, but they are two aspects of the same event. The Spirit is "the permanent character of faith as a gift." [55] If Ebeling means that the Spirit is the source of man's faith-experience, he is affirming what historic Christian thought has normally held. However, his language is ambiguous, opening the way to confusion regarding the relation between God and man in faith, and shedding little light on their distinctive roles.

2. Likewise equivocal is his related denial that there can be any true knowledge of God in himself. Ebeling definitely asserts that faith has to do with actualities, and he assumes the ontological reality of God. Nevertheless, he insists that we can speak of God only as he is "with us and for us." By this he may sometimes mean simply the tautology that any knowledge of God attainable by man is human knowledge, and that in thinking about God we cannot transcend our human categories or conceive God as he might be imagined by some nonhuman theologian. There can be no quarrel with this judgment, although it is still in order to ask what relation this "God for us" may bear to the real God whose existence does not depend on us. However, Ebeling seems to mean primarily that we can know God truly only in terms of what he does for our salvation. Knowledge of God "in himself" would be "neutral, objective knowledge of God which sets him at a distance." [56]

---

[54] *Word and Faith*, pp. 320, 327.
[55] *The Nature of Faith*, pp. 105 f.
[56] *Ibid.*, p. 108.

But may not the man of faith seek truth regarding, for example, God's creative activity in nature, and the implications of such activity for the nature of God himself, without thereby adopting an attitude of disinterested neutrality? May not faith itself prompt the sincere believer to attempt to broaden and deepen his understanding of God in order to serve him more intelligently? If reality, as Ebeling believes, has language-character, is it not likely to say something to us about its own nature?

The biblical writers seem to assume that God through his Word utters truth about himself. Centrally, of course, they do deal with those actions of God which concern the redemption of man—righteousness, judgment, love, forgiveness, mercy. Yet they also speak of God's creative power, his wisdom, his majesty, his unity and sole existence, and his sovereignty in nature as well as in history. Though they would not separate such disclosures from the faith-relation to God, they believe they are proclaiming God as he really and eternally is. Similarly, the chief historic statements of Christian faith, though they do not pretend to know everything about God, do claim to refer truly to him as he exists independently of our belief.

3. Objection must be entered to Ebeling's radical differentiation between faith and religion. Religion to him means human self-assertion which moves from man to God, along with appropriate cultic and institutional activities. Faith he regards as basically the event in which the whole person enters a relation of transforming trust to the ground of his existence. Such faith occurs only within Christianity. It is closely akin to Bonhoeffer's "religionless Christianity." [57]

Though the distinction between God-centered trust and man-centered works is valid, it is misleading to tie it to Ebeling's highly specialized use of the terms "faith" and "religion." Both words have much broader meanings which are long established and widely accepted. Ebeling is entitled for his own purposes to adopt different connotations, but not to treat them as normative in scholarly discussion.

Religion may be broadly described as man's total relation to whatever he regards as most worthy of reverence or devotion. There are different ways of conceiving and practicing this relation, one of which is that which Ebeling calls faith. As Christians we may regard Christian faith as unique, exclusive, and the sole way to true salvation. Nevertheless, it remains a

[57] Eberhard Bethge (ed.), *Prisoner for God; Letters and Papers from Prison*, tr. Reginald H. Fuller (New York: The Macmillan Company, 1954), pp. 62, 122, 145-47, 163 f.

religious attitude in the broad sense indicated, and also in the sense that it has to do with man's ultimate concern, as distinguished from more limited interests such as those which are political, economic, or esthetic in nature.[58]

Nor can the term "faith" be confined to biblical faith. Men obviously place varying degrees of trust in a wide variety of objects, and sometimes commitment is as complete as that which marks the justifying faith of the Christian. We may have faith in party, country, dictator, class, race, money, a bank, an automobile, a cosmetic, another person, or ourselves—to mention only a few of the claims which win human allegiance. We may think of Christian faith as being so superior to all of these as to be figuratively in a class by itself. Yet is it not still a kind of faith? It is *religious* faith as distinguished from other types, and among religious faiths it is uniquely related to Jesus Christ rather than Buddhist or Muslim in orientation. To treat this broader usage as illegitimate involves a change in linguistic meanings which is as confusing as it is unnecessary.

4. Finally, several questions should be raised regarding the relation of faith to ethics and the life of the Christian in the world. Ebeling protests against "the moral misunderstanding" of the biblical view of sin, insisting that what is called sin from an ethical standpoint is "no more than" a result of man's real sin, unbelief.[59] Obversely, in faith the believer is assured that he is loved, and this assurance liberates him from self-love to neighbor-love.[60] Thus faith and unbelief both exert effects in the moral realm, producing either the capacity or the incapacity for disinterested love, but they are not themselves to be morally interpreted.

Here as elsewhere Ebeling is rightly concerned with insisting that the Christian lives by the power of God, not by his own strength. He is true to the biblical witness in locating the center of sin in man's trust in himself rather than God. He is also sound in refusing to limit man's relation to God to the realm of moral obedience. Nevertheless, his position entails a misconstruction of the ethical dimension of faith. In biblical perspective faith is inherently ethical because the God whom the believer trusts is revealed to him as righteous and loving. "The Lord of hosts is exalted in righteousness" (Isa. 5:16). Hence acceptance of the claims of righteousness is not so much an addition to belief as an integral part of it. Similarly,

---

[58] Ebeling himself has apparently recognized this usage by contributing several definitive articles, including one on Luther's theology, which centers in faith, to the third edition of the standard German encyclopedia of religion, *Die Religion in Geschichte und Gegenwart* (*Religion in History and the Present*) (ed. Kurt Galling; Tübingen: J. C. B. Mohr [Paul Siebeck], 1957-62).

[59] *The Nature of Faith*, pp. 135, 117.

[60] *Ibid.*, pp. 137, 145; *Word and Faith*, pp. 432 f.

faithlessness is often identified with rejection of God's good will; disobedience constitutes unbelief rather than resulting from it.[61]

Ebeling rightly reminds us that the requirement to serve God alone is the first commandment. However, we also need to remember that it is followed by nine others, six of which are ethical in content.[62] These six, moreover, are not regarded only as consequences of the first. All ten, integrally related, constitute the law of God. Adultery and murder are "real sins" too; they not only spring from, but are forms of, unbelief. We do not first deny God, then covet or steal; rather we deny God by coveting and stealing—by putting ourselves in the center in the ways which these sins involve.

Moreover, the believer is not only "free to love his neighbor"; he is commanded to love him (John 13:34). Faith has its imperative as well as its indicative. The imperative presupposes the indicative, but since the God in whom we trust acts in love to redeem men, the faith to which he calls us implies by its very nature acceptance of the obligation to love all whom he loves. By the same token, the unbelief which for Ebeling is the essence of sin includes by its very nature rejection of the command to love.

Ebeling's nonmoral view of sin is implied in his discussion of the role of faith in the "de-divinization of the world." The secular order is de-divinized when we see that our good works there have no bearing on our salvation, which depends on faith alone. However, Ebeling also calls for "worldly talk of God." The Word brings God and the world together, so that we cannot speak of one without the other.

It is hard to avoid the impression of incongruity between these two emphases. How can we consistently regard as the locus of de-divinization a world which God himself addresses and affirms, and in which he is actively and intimately present? If to talk truly about God is to talk in worldly fashion, then God must be concerned about our worldly actions, and those actions must have something to do with our relation to him—even with the genuineness of our faith in him.

---

[61] In Isaiah, for example, Judah's faithfulness to the Holy One of Israel consists in her calling "evil good and good evil," or in her formation of a military alliance with Egypt in violation of the divine command (Isa. 5:20; 30:1-3; 31:1-3).

[62] In the Deuteronomic version the fourth commandment also has a strong moral flavor: Israel is enjoined to provide a day of rest for servants and animals as an act of grateful remembrance of her own deliverance from servitude (Deut. 5:12-15).

Section III: Neo-Lutheran Theologies

7. EDMUND SCHLINK

The theology of Edmund Schlink is peculiarly interesting because he combines a profound commitment to traditional Lutheran doctrinal emphases with vigorous participation in ecumenical theological endeavor. Actively involved in the struggle of the Confessing Church against Hitler's totalitarianism, he was deeply strengthened by the confessions of the ancient church and the Reformation. Simultaneously he was drawn close to representatives of other Christian traditions; facing a common enemy, in their refusal to deny Christ they were brought together into the presence of their common Lord.

These events provide an important clue to Schlink's later life and work. He regards the confessional writings of the Book of Concord [1] as a definitive and essentially sound explication of the truths of Scripture. He has also been actively engaged for many years in ecumenical enterprises, and is now working on an ecumenical dogmatics which aims to expound

[1] The Lutheran Confessions are contained in the Book of Concord (1577), consisting of the Apostles', Nicene, and so-called Athanasian Creeds; the two Catechisms of Luther; the Augsburg Confession with its Apology; the Smalcald Articles; the Treatise on the Power and Primacy of the Pope; and the Formula of Concord in two parts, Epitome and Solid Declaration.

from his own perspective the truths held in common by the three major branches of Christendom. In interpreting his thought we shall consider first his view of the relation between the Lutheran Confessions and dogmatic theology, secondly, his approach to ecumenical theology, and thirdly, several of his major doctrinal emphases.

The Lutheran Confessions and Dogmatic Theology

Schlink points out that the Confessions "aim to summarize the multiplicity of statements from Scripture in doctrinal articles directed against the errors of their day and designed for the protection of the correct proclamation then and for all time to come." [2] Explicit or implicit in this statement are four affirmations.

1. The Confessions are a normative exposition of biblical truth.

2. In them it is the historic church, the whole congregation of believers, which expounds Scripture. It always precedes the individual Christian, giving him, through the Word of God, new birth as a child of God and instructing him before he himself is able to believe. The modern Christian is therefore called upon to submit as a pupil to the instruction and discipline of the teaching church and approach the Bible "together with the fathers in a common act of hearing."

3. The Confessions claim to speak authoritatively for "the whole Christian church on earth." They specifically repudiate the designation "Lutheran," and declare rather that "the one holy catholic and apostolic church" has spoken. Their claim is therefore comprehensive. They are far more than historically conditioned responses to the specific problems which occasioned them; they are rather "designed by the church to bind once for all the proclamation of all subsequent time." [3]

4. Their purpose is proclamation, not the formulation of theoretical dogma. They seek to guard the purity of the gospel of salvation, to which they bear witness by distinguishing it carefully from the law.[4] They are offered as a model not for correct belief in the abstract, but for the teaching and preaching of the church.[5]

---

[2] Schlink, Theology of the Lutheran Confessions, tr. Paul Koehneke and J. A. Bouman (Philadelphia: Muhlenberg Press, 1961), p. xvi. The German edition is Theologie der lutherischen Bekenntnisschriften (3rd ed. München: Chr. Kaiser Verlag [1940], 1948). Hereafter this book will be designated as Theology.

[3] Ibid., pp. xxiii, xvii-xix.

[4] "The Significance of the Eastern and Western Traditions for the Christian Church," Ecumenical Review, XII (1959-60), 139.

[5] Theology, p. 26.

The church today must take cognizance of these claims of the Confessions, interpreting their enduring truth in the light of the circumstances of their origin, and especially in relation to each other. Such interpretation must also judge whether they may be rightly regarded as the church's normative exposition of the Scriptures. To do this, we must critically retrace their exegesis of Scripture, measuring their teaching against Scripture, then presenting their doctrine systematically as scriptural teaching. This is part of the task of dogmatics.

Schlink recognizes that the Confessions have bypassed or abridged important biblical truths, and that they have no answers to some urgent concrete questions which confront us today. Nevertheless, for him the statements of the Confessions are confirmed by recent exegesis to a surprising degree; moreover, the Confessions disclose "the meaning of Scriptural texts and contexts which today are commonly overlooked." [6]

Confessional theology, then, is the necessary prolegomenon to dogmatic theology. Since our faith is called forth by the church's proclamation, our interpretation of that faith must start with the church's confession. The priority is logical as well as empirical. The Confessions are the voice of the church as a whole witnessing to the scriptural gospel of salvation. The dogmatician is therefore obligated to give them precedence over all other commentaries on Scripture. His proper task is that of thinking them through "to their logical conclusion in the act of critically retracing the Reformation's exegesis of Scripture." [7] This involves two responsibilities.

1. Dogmatics cannot be simply a blind restatement of the doctrines of the Confessions; rather it must test and if necessary correct them by the Scriptures. This requires painstaking exegetical work which reexamines all of the Scripture references of the Confessions and relates every doctrine of the Confessions to all pertinent texts of Scripture. The result is a dogmatic conversation between Scripture and Confession which Schlink suggests should proceed according to the following rules:

a. We should understand the assertions of the Confessions from their center, the doctrine of justification, and ask whether Scripture itself makes justification central, regarding it as a summary of its witness.

b. We should interpret each Scripture passage in its own immediate and total context, as part of the history of salvation, "a word of the entire Scriptures of both testaments."

[6] *Ibid.*, pp. xviii, xix f., xxix.
[7] *Ibid.*, pp. xxiii, 34-36.

c. We should carry out our exegetical study "in concert with the fathers and brethren," listening carefully to both older and more recent exegesis, including work done in other denominations than our own.

d. We need to recognize that the criterion of the scripturalness of a confession is not its verbatim agreement with the Scriptures. A confession may be fully scriptural, yet couched in nonbiblical terms, like the doctrine of the Trinity. What, then, does "scriptural" mean? Questions like the following must be asked: Are there Scripture passages which teach what a given confessional statement asserts? Are there none which contradict it? What point of view determines the selection of texts? Which passages are particularly normative because they state the *sum* of Scripture? Which extrabiblical concepts may be included to attest the fullness of the biblical witness? To what degree may logical deductions from biblical statements be employed? Throughout the process we must remember that the church's dogmatics, like its confessions, is always the servant of the church's proclamation, not an end in itself.[8]

2. Dogmatic theology is responsible for expounding systematically the truths of Scripture. In performing this task, however, it is "bound by the Confessions"; that is, it must move within the framework which they provide. This relationship yields guidelines for the work of the dogmatician.

a. The sole norm of dogmatics is Holy Scripture. "All dogmatic statements must be derived from God's revelation in His Word." Hence dogmatic theology must be the exposition of Scripture.

b. Within the Scriptures the all-controlling norm is the gospel—"the promise of forgiveness for the sake of Jesus Christ." Only those assertions are properly founded on Scripture which find their normative center in the eternal Word made flesh, whose work opens the way to our justification by grace through faith.

c. The gospel involves the ever present bestowal of forgiveness; it is "the Word by which God today forgives the sinner all his sins." This takes place through the preaching of the Word and the administration of the sacraments. Therefore dogmatics must always be carried on in close connection with this twofold proclamation of the gospel. It exists to serve such proclamation by an exposition of Scripture which guards it against false doctrine.

d. Man cannot know or believe the gospel except through the Holy Spirit—the witnessing and re-creating activity of the triune God. Dog-

[8] *Ibid.*, pp. 297-99, 314 f.

matics must make certain of the strictly trinitarian basis of its own epistemology and of biblical hermeneutics as well.

e. Dogmatics must beware of elevating the teachings of individual leaders—even the writings of the young Luther—to a status equal to that of the Confessions. They alone represent the consensus of the church, hence they "are incomparably and uniquely binding."

f. Dogmatics is responsible for continuing the work of the Confessions by exposing and refuting later heresies. Hence new confessions are always possible, and the work of dogmatic theology is never finished. "The Scripture must be heard ever anew." [9]

Toward an Ecumenical Theology

In view of the confessional nature of Schlink's theology as so far examined, the extent of his ecumenical interest may occasion surprise. The combination is best explained in his own words: "Far from widening the historic splits in Christendom, a concern for the right kind of confessing rather recalls the separated churches to the one Lord from whom alone they receive life." He therefore voices the hope that the English translation of his work on the Lutheran Confessions "will not lead to an anxious and aloof repristination but to a concern for genuine confession in our time and that it will encourage a loving approach to the other churches." [10] This attitude is manifest in Schlink's view of the importance of the Eastern tradition for Western Christendom. "Our *first* question must be what fruits of the Spirit we can perceive in *other* traditions, which are based on the common foundation of all churches, namely the message of the Apostles." [11]

Schlink's ecumenical concern is best understood in the light of his "morphological" approach to the structure of dogmatic statements.[12] He notes that Christians of different traditions can express together in prayer and preaching convictions—christological, anthropological, soteriological, or ecclesiological—which they cannot readily formulate in mutually acceptable dogmatic statements. He therefore inquires into the structural

---

[9] *Ibid.*, pp. 26-33, 316.

[10] *Ibid.*, pp. v-vi.

[11] "The Significance of the Eastern and Western Traditions for the Christian Church," *Ecumenical Review*, XII (1959-60), 142.

[12] "Die Struktur der dogmatischen Aussage als ökumenisches Problem," in *Der kommende Christus und die kirchlichen Traditionen* (Göttingen: Vandenhoeck und Ruprecht, 1961), pp. 24-79. Hereafter this book will be cited as *Der kommende Christus*.

differences between the two kinds of expression and the effect these differences have on the content of theological assertions.

Analysis reveals five basic forms of theological statement, all of them answers of faith to God's saving action in Jesus Christ: prayer, doxology, witness, teaching or doctrine, and confession. The last two of these crystallize into fixed formulas more easily than the others. In peculiar fashion all of the first four are concentrated in confession. For example, confessions of faith like the Apostles' and Nicene Creeds are doxology, prayer, and witness all in one.

Dogma roots in confession. Its history began with primitive confessions like "Jesus is Lord." However, as time passed, the structural elements in confession became independent and differentiated, and doctrinal elements tended to become dominant. Faith affirmed gradually became doctrine believed, then doctrine *to be* believed—true doctrine, the acceptance of which separated believers from nonbelievers. For example, the Chalcedonian Decree is not a confession in the spirit of worship, but a statement of truth agreed to; it begins not with "We believe in . . . ," but with "We teach that to be believed is . . . ." The Athanasian Creed carries the process further; in it the distinction between true and false belief which is implicit in all confession becomes explicit in the declaration that acceptance of the catholic faith is necessary for eternal salvation. Another change in the direction of greater rigidity is that an initial variety in confessional formulas gradually gave way to uniformity. The further the church moved from the apostolic age, the more definite became the formulations of the doctrinal content of its faith. Moreover, just as confession was the root of dogma, doctrine became the source of dogmatics, which is teaching *about* realities like faith, repentance, prayer, and witness, which result from God's saving act.

Such circumstances make plain that dogmatic theology must deal with the whole range of the answers which faith has given to the gospel. Doctrine has its important place, but distortion results if it oversteps its limits and silences the voice of sermon, exhortation, prayer, doxology, or confession. Falsification also ensues if any of these forms claims superiority and attempts to suppress the others.[13]

In addition to being one of the basic forms of *theological* assertion, the dogmatic statement is also one of the basic *anthropological* forms of ap-

[13] *Ibid.*, pp. 24-47. Cf. Schlink, "Changes in Protestant Thinking about the Eastern Church," *Ecumenical Review*, X (1957-58), 398.

prehension. Here structure is determined not by the divine address and the manifold responses of faith, but by the natural differences in the men encountered. These include differing religious and philosophical presuppositions, hence varying understandings of God, man, and self; different environmental experiences and social connections; different languages; and differences in psychophysical makeup. There are four basic forms of apprehension—the I-object consciousness, the consciousness of existence, picturization, and thought movement.

Because of such variations the gospel strikes different persons differently. It comes to each man in his concrete situation, and through the capacities and attitudes which are peculiarly his. His answers reflect his own singularity; it is *he* who is called into service; it is *he* who prays, witnesses, and confesses. Inevitably, therefore, differences in anthropological apprehension affect men's formulations of belief.[14]

Relating the basic forms to each other, Schlink draws three conclusions:

1. Where one theological form is isolated from the others or dominates them, it is easier for the corresponding anthropological forms to maintain themselves in spite of revelation and to intensify one-sidedness in theological statements.

2. Where the answer of faith is clearly expressed in the full range of theological forms, the anthropological forms are made more resilient and open to each other, human rigidities are overcome through the gospel, and men are saved from the sinful exaggeration of their differences.

3. The basic theological forms are of much greater significance than the anthropological ones.[15]

Where do these considerations lead with respect to the disparity in the dogmatic statements of separated churches over against their relative unity on the level of prayer and preaching? When assertions originally made in prayer and witness are translated into dogmatic statements, changes occur which are accentuated by the basic forms of anthropological apprehension. However, it would be erroneous to conclude that church unity can be attained by treating dogma as superfluous to real unity in Christ. True unity must be unity at all levels. The church's answer to the gospel in prayer and witness alone, without confession, would not be a complete answer of faith. Hence dogmatic statements must be taken seriously in ecumenical discussion. Through new formulations of questions and new methods we must

[14] *Der kommende Christus*, pp. 47-64.
[15] *Ibid.*, pp. 73 f.

strive for that unity of dogmatic utterance which is part of the unity of the church.

The New Testament canon is one, but it contains a variety of witnesses to Jesus Christ. Within the canon the one gospel was transmitted in four "Gospels." In the first centuries a variety of local confessions existed side by side, and their unity consisted in their mutual recognition by different congregations. Thus dogmatic unity does not require agreement on one formula; it may consist equally in "the fellowship of the reciprocal recognition of different dogmatic formulations." On this basis the problem of determining and expressing dogmatic unity is more complicated than when uniformity exists. Uniformity demands only a yes or no answer, whereas the unity of reciprocal recognition raises the question: In which statements can the one dogma be recognized? Though this question can be adequately answered only by an ecumenical dogmatics as a whole, certain preliminary suggestions regarding method can be made.

The different dogmatic formulations need to be investigated philologically, historically, and anthropologically. Special attention must be given to the place which they occupy among the basic forms of theological assertion and the degree to which they have cut themselves off from their confessional roots and changed the meanings originally intended. Also relevant is the quality of *actual* acceptance accorded different declarations by different communions; e.g., are they recognized as currently normative, as models of past belief, or merely sociologically, as symbols of fellowship? Full consideration must be given to the human differences which unconsciously affect men's formulations of belief. In all these areas careful scrutiny may bring to light an underlying unity or lack of unity not previously apparent.

If we also investigate the doctrinal statements of the separated churches morphologically, in connection with the entire range of their expressions of faith, we discover much more unity than could be expected from doctrinal assertions alone. Many statements of dogma are basically prayers or sermons which have been transposed into doctrinal form, whereas others are originally doctrinal. All must be interpreted according to their basic form. We then see both the rich variety of the forms and the true unity and fullness of dogma in its original configuration as confession, in which all forms are concentrated. Thus we discern the true unity-in-diversity of the church.[16]

[16] *Ibid.*, pp. 76-79.

From this perspective, moreover, we can understand how firm commitment to the Lutheran Confessions can stimulate ecumenical activity, which for Schlink now includes the writing of an "ecumenical dogmatics." A few features of this project may be mentioned.[17]

The work begins with an introductory section on the gospel as the ground of all dogmatic affirmation. Then follow three major parts which in a trinitarian structure deal with creation, reconciliation, and the new creation. A fourth part treats the doctrine of God, while a concluding section discusses God's loving decree. Although Schlink comments that this structure is "astonishingly traditional," it departs at several points from traditional patterns. The doctrine of man has no special section, but is treated under various other headings. Likewise, eschatology appears at several points instead of at the end as is ordinarily the case. Predestination, which Schlink insists should be indeterministically developed, is dealt with in the closing section. Questions having to do with the biblical canon and hermeneutics, instead of being treated under prolegomena, are not considered until Part Three in connection with the doctrine of the church.

Implicitly opposing Bultmann, Schlink insists that the hermeneutical question, rather than having priority over the canon, can be considered only when the canon already exists. The canon in turn is determined by the church. Christian doctrine exists to clarify and transmit the meaning of the proclamation of the mighty deeds of God which center in Jesus Christ. It must therefore speak not only of what God does, but also of God himself. Doxological confession implies a divine character, and therefore dogmatics rightly deals with those aspects of God's nature which he has revealed in the gospel. Similarly, dogmatics includes teaching concerning man and the world as they are in themselves, inasmuch as they are involved in teaching concerning God.

Characteristic Doctrinal Emphases

We now turn to an exposition of Schlink's views on three representative issues.

Law and Gospel

Schlink repeatedly refers to the distinction between law and gospel as central in Christian doctrine. The "decisive theme" is "sin and grace, law

---

[17] These comments on Schlink's projected ecumenical dogmatics are based on a lecture which he gave before the theological faculty of the University of Heidelberg on February 26, 1960, and on an extensive duplicated outline.

and gospel, judgment and forgiveness, God's wrath and God's mercy." The "proper" distinction, moreover, is one which recognizes the supremacy of gospel over law. Hence it can be said equally well that the central doctrine of Christianity is justification by grace through faith.[18]

Schlink points out three ways in which the difference between law and gospel in both temporal order and content appears. 1. The basic antithesis is that between the Old Testament law and the New Testament gospel. As God's Word through Moses to the people of the old covenant, the law demands works as the condition of life and discloses the power and extent of sin, but actually it brings death and is helpless to save. As God's Word to the people of the new covenant in Jesus Christ, the gospel calls men to faith, justifies the sinner, brings eternal life, and is the power of God for salvation to all who have faith. The law demands, the gospel gives.

2. Already in the Old Testament, law is a double Word of God; it includes both assurance and demand. Those who believed shared in the promised gifts although these gifts awaited fulfillment in Christ. The promise to Abraham and his descendants was based not on the law, but on the righteousness of faith in God's grace (Rom. 4:13; Gal. 3:18).

3. Also in the New Testament gospel, a distinction must be made between assurance and claim, God's gift and God's command. The apostolic proclamation includes both an indicative and an imperative. But the imperative is grounded in the indicative—the act of salvation which God accomplishes in the believer. God demands nothing from the man of faith which he has not already presented to him through the gospel. The believer is called on simply to live as one who has been forgiven, freed, newly created—a member of the body of Christ. The Christian imperative is well expressed by Paul's term *paráklesis,* which means both summons and comfort.[19]

Law and gospel cannot be truly understood apart from their underlying unity; both are the Word of one triune God, and both are acts of his love. Even Paul combines paradoxically the eschatological judgment of justification, which is received by faith independently of works, and judgment according to works. One gospel announces both the judgment which sinners deserve and the Christ who takes this judgment on himself. The fruits of the Spirit which result from the gospel correspond to the content of the law.[20]

[18] *Theology,* pp. xxii, xxv, xxix, 55. Cf. *Der kommende Christus,* p. 159.
[19] *Theology,* pp. 127-32; cf. pp. 117, 139.
[20] *Ibid.,* pp. 133-38.

Nevertheless, the distinction must be clearly maintained. The whole human race, whether it knows it or not, is moving toward the day when Christ will come to judge the living and the dead. He who is the Word of God will pronounce two different words, "Come," or "Depart from me" (Matt. 25:34, 41). Only one of the two will apply to each individual. Until then the church must offer men the choice between acquittal through faith or judgment according to works, calling everyone to repentance and faith. In view of this call, the distinction must always make plain the superiority of the gospel in its positive offer of salvation. No recognition of the weight of sin or the lostness of men should prevent the preacher from proclaiming above all the loving will of God who in Christ has destroyed the power of sin, death, and law.[21] Gospel, not law, is God's "proper" Word.

The Church

In accord with the Augsburg Confession, Schlink views the church as "the congregation of all faithful men, in which the gospel is purely preached and the holy sacraments administered according to the gospel." Stress is laid on the oral event of preaching or teaching,[22] not on possession of a doctrine; on actual administration of the sacraments, not on knowledge about them. "According to the gospel" connotes the offering and reception of the sacraments with the use of the words of institution found in the gospel, and in connection with sound interpretation. Schlink points out that by conceiving gospel and sacraments as essential to the church, the Augsburg Confession locates in the nature of the church the sole means by which God imparts the Holy Spirit and by which the Holy Spirit operates. He also comments on the absence of any mention of the Bible. The Scriptures are indeed the sole norm of all churchly teaching, but they have this status on the basis of the prophetic and apostolic gospel to which they bear witness, the center to whom both testaments testify, Jesus Christ.[23]

The church is the people of God gathered out of the world by the call of Christ, but equally the prophetic-priestly-royal people sent by him into the world to proclaim his lordship. This double movement centers in the worshiping assembly, in which Christ continually acts in Word and sacrament, and in which we offer our confessions, petitions, and doxologies, and

---

[21] *Ibid.*, pp. 138-43.

[22] In the Latin and German texts of the Augsburg Confession *preach* and *teach* have essentially the same meaning.

[23] "Die Weite der Kirche nach dem lutherischen Bekenntnis," *Der kommende Christus*, pp. 106-9.

respond to his call to service to one another and in the world. The church is the bride of Christ who awaits his coming, yet in worship already participates in the wedding feast. It is also the body of Christ which in worship is built up into "the fulness of him who fills all in all" (Eph. 1:23), bringing creation to its goal. The church is one, because of the unity of him who acts in all its members; holy, because the holiness of Christ is imparted to it and the Holy Spirit sanctifies his people and dwells in them; catholic, because the Ruler of all acts in its midst, empowering and commissioning his people; and apostolic, since Christ in truth encounters the church only in the apostolic witness. The church is also indestructible and visible. Finally, the church stands under judgment for its errors, unbelief, disobedience, narrow orthodoxy, legalism, and self-seeking, and so is called to repentance; at the same time it has the promise of rescue, glorification, and consummation through the Christ who is coming again in final victory.[24]

The character of the church's ministry is determined by the church's nature and task.[25] Through the gospel and baptism all believers are called to the life of the Spirit among the new people of God, and all are sent to minister according to their peculiar spiritual gifts. Some, however, are called to a particular service and specifically empowered to perform it. In the New Testament their ministry is primarily that of the missionary founding of churches and pastoral and administrative leadership. They are commissioned to this service by the laying on of hands, or ordination, which is not merely a form but an act in which the special gifts of God's grace are transmitted.[26]

From the beginning special authority has resided in the apostles, eyewitnesses of the resurrection who were commissioned to preach the good news of salvation. Their status is unique and unrepeatable, and their teaching is normative for all time. The entire ministry of the church, whether of ordained pastors or of other baptized persons, roots in the apostolic witness and in different ways carries it forward. Ordination through the laying on of hands of a bishop, whose authority may be traced back to the apostles, is to be sought as a valuable external sign of the continuity of the church and its ministry. However, it must not be separated from the substance

---

[24] "Christus und die Kirche," *Der kommende Christus*, pp. 88-105. This christological interpretation is Schlink's clearest account of the nature of the church. However, he rejects the equation of ecclesiology with Christology, insisting that the church can be understood only in its fully trinitarian context.

[25] Schlink's most careful study of the ministry appears in his lecture "Die apostolische Sukzession," in *Der kommende Christus*, pp. 160-95.

[26] *Ibid.*, pp. 165-68.

which it signifies—the transmission of apostolic teaching, which is neither dependent on nor guaranteed by the laying on of hands.

Specifically, apostolic succession for the church as a whole consists in (1) faith in the apostolic message and obedience to the apostolic instructions; (2) the witness to the apostolic gospel which each Christian is called to make according to his gifts; (3) a thrust into the world, combined with the building up of the congregation; and (4) the nurture of a sense of community with Christians everywhere, since the apostles are the bond of unity of the church in all times and places.

Apostolic succession for the pastor means that (1) he adheres to the apostolic model in preaching, teaching, guidance, and administration; (2) like the apostle, he is in the church the voice and representative of Christ; (3) like every other member of the congregation, he must turn each day anew to the grace of Christ; and (4) he tends the church in fellowship with other pastors, as well as with other Christians equipped to perform charismatic ministries.

Apostolic succession in both senses must carry on the relationship of apostle and church in the community of reciprocal service and common service to the world. Hence in our effort to understand the unity of the church we must recapture the primitive Christian category of community. In both faith and order the early church manifested far greater diversity than was later realized, mainly because the first Christians, amid their differences, were aware that they belonged to one another. This sense of our oneness in Christ is apostolic, and basic to Christian understanding and unity in all epochs.[27]

Eschatology and Historical Society

Eschatological overtones have been heard at various points in this chapter. Likewise, Schlink's concern for responsible action by Christians in society has become clearly apparent. To many Americans it may seem strange to consider together these two aspects of his thought. Yet Schlink often does just this. In his view the expectation of God's victory at the end of history is dialectically related to the struggle for righteousness in history.

Schlink emphasizes that the real threat to our world comes not from men or nature but from God, whose judgment none can escape. Conversely, our hope is not in the preservation of this world, but in Jesus Christ. He is the hope of the world because he frees us from its binding ties, calling men out of it to become a people whose citizenship is in heaven; because he

[27] *Ibid.*, pp. 108 f., 171-73, 182-86, 192-94.

makes possible its transformation through repentance and faith; and because he is its end, bringing to birth a new creation. In the church this new creation is already real; Christ is already gathering his faithful people. Thus we are now living in the "last days." In his resurrection Christ has been elevated to lordship over the world. On his return he will make his victory clear. The passage of two thousand years is "no refutation of His promise. ... Rather, this time in which we live is the time of God's patience; ... the time of the Church, of the growing body of Christ." When the body has reached its full stature and the number of the elect is complete, the world will pass away and the new creation will be realized.[28]

In discussing the threat of nuclear war Schlink similarly declares that in Christ the world has already come to its end; it is now subjected to him as its Lord. World history can bring forth nothing new; the genuinely new occurs only as the dead are given new life through the gospel and growth takes place in the community of believers. God allows history to continue because he purposes the salvation of additional multitudes. The final end of history will come with the return of Christ, the judge of both the world and the church. In this perspective, the preservation of earthly life at any price can never be for Christians a norm of ethical decision. Men who have rejected God are dead even though physically alive, and men with faith in Christ live even in death.[29]

Nevertheless, the present period is a time of action rather than passivity; Christians carry on their work "with the most intense expectancy." Two tasks in particular are theirs: preaching the gospel for the whole world and accepting responsibility for a just society. Though the former task is primary, the God we preach and in whom we hope is Sustainer as well as Creator and Redeemer; he "sustains men in order that they should make, under Him, a responsible decision." Such a God

demands that we take responsibility for the preservation of all human life regardless of whether that life be Christian or not, that we take responsibility for all men, regardless of their nationality, race, or social status, and He also demands that we accept responsibility for their freedom. ... Accepting the obligation ... means taking responsibility for justice and peace on earth—peace among men, classes, races, peoples, and nations. And it means having an active concern, in the fullest sense of that word, for the right ordering of society.[30]

---

[28] "Christ the Hope of the World," *Ecumenical Review*, VII (1954-55), 127-32.

[29] "Die Atomfrage in der kirchlichen Verkündigung," in *Atomzeitalter, Krieg und Frieden*, ed. Günther Howe (Witten and Berlin: Eckart-Verlag, 1959), pp. 204-8, 212.

[30] "Christ the Hope of the World," p. 134.

Knowing himself saved by Christ, the Christian in struggling for a just order will be selfless regarding his own interests, but "adamant in his concern for the enslaved, the hungry, and the forgotten." Hidden in God's care, believers are freed for real encounter with their fellow men, for discovery of the thou and the neighbor even in their enemies.[31]

The life-giving center of the church's activity in the world is its worship. Here the Lord purifies and strengthens his people, unites them with himself, and sends them out to serve. If the congregation's sacrifice of praise and devotion is genuine, it "breaks out into the world, and the whole life of the members becomes that sacrifice of praise that is extolled by Christ." [32] From this perspective Schlink points out that

the Western churches regard the Eastern Church's concentration on the holy liturgy as a way of eluding responsibility in the world, and its hymnic emphasis on the eschatological presence as tantamount to abandoning this world to its own devices without attempting to influence society or promote justice. Does the Eastern Church seriously realise that obedience to God implies something more than witness and worship, but also demands active efforts to promote justice and freedom in human society? For it is not only as our Redeemer, but also as the Sustainer of the world, that God requires our obedience! [33]

Christians must with all their strength oppose the use of weapons of mass destruction and work to prevent nuclear war. However, Schlink is not a nuclear pacifist. He maintains that at present the threat of the use of atomic weapons hinders their actual use, so that possession of them to this degree contributes to the preservation of life. In this precarious situation the church, while calling the world to repentance and faith, must seek to arouse an international conscience against the resort to atomic weapons, and do everything possible to prevent war itself.[34]

While pleading for active effort for social justice and peace, Schlink repeatedly insists that this is not the primary concern of the Christian or the church. "Peace on earth is not peace with God." The justice and freedom attainable here are limited and transitory. "This life is not eternal life. Our striving for a just order in society does not bring in Christ's Kingdom nor does it fashion the new creation. Christ's Kingdom enters only

---

[31] *Ibid.;* "Die Atomfrage," p. 215.
[32] "Worship in the Light of Protestant Theology," *Ecumenical Review,* XIII (1960-61), 151 f.
[33] "The Significance of the Eastern and Western Traditions for the Christian Church," *Ecumenical Review,* XII (1959-60), 140.
[34] "Christ the Hope of the World," p. 134; "Die Atomfrage," pp. 211, 215, 217, 222 f.

through the gospel; the Communion of Saints is the new creation." Our chief task is to tell men of the peace of God.[35]

The atom bomb is not our basic trouble, but "only a symptom of an all-embracing sickness of human society which lies much deeper." Man has usurped the place of his Creator, sinfully claiming the created world for his own and thereby perverting the God-intended relation of man to man and man to nature. Since he seeks domination over his fellows instead of community, the exploitation of nature rather than stewardship over it, he is enslaved by anxiety and fear. By assuming power over his own life he has chosen the way of death.[36]

Above all, therefore, the church must proclaim to a world under judgment the way of redemption. This command of God the Redeemer cannot be separated from the command of God the Sustainer to seek the establishment of earthly justice. But their relative order must be kept clear.

God preserves this world in order that through the Gospel salvation may be offered. He does not offer salvation in order that the world may be preserved. We do not preach the Gospel in order to bring about earthly justice. On the contrary, we try to establish justice in order that we may preach the Gospel.[37]

Facing the menace of atomic destruction, Christianity places its hope in the lordship of Christ. This world is inescapably under the rule of him who on the cross won victory over all evil and is coming again at the end of time. He is also present in the world now, calling it to repentance and faith, gathering his people and sending them out with his saving message. Through his Holy Spirit God guides us as to what we shall do, and uses our action to lead men "in the way of salvation through guilt, need, and suffering to the eschatological time of consummation." [38]

Critique

Values

1. Schlink is to be commended on his combination of high regard for his own heritage with openness to the convictions of other traditions. His own work demonstrates eloquently that concern for scripturally grounded confession, instead of erecting barriers, may lead separated churches closer

---

[35] "Christ the Hope of the World," p. 135; "Die Atomfrage," pp. 214-16.
[36] "Die Atomfrage," pp. 211 f.
[37] "Christ the Hope of the World," p. 135.
[38] "Die Atomfrage," pp. 224 f.

together because it recalls them to the one Lord proclaimed in the apostolic message. Illustrative of this truth are Schlink's acceptance of some of Barth's emphases, his warm relationships with Roman Catholic and Eastern Orthodox theologians, and his constructive participation in ecumenical enterprises.

2. Schlink's morphological approach to the structure of dogmatic statements is an illuminating scientific contribution to ecumenical understanding. The identification of Christian beliefs as expressed in prayer, doxology, witness, and confession as well as formal doctrine should promote mutual appreciation and awareness of existing unity among Christian bodies, and respect for seriously held doctrinal differences. Knowledge also of the powerful influence on belief of psychological, linguistic, and environmental differences makes it easier to deal constructively with dogmatic disagreements.

3. In opposition to Bultmann and some other theologies of existence, Schlink maintains that dogma is concerned with God, man, and the world as they really are. In this he has the support of the biblical witness and the major historic expressions of Christian faith. With Bultmann, Schlink stresses proclamation and personal encounter. However, he rightly insists that since the gospel proclaims the mighty acts of God revealed in Jesus Christ, dogmatics must speak of God himself as thus disclosed, not only of what he does. Similarly, it must deal with the nature of the man whom God acts to save. The encounter, moreover, is not an isolated event, but a relation between God and man, both of whom exist before and after each encounter.

4. Schlink's interpretation of the relation between law and gospel is both clarifying and irenic. In typical Lutheran fashion he emphasizes the fundamental importance of this distinction and elucidates its nature, adhering to the traditional order rather than accepting Barth's gospel-law reversal. Nevertheless, he is close to Barth in making plain the underlying unity of law and gospel and in asserting unequivocally the primacy and superiority of the gospel as God's "proper" Word. He thus increases the possibility of understanding between two major theological orientations.

5. Schlink renders an important service by making plain the relevance of a prominently eschatological perspective to social responsibility. While insisting that world history must be seen in the light of its end, he shows convincingly that God, by continuing to sustain his world, requires us to accept responsibility for the preservation of life and for the maintenance of freedom, justice, and peace among men. This insight is a valuable corrective for opposite forms of one-sidedness: the this-worldly activism which

regards eschatological belief as inherently devoid of concern for life here and now; and the otherworldly pietism which accepts no obligation for the right ordering of earthly society.

Difficulties

1. Open to question is Schlink's assumption that the confessional writings above all else provide the necessary prolegomena to systematic theology and the guidelines within which it must proceed. He does assert the responsibility of dogmatics to deal with new heresies, and he acknowledges that new confessions may sometimes be needed. However, apart from such new statements the existing Confessions are "incomparably and uniquely binding" above all other pronouncements. Schlink is certainly right in regarding them as an essential foundation for systematic theology, and in recognizing their unique worth derived from their expression of a corporate rather than a merely individual witness. But there are weighty objections to his supposition that in the interpretation of Scripture the Confessions are second only to the Scriptures themselves in the guidance they provide.

a. As Schlink himself admits, the Confessions omit some important biblical truths while greatly abbreviating others.

b. As he also concedes, they shed no light on many pressing issues which confront Christian theology today. Instead of giving priority to documents the latest of which are four centuries old, should we not seek mainly for the fresh guidance of the Holy Spirit as we attempt to interpret the gospel in our own intellectual and cultural situation?

c. The confessional statements, highly condensed, cannot match the thoroughness with which important issues are explored in the writings of many individual theologians who also represent the thought of the church, and whose ideas have often evoked the confessional definitions. In some instances Irenaeus, Augustine, Anselm, Thomas Aquinas, Luther, Calvin, or Wesley may prove to be better guides than the tight formulas of the Nicene Creed, the Augsburg Confession, or the Smalcald Articles.

d. In the interest of doctrinal unity and conformity, the Confessions sometimes attempt a harmonization or leveling down of scriptural statements which obscures the real diversity of the biblical witness.

e. There are obvious discrepancies between different Confessions of the same period, making necessary some discrimination between them.

2. In Schlink, as in Luther, there appears an unresolved dialectic between adherence to the ontology of the ancient creeds and concern for the personal appropriation of truth demanded by the doctrine of justification. However,

as Hermann Diem has shown, this is a false antithesis, intensified for Schlink by the current theological conflict between essentialist and existentialist points of view. In the perspective of the trinitarian action of God affirmed by the creeds, the whole opposition between ontology and "personalism" is seen to be false, since it is only through this action that man becomes fully a person and receives in faith the gift of salvation.[39]

3. Though Schlink makes a strong case for Christian social responsibility on the basis of the activity of God as Sustainer, he fails to bring to bear on this problem the full implications of his trinitarian faith. The doctrines of creation and redemption also have profound social significance. Christians are summoned to seek each other's welfare and a just social order because all men are children of one Father, who has created them in his image for fellowship with himself and one another, and because all men are objects of his redeeming love manifest in Jesus Christ. The gospel, which is rightly central in Schlink's theology, declares that God has acted to redeem sinful men and fulfill his purpose in creation. The salvation made real as men respond in repentance, faith, and love concerns life now as well as hereafter, and it is inherently social, involving persons in their wholeness, interrelated with other persons in manifold ways. Moreover, it is realized within a community which is called to a ministry of reconciliation of man with God and man with man. Possibly the sharpness of Schlink's distinction between law and gospel, coupled with his separation between the earthly and the heavenly realms, obscures for him such social connotations of faith in God as Creator and Redeemer.

4. Although Schlink's strongly eschatological orientation allows no room for social irresponsibility, it lacks any positive estimate of earthly history or man's temporal activities. Present history is significant only as a time of waiting for the consummation to come in the return of Christ, and hence especially as a time for the proclamation of the gospel of salvation. This view was quite appropriate for first-century Christians for whom the *parousia* was imminent, but it is hardly adequate now, in view of the prolongation of history for more than nineteen additional centuries. Inevitably questions arise concerning the purpose of creation and the meaning of history which are much too large to be dealt with here. It is hardly likely, however, that God created the world only in order that men might sin and be saved. If creation was good, as biblical faith affirms, and if

[39] Diem, "Dogmatik zwischen Personalismus und Ontologie," *Evangelische Theologie,* XV (1955), 414.

God's purpose is placing men on this earth has been flouted, as it has, may not his will for men include the greatest possible fulfillment of his original ends within history as well as their consummation beyond history? Such a view seems implied in the prayer, "Thy kingdom come, thy will be done on earth as it is in heaven."

It is also clear that God has created us capable of high values—social, intellectual, moral, esthetic, and religious. Such experiences have positive worth, now as well as eternally. Schlink is right in making all-important the new relation to God which the gospel offers, and in placing all life in the perspective of God's everlasting kingdom. Yet that very perspective gives exalted meaning to the things that are "true, honorable, just, pure, lovely, and gracious" here and now, and it assigns positive value to the historical institutions and relations which provide a structure within which such values may be attained.

8. GUSTAF WINGREN

Immediate Background

About the same time as the dialectical theology appeared in Switzerland and Germany, fresh theological winds began to stir at the University of Lund in Sweden in the work of Gustaf Aulén and Anders Nygren. Although both movements opposed the then dominant liberal theology, in other respects they were opposed to each other. Barth and his supporters, strongly influenced by Kierkegaard and existentialist philosophy, initially rejected every attempt to ground dogmatics in anthropology or philosophy of religion. In contrast, the Lundensians, approaching theology from the perspective of a Kantian-Schleiermacherian interpretation of religion, sought to free dogmatics from any connection with metaphysics and to demonstrate its independence and scientific nature. A particular concern was the definition of the essence or distinctive nature of Christianity. The method developed to achieve this purpose was that of motif-research, which sought to identify the basic motif of Christianity in relation to the motifs of other historical religions and ethical systems.

Aulén has exerted great influence, particularly through two of his works, *Christus Victor* [1] and *The Faith of the Christian Church*. [2] In the

[1] Tr. A. G. Hebert (New York: The Macmillan Company, [1931] 1951).
[2] Tr. Eric H. Wahlstrom and G. Everett Arden (Philadelphia: Muhlenberg Press, [1948] 1960).

former, a primarily historical study of atonement theories, he champions the "classical" view of Irenaeus and Luther (in Christ's death and resurrection God frees man by defeating the power of evil) over against the Latin or objective theory of Anselm and the humanistic or subjective view of Abelard. The latter, one of the very few one-volume systematic theologies available in English, is widely used in American seminaries.

It is Nygren, however, who has developed the characteristically Lundensian method of motif-research, or typological or structural research. In Nygren's view the questions of both religion and ethics are concerned with man's relationship with other persons and his more ultimate relationship with the Eternal, or God. Behind particular doctrinal formulations are more basic answers to such questions which synthesize many individual values, judgments, and decisions. These are what Nygren means by fundamental motifs or structures. Underlying these, moreover, may be found in each religion the basic motif which distinguishes it from all others.

In his *Agape and Eros*[3] he defines three motifs in religion and ethics— *agape, eros,* and *nomos.* In the *agape* motif the dominant factor is the spontaneous, unmotivated, other-regarding, self-giving love disclosed in Jesus Christ. The *eros* motif is marked by love which desires primarily to possess the good or to attain the higher values. Uppermost in the *nomos* motif is fulfillment of the law, including a system of rewards and punishments. The three are respectively characteristic of Christianity, Hellenistic thought, and Judaism. Nygren's book deals mainly with the two love motifs. Proceeding historically, he shows that Christian thought concerning love has tended to adulterate the *agape* of the Christian revelation with the *eros* of Hellenism. In his view the Reformation rightly brought this attempted synthesis to an end and preserved the uniqueness of the Christian faith.

Theological Position

Nygren was succeeded at Lund by Gustaf Wingren, formerly one of his outstanding students. Significantly, Wingren began his scholarly work with research into the thought of Irenaeus and Luther, the two theologians believed by Nygren to have stated the *agape* motif most clearly. The results appeared in his doctoral dissertation, *Luther on Vocation,*[4] and *Man and the Incarnation,*[5] an investigation of the biblical theology of Irenaeus.

[3] *Agape and Eros; a Study of the Christian Idea of Love,* tr. A. G. Hebert; 2 vols. (New York: The Macmillan Company, 1932-38. One-volume edition, 1953).

[4] *Luthers lära om kallelsen,* 1948.

[5] *Människan och inkarnationen enligt Irenaeus,* 1947.

Then followed a series of related volumes: *The Living Word*,[6] a study of the preaching of the classic themes of the Christian faith in relation to the nature and mission of the church; *Theology in Conflict*,[7] a critical examination of the anthropological and hermeneutical presuppositions of Nygren, Barth, and Bultmann, which yields important clues to the author's own views; *Creation and Law*;[8] and *Gospel and Church*.[9] The two latest books are integrally related, and together provide the best constructive statement of Wingren's dogmatics. We now turn to an exposition of his basic theological position as disclosed primarily in these four related volumes.

Creation

According to Wingren, Nygren and Barth are in different ways guilty of the same error—that of beginning with the second article of the ancient three-part Christian creeds instead of the first. Nygren defines Christianity solely in terms of the *agape* of the New Testament, out of all relation to the *nomos* motif which is dominant in the Old Testament. But this leaves *agape* in a vacuum. The New Testament gospel cannot soundly be separated from the law, since the law poses the question of guilt which the gospel answers with the proclamation of forgiveness through Christ.[10] Nygren fails to see this because he mistakenly treats the Christian faith as an answer to the philosophical question regarding the essence of Christianity. Barth's christological approach assumes that we can understand God's work in creation only in the light of the gospel of his incarnation. But this attitude places "man and his knowledge, rather than God and His works in the centre"; and it forgets the biblical recognition that man as continually created by God knows, quite apart from the gospel that he is subject to law, guilt, and judgment.[11]

Wingren believes that such misinterpretation can be corrected only by keeping the Old and New Testaments together, and by beginning with

[6] *Predikan*, 1949.

[7] *Teologiens metodfràga*, 1954.

[8] *Skapelsen och lagen*, 1958. The five works listed were published in Sweden by C. W. K. Gleerup, Lund. The English translations were published by Muhlenberg Press (now Fortress Press, Philadelphia, 1957-1964).

[9] *Evangeliet och kyrkan* (Lund: C. W. K. Gleerup, 1962). This work has not yet been translated into English. References in this chapter are to the German edition, *Evangelium und Kirche*, tr. P. Gerhard Klose (Göttingen: Vandenhoeck und Ruprecht, 1963).

[10] *Theology in Conflict*, pp. 66 f., 69; *Creation and Law*, p. 58, n. 39.

[11] *Creation and Law*, pp. 11 f.; *Theology in Conflict*, pp. 42, 73 f., 115; *Evangelium und Kirche*, pp. 39 f., 119.

God's work of creation, as do the trinitarian creeds.[12] According to the Bible the original basis of man's relation to God is creation itself, "the fact that man lives." [13] Quite apart from the incarnation, creation itself shows man's complete dependence on his Creator for his existence. No aspect of man's life can be isolated from this relationship (Ps. 139:5). Moreover, creation is not a one-time affair; it continues in the present, and it includes each individual person. Every man's birth is a result of the continuing creative activity of God, who gives him life and responsibility for fulfilling certain functions which he has not himself determined.[14] The primary human realities of conception and birth, love, work, and death are established by God, not man. In short, man's life is the work of God. This view is not only affirmed by the Old Testament but espoused by the New Testament writers and by the early church, which accepted both collections of writings as its canonical Scriptures.

However, the Bible speaks also of man's rebellion against his Creator. Yielding to the temptation to trust himself instead of God, he sins, and his disobedience disrupts his relation to created nature and his fellow men as well as to God. As a result, he faces the judgment and wrath of God and falls under the dominion of death.[15] There are thus two aspects of the status of man in creation. First, even as fallen man he retains a certain power over the natural order which God has created good. Secondly, he disobeys God's will for him in relation to his neighbor and misuses his authority over nature. Therefore, he experiences the will of God as threat and constraint; commanded to do it, he finds himself in a relation of compulsion and bondage to his fellows and to the work he is given to perform.[16] This is the situation of all men on earth.

The answer to man's plight is the gospel of the birth, life, death, and resurrection of Christ. However, the gospel is not preached to men who have no prior awareness of their need. On the contrary, it is always proclaimed to men with the story of Genesis 1-3 behind them. "Creation is repeated in every birth, the fall in the egocentric attempt made by every man to guarantee his own safety. The condemnation of the Law is felt by all men in the bondage and constraint in which they are imprisoned." Men are still free to respond either affirmatively or negatively to God's offer of

[12] *Creation and Law*, pp. 16, 9, 126 f.; *Evangelium und Kirche*, pp. 10 f., 93, 109 f.
[13] *Creation and Law*, p. 67.
[14] *Ibid.*, pp. 26, 47, 49, 89; *Evangelium und Kirche*, p. 49, n. 2.
[15] *Creation and Law*, pp. 40 f., 44, 49-51, 117 f.
[16] *Ibid.*, pp. 95, 123.

salvation. They may refuse to admit that they have wasted the lives given them by God, or they may say in penitence, "I am God's lost Creation. I believe—help Thou my unbelief." [17] In either case, they speak out of a universal human condition which already roots in the creative activity of God—the same God who in Christ acts redemptively to heal the sinful disorder of that condition.

If in this way we place creation first, we may still speak with Barth of the "creation of the world in Christ" (Col. 1:16 f.; Heb. 1:2; John 1:1-14). This concept is best understood if we put the creation of man rather than that of the world in the center. By his very existence as the creature of God man is "destined for Christ," made in his image. Even before the gospel God fashioned his external creation, giving men life and calling them to goodness and love. Thus that creation speaks basically the same language as does Christ, in whom God gives newness of life and reconciliation with himself.[18] Man's creation points beyond alienation to his new creation through the work of him who is both Creator and Conqueror.

The Law

The doctrine of creation is also the clue to the biblical conception of the law. Fundamentally the law is inherent in the fact that God has created the world and governs it. The law with its pressure and compulsion is built into the nature of man's corporate life, whether men recognize it or not. For example, the demands of community living, such as those connected with the need for food, clothing, and shelter, proceed from our relation to other men. These social pressures are empirically given, and the neighbor is present in them from the start.[19]

Further, the law is peculiarly related to man's sinful distortion of the divine purpose in creation. It is God's creative will as disclosed in his conflict with human sin. It is thus correlative with sin. God "governs the course of events in accordance with his will in opposition to that hostile resistance in whose destructive work man has become involved because of his sin. The sovereignty of the law is the direct result of the corruption of life." [20] The law is good, since it mediates God's mercy. However, it is

---

[17] *Ibid.*, pp. 119 f.

[18] *Ibid.*, pp. 35, 42.

[19] *Theology in Conflict*, pp. 140 f., 81 f.; *Creation and Law*, p. 43; *Evangelium und Kirche*, p. 179.

[20] *Theology in Conflict*, pp. 141 f., 82; *Creation and Law*, p. 125.

also in part the "alien" or "hardened" will of God, operating with greater severity than God would have displayed if men had not sinned. Nevertheless, "it is still the same divine will which God revealed in His pure gift in the primal act of Creation." [21]

Thus the law is grounded in the total life of man as a disobedient creature of God. Its ethical content is here, and neither needs to be nor should be derived solely from the gospel—as Barth seeks to do by reversing the biblical order and moving from gospel to law. Such a reversal, Wingren believes, makes the world profane and the New Testament legalistic, since then we must somehow discover in the message of God's act of forgiveness the ethical norms which we have refused to find in creation itself.[22] Men experience law, temptation, and guilt before they hear the gospel preached. The sacrificial love called for by the gospel does indeed go beyond the demands of the law, but rather than being antagonistic it is a fulfillment of the regard for the neighbor which is required by man's participation in society. The biblical order of law and gospel is therefore sound.

Wingren adopts Luther's distinction between the two functions of the law, "civil" and "proper," designating them respectively as the first and second uses,[23] and relating them concretely to twentieth-century life.

In its first or "civil" use the law points man primarily outward toward the world, and concerns chiefly his responsibilities there. It commands man to fulfill the needs of his neighbor, and backs up its demands with the power of enforcing its norms. Thus it functions in the compulsion and the condemnation and restraint of evil which are necessary for orderly life in society. It operates by constraint rather than by persuasion, forcing all men to recognize its demands, and retaining its authority even where love of neighbor is missing. We are obligated to our neighbors just because they are there, created by God. Positively and negatively, therefore, the law functions to produce the works of "earthly righteousness" [24] which pre-

---

[21] *Creation and Law,* p. 138.

[22] *Ibid.,* pp. 71 f.; *Evangelium und Kirche,* pp. 39 f., 119. Moreover, Wingren rejects Barth's accusation that his view of law is merely "a conventional Lutheran accentuation" (*Creation and Law,* p. 82). Indeed, though he frequently cites Luther's views on the law-gospel relation and for the most part agrees with them, he insists that what is required is not simply a restudy of Luther, but a direct study of the biblical documents themselves, so that we can do for our day what Luther did for the sixteenth century. The alternative would be to "assume that the Weimar Edition is God's Word which we are now to proclaim" (*ibid.,* pp. 72 f., 76 f., 80, 82, 104 f.).

[23] *Usus civilis* and *usus proprius.* Luther himself does not use numerical designations.

[24] Luther, *Commentary on Galatians,* Weimar edition of Luther's *Werke,* vol. XL, part I, p. 45, l.27–p. 47, l.14.

serve and advance human life. In both respects it is part of God's continuing creation of the world.[25]

Wingren is convinced that the first use of the law must not be restricted to civil government alone. The good works demanded relate also to family, education, science, art, economic life, the administration of justice, and international relations. All of these serve the needs of men, and our involvement in them arises much less from choice than from the fact that as created beings we are members of a society to which they are essential. The acts we perform in relation to them may be other-regarding or self-centered, but the need of some action is forced on us to a considerable degree by social pressures. These pressures are an embodiment of the first use of the law.[26]

In its second or "proper" use the law concerns man himself, who even in performing what is demanded of him often renders only superficial obedience through compulsion alone. The law confronts man with his guilt before God, accuses and convicts him of sin, judges and condemns the evil in his heart. It reveals to man his stark failure to conform to God's will, saying to him in unmistakable terms, "You are not the image of God you were created to be." This is the principal or essential function of the law, since it operates at the deepest level of man's being, burdens his conscience, and sets him before God as a captive and sinner.[27] It thus makes him aware of his need for redemption, which if accomplished transforms his motivation for furthering the interests of men in society—the concern of the civil use of the law.

However, the two uses cannot be separated. The guilt disclosed springs from evil committed in the world in relation to man's neighbor and the created things which he has made his idols. He has refused to give what was required of him—trust in God, love toward his neighbor, responsible use of the resources of nature. Hence the compulsion involved in the first use is constantly passing into the accusation which functions in the second. The law operates in both ways at once. In the former I am required to look out on the world, which rightly commands my service, and which is "purer" than I because it has not fallen and is still doing God's will. In the latter I am required to look inward at myself, recognizing that I am actual-

[25] *Creation and Law*, pp. 149-55, 160, 111.
[26] *Ibid.*, pp. 153-56.
[27] *Ibid.*, pp. 149-51, 174, 181-83, 195.

ly less "pure" than the world. Thus the two uses are but two sides of the same coin.[28]

Law and Gospel

The accusatory use of the law is fulfilled, however, only when Christ is proclaimed in the gospel. It is true that the proclamation comes to men who because of the law are already aware of their distress. Jesus himself went to sinners who knew of their captivity before they heard the good news of release. We know of our sickness and our need of a physician simply because we are men. The guilty conscience which we experience before the witness to Christ is in principle the same as that which we know afterward. In each case it is the work of the law. Without the background of the law, the gospel would be "made to answer a question from which the idea of guilt has been removed." [29]

Nevertheless, the full extent of our need is disclosed only when we hear the gospel. Then our sense of guilt is broadened until it includes our whole existence. No commandment can make its accusation so particular and personal as the specific human life of the Incarnate One. Here concretely we see the gulf between this true image of God and the broken, distorted images which we have fashioned by our sin.

We see our total guilt because we now stand outside ourselves, glimpse the meaning of total forgiveness, and learn that we can become new creations. At its best the law remains basically a summons to works; it cannot bring salvation. But the gospel offers a new beginning which will ultimately transform the rule of law. It points away from works to another kingdom which is not of this world. The deepest function of the law, that of putting man "to death," is both revealed and brought to completion when men through the gospel are led out of the bondage of sin into the freedom of new creatures in Christ.[30]

Jesus Christ and the Gospel

Wingren makes clear that the redemptive action of God in Jesus Christ is central for Christian faith. "This is the gospel, the Word with which the church stands and falls." The second article must not be isolated from the first or allowed to become the sole starting point. Nevertheless, it announces a *new* divine act by which the reign of law is broken and a new

[28] *Ibid.,* pp. 180 f.
[29] *Ibid.,* pp. 160, 177 f., 184 f., 98 f., 103 f.
[30] *Ibid.,* pp. 182 f., 194 f.

community of forgiven men is established.[31] This occurs through him who unites humanity and divinity in himself.

As man under the law Christ experiences the full reality of human life, including temptation, suffering, deprivation, and death.[32] However, his abasement is in itself his victory, for it represents the opposite of our attitude. He recapitulates the life of "Adam" in reverse. By emptying himself and taking the form of a servant he realizes the true image of God, which is true humanity. Whereas Adam (we) ruined human life by trying to become like God, Christ by becoming man—renouncing his divine rights and rendering the obedience of a servant, even to the cross—overcomes the reign of law and its wrath, while in his resurrection he also conquers death.[33]

Christ acts *as God* when he gives life to others, creating it in those who do not of themselves possess it. Only God can really create, bringing the new into being. The divinity of Christ is expressed decisively in the forgiveness of sins, by which he annuls the judgment based on God's law. Even before his death he begins to break the power of the law; however, his resurrection extends this divine forgiving action to all men. Far from being simply the return to life of a dead man, the resurrection is centrally the conquest of the law and thus the renewal of creation through the forgiveness of men's guilt.[34]

Wingren believes that this understanding of Christ best preserves both the reality and the union of his two natures. If his divinity is seen in his forgiveness of sins, then it is manifested on the cross when a man who has plumbed the depths of human agony prays for his enemies. Thus the divine qualities are "communicated" to the human nature. God's power to overcome the law operates in and through the human struggle of one who is himself under the law.[35]

Wingren's strong emphasis on the humanity of Christ leads him to modify while basically accepting Aulén's "classical" theory of the atonement. In his judgment Aulén overemphasizes the divine character of Christ's victory over the powers of evil and death and diminishes the im-

[31] *Evangelium und Kirche,* pp. 10 f., 77, 109 f.

[32] Repeatedly Wingren attacks the "monophysite Christocentricity" which fails to assign to the real humanity of Christ the central role which it plays in New Testament soteriology. This failure he traces mainly to the antiliberal attitude which has dominated European theology since World War I (*Evangelium und Kirche,* pp. 52, 54, 58, 264).

[33] *Ibid.,* pp. 44 f., 56-59, 104.

[34] *Ibid.,* pp. 75, 91 f., 104 f.

[35] *Ibid.,* pp. 51, 105.

portance of his real humanity. We must see the self-emptying of Christ and his obedience unto death as the opposite of the disruption of creation through Adam, and therefore as the restoration and deliverance of man created by God. However, Wingren accents with Aulén the radical nature of the conflict in man and the world. Humanity is the battleground of a cosmic duel in which a life-and-death struggle is being fought between God and Satan. The Old Testament portrays this conflict in the history of Israel, and the gospel presupposes that the man who hears is enslaved by "an active, evil power" which must be killed in order that a new man may appear. "An evil activity against a good activity, a conflict—that is the basic conception of the New Testament." Each man's existence, with its daily experience of light and darkness, evidences both God's goodness and the destroyer's evil. Caught in this grim battle, humanity cries out for release from the power of the devil.[36]

This release occurs through the death and resurrection of Christ. The atonement is not the payment of a penalty or a subjective change in the sinner. It is rather the decisive victory of Christ over Satan. In his cross and resurrection he routed the forces of evil and broke the power of sin and death.[37] In this triumph he conquered our enemies as well as his. "The victory over Satan is Christ's death and resurrection which took place that redemption might be ours through the Word and baptism." We are freed from the threat of death by the power of Christ's resurrection flowing into our lives, breaking down the barriers, and refashioning in us the image of God in which we were created.[38]

In opposition to Bultmann, Wingren affirms the factual nature of both the cross and the resurrection. Apart from such factuality there would be no valid ground for preaching. *"Not faith but only the fact in which faith believes is a valid ground."* The gospel is truly the gospel because the events it proclaims really *took place* in history independently of their acceptance in faith. He recognizes, however, that the factual nature of these events may not be treated as a purely scientific question without radically altering their central meaning. *"The fact in which faith believes is no longer the same fact if faith is absent."* But belief in the outwardness of

---

[36] *Ibid.,* pp. 54-56; *The Living Word,* pp. 49, 112 f., 53, 91; *Creation and Law,* p. 114. Wingren finds a major weakness of Barth's theology in his failure to recognize the reality of the enemy in the total event of salvation through Christ. For Barth there is "no active evil power"; "evil has no objective existence" (*Creation and Law,* pp. 112 f., 124).

[37] *Theology in Conflict,* pp. 25, 34, 37, 122 n.; *Evangelium und Kirche,* pp. 53-55, 66 f., 96.

[38] *The Living Word,* p. 78; cf. pp. 53 f., 91 f.; *Creation and Law,* p. 73. Wingren interprets "death" broadly to include "the whole dislocation of God's life-giving activity" (*ibid.,* p. 49).

the events of Christ's death and resurrection cannot be given up any more than faith in God's creation of the external world. Salvation does not occur in a vacuum or in a purely I-thou relation of man to God. It is mediated by God's action in the material world which he made and rules.[39]

The Church

The freedom won by Jesus Christ is never completely attained by men in this life. Since we are human the conflict continues, and our release depends on our perseverance until victory comes through our incorporation into Christ's death and resurrection. Therefore the gospel proclaimed in the second article of the ancient creeds carries over into affirmations concerning the Holy Spirit, the church, and the resurrection which comprise the third article. The church continues the restoration of creation which Christ began. Through the Word, the sacraments, and the other means of grace we grow toward "mature manhood" and the "fulness of Christ" (Eph. 4:13) until "the enemy of man has been slain and sin driven out— that is to say, in the resurrection of the dead." [40]

Like Christ, those who comprise the church recapitulate in reverse the experience of fallen men, moving through the alienation of temptation, suffering, and death to the victorious life of the new creation. It is therefore highly appropriate that we enter the church by baptism. To be baptized means to be incorporated into the body of Christ by participating in his death and resurrection. For this very reason, however, baptism is far more than a rite of initiation. It is rather "the great sacrament in which the whole Christian life is contained." Just as the baptism of Jesus led him to Gethsemane and the cross, so ours draws us into a series of events which continue throughout our earthly life, re-creating us in God's image. The death of the old through testing and self-discipline and the birth of the new in trust and joy are for the Christian daily occurrences. As Luther says, the Christian "walks clothed in his baptism." [41]

Here lies the clue to Wingren's view of the relation between baptism and the Lord's Supper. The entire life of the baptized person, including his death, is enclosed in the death and resurrection of Christ. Therefore baptism occurs once for all, and is not repeated. However, the same Christ gives himself as the crucified and risen Lord in a meal—an event which

---

[39] *The Living Word*, p. 120; *Theology in Conflict*, pp. 65, 132, 134-49; *Evangelium und Kirche*, pp. 29 f.; *Creation and Law*, p. 91.

[40] *Creation and Law*, pp. 24, 196 f.; *Evangelium und Kirche*, pp. 111, 115 f.; *The Living Word*, pp. 78 f., 175.

[41] *Evangelium und Kirche*, pp. 15, 18-21, 149-54.

is constantly repeated. Baptism is the first and greater sacrament, since it comprises all, including the Lord's Supper, but the Supper is needed in order that what has already been conferred by baptism may be regularly renewed. Thus the two belong together.[42]

Important though the sacraments are, the full life of the church is much broader. Baptism must be followed, for example, by instruction and confirmation. Christians must repeatedly participate in worship, including the hearing of the Word and the celebration of the common meal, in study, and in private prayer. They must practice the living *koinonia* of the body of Christ and submit themselves to its guiding and healing disciplines. But beyond all these they must relate themselves responsibly to other men through mission and *diakonia*.

The church is not truly the church unless it follows its Lord in this twofold movement of redemptive love toward the whole creation. It is sent to preach the Word of life and baptize those who respond, and to give itself in service for the sake of men. Wingren laments that both forms of outreach are so frequently missing in today's churches—especially, he feels, in state-supported churches. In particular he relates the numerical and spiritual emptiness of the churches to their willingness to allow baptism to become a mere formality, while placing exaggerated stress on the Eucharist and treating its administration as the special badge of the clergyman.[43] Actually, the total worship and life of the Christian community should so reproduce the victory-in-defeat and the resurrection-in-death of Christ's own life that its members are driven forth to share the good news in word and deed.

The mission of the church requires a specially chosen ministry to proclaim the living Word entrusted to it. What is involved, however, is "the ministry of the Word," not "the word of the Ministry." The minister's authority is derived wholly from his message, not vice versa. Ordination is not the impartation of power by the laying on of hands; it is simply the commissioning of a person with special gifts for a task to which the church is called.[44] Empowered by the Holy Spirit, he then declares the Word of salvation to all who can be reached. However, he is a priest among priests. His preaching is addressed to people who themselves have ministries and

---

[42] *Ibid.*, pp. 20-22. Wingren frequently deplores the priority ordinarily accorded the Lord's Supper by both Protestant and Catholic churches. He points out, for example, that the apostles were commissioned to preach and baptize, but not commanded to administer the Eucharist to the new converts (Matt. 28:19; Mark 16:15 f.). *Ibid.*, pp. 134 f.

[43] *Evangelium und Kirche*, pp. 134-39, 143-45, 162, 167, 176 f.

[44] *The Living Word*, pp. 98, 101-3; *Evangelium und Kirche*, pp. 156 f.

vocations from God according to their own capacities and situations. They too are called to witness; "*diakonia* is the daily work of all baptized persons."[45]

Christian Ethics

Wingren maintains that when we rightly understand the relation between law and gospel, we discover that systematic theology really has two starting points: creation and redemption, judgment and grace. This discovery makes possible a Christian ethic, social as well as individual, which fully recognizes the validity of universal law while also utilizing the distinctive truths of the gospel.[46] The ethical life of the Christian is grounded in both creation and redemption in intimate connection.

Wingren observes that recent Protestant theology in Europe, when it has not been simply noncommital, has tended to answer the question of the relation between the Christian faith and culture in one of two ways. On the one hand, it has said "yes" to its cultural environment, surrendered the uniqueness of the gospel, and identified itself with contemporary philosophies. On the other, it has pietistically walled itself off from culture, said "no" to its environment, and stressed the opposition between the gospel and other interpretations of reality. Although Barth has shown a "remarkable ability" to relate his theology to the contemporary situation and Nygren has given much attention to philosophy, both of them have reinforced the pietistic tendency. Barth views idealistic ethics purely as an activity of natural man which must be rejected by the gospel, while motif research treats it as an expression of *eros* which is quite at variance with *agape*. Such a gulf could be avoided, Wingren believes, if Barth did not make the law completely subsidiary to the gospel and if Nygren interpreted idealistic ethics as *nomos* (though in a sense much broader than the Hebrew law) rather than *eros*.[47]

Christian thought can relate itself positively to much in modern culture, without sacrificing its own uniqueness, by construing culture in terms of the first or civil use of the law. In the second century Justin Martyr cited the universal condemnation of murder, fornication, and adultery as evidence that the whole human race stands under the law, and Irenaeus saw the natural ethical laws and the provision for earthly rulers as part of God's work in creation. In the sixteenth century the Reformers found God's

---

[45] *The Living Word*, pp. 135 f., 104; *Evangelium und Kirche*, p. 167.
[46] *Creation and Law*, pp. 187, 192.
[47] *Theology in Conflict*, pp. 78 f.; *Creation and Law*, pp. 172 f., 176.

demands expressed in the rule of "the prince" or "the secular government." Similarly, many of the values recognized today in the environment where the gospel is preached serve to force men into or restrain them from particular forms of conduct. In particular, where idealistic ethics is accepted many acts are encouraged which serve the neighbor and advance helpful human relations, while antisocial drives are restrained and many selfish acts are prevented. In short, such cultural factors function as law in the biblical sense. There are dangers in this view, since some of the values cherished by society appear in the context of ideologies or quasi-religious attitudes which are alien or hostile to the gospel. But if the norms upheld have the effect of making men better *"in their outward works on behalf of their neighbor,"* they serve the function of the law in relation to the gospel, and should be so regarded. In this way Christianity and culture meet in the law.[48]

There is also profound ethical and social significance in Wingren's conception of the gospel, the church, and the sacraments. In his view, as in Luther's, the death and resurrection effected in baptism are re-enacted daily in the crucifixion of the old man and the birth of the new which occur as we fulfill our ordinary calling in faith. Our baptism is realized in our work, where we are exposed to all the temptations of earthly life yet win victory and renewal in Christ. Our fellowship with him cannot be genuine if it is sought in isolation from the world he came to redeem. It can "endure only when it is simultaneously a *communio* between the baptized person and other men.[49]

Wingren goes beyond Luther to draw similar conclusions with respect to the Lord's Supper. The same Christ who has come in baptism comes to men also in the sacramental meal, drawing them repeatedly into the event of death and resurrection. God gives himself ever anew to the communicants, who in turn must give themselves to their neighbors in their earthly callings.[50]

"To live in the church means to live from the sacraments, and just for this reason to be open for all men, for death—and the resurrection of the dead." Since both sacraments celebrate the present action of the Christ who in his humanity shared the whole range of our earthly experience, they flow into events outside the place of worship, moving the recipient to offer himself as a "living sacrifice" amid the demands of every day (Rom. 12:1-

---

[48] *Creation and Law*, pp. 168-75; *Theology in Conflict*, pp. 76-79.
[49] *Evangelium und Kirche*, pp. 59, 228; cf. pp. 231 f.
[50] *Ibid.*, pp. 23 f., 59.

21). "The inner connection of baptism and Lord's Supper and the connection of both with the gospel and the church would probably become
clearer if the sacrifice of daily work and that of worshipful praise were
theologically viewed together as one." True worship implicates the worshiper in the struggles and sufferings of men in society. There he is called
to mediate the love of Christ to his neighbor.[51]

In some respects Wingren's position regarding the church's social responsibility is conservative. He attacks Barth because he finds that Barth,
on the basis of the primacy of the gospel over the law, assigns to the church
alone the human initiative on the political level.[52] In Wingren's view Barth
thus uses the second article of faith as a weapon against collectivist political systems, but in so doing makes the church itself a collective over
against other collectives and artificially separates Christians from their
neighbors outside it. Instead, the church

must respect the existing relationships of those outside, and recognize that these
are divinely appointed. . . . The less the Church respects the world for what it is,
in other words, the more the Church feels it has to interfere in the world and
regulate it, the more legalistic its attitude becomes, and the more it loses what
characterizes it as the Church, viz. the Gospel.[53]

It is within the given secular relationships that men who know their sins
forgiven are to live in obedience to God. "Where his calling is shall each remain. There he stands beside his neighbour. 'Programmes' avail nothing
if this place is abandoned." The Bible puts forward "no proposal for any
social reform, or for any new type of society." Christ's Word is "first and
last the Gospel, the Word of resurrection, the Word of forgiveness, which
is not intended to improve the earth but to open heaven." [54]

Wingren points out that when the use of force by earthly governments
becomes necessary to prevent injury to life, it is the Creator's force which
is utilized and the good of the neighbor which is conserved. It is thus an
act of love to take up arms in defense of one's neighbor. In this connection
Wingren admits the difficulty involved for the soldier in loving one's
neighbor while shooting him, and the possibility of a meaningless war

[51] *Ibid.*, pp. 23, 59 f., 232 f., 237.
[52] Barth, *Christengemeinde und Bürgergemeinde* (Zollikon-Zürich, 1946), pp. 21-25 (*Against the
Stream*, pp. 32-34). Wingren, "Evangelium und Gesetz," in *Antwort, Festschrift für Karl Barth*,
pp. 311 f., 319; *Creation and Law*, pp. 12 f., 92 f., 126, 156-59.
[53] *Creation and Law*, pp. 92 f.
[54] *The Living Word*, pp. 140, 185 f.

which will benefit nobody but injure many. Yet he adds that refusal by the soldier to take up arms would make that possibility a reality.[55]

Other utterances of Wingren disclose a genuine concern for social change and renewal. He observes, for example, that Protestant ethics has either shown a relative indifference to existing social structures or accepted them too uncritically. Seldom has it "combined a positive interest in man's position in the world with a comprehensive criticism of the development of the power of collective groups." The very fact that earthly institutions like the family and the state are seen as purposed by God increases rather than lessens the obligations of those responsible for them. "The existing structure of the earthly government must continually be re-examined and criticized. . . . Undeviating allegiance to an outmoded and rigid order of government can often be as lacking in love and consideration as calculated ill-will." [56] Indeed, in the very passage where Wingren asserts the Bible's lack of interest in social reform he stresses that the kernel of its message is love for one's neighbor and uprightness in all one's affairs. Though he declares that the conception of ethical improvement is entirely absent from the Bible, he makes plain that what he means is improvement "apart from man's obedience to God's will in his own concrete relations with his neighbour." Elsewhere he suggests that if the evangelical churches had accepted the first use of the law as a living doctrine they would have been more closely associated with the popular movements in temperance and education in the past century. Lacking that doctrine they have become ingrown groups separate from the world, thereby making the church an idol and making it easier for other human associations to become idols.[57]

Wingren also laments the tendency to conceive the continuity of the ordained ministry, particularly in its eucharistic office, as the peculiar channel of the work of the Holy Spirit, while the care of the neighbor is assigned to secular society. This extreme form of the necessary separation of the spiritual and worldly realms places two closed collectives, one churchly and the other political, over against each other, overlooking that the same individual person is involved in both. Only when the doctrine of creation and the doctrine of the church intersect in the individual can either retain its meaning.[58]

Our relation to God and neighbor is "one and the same reality, seen

[55] *Creation and Law*, pp. 152 f.
[56] *Ibid.*, pp. 117, 144.
[57] *The Living Word*, pp. 185, 169 f.
[58] *Evangelium und Kirche*, pp. 126 f.

from two different sides." Therefore Christians should be sent out by the church to participate in the life of the world as "baptized persons who live from their baptism." Thus the secular relationships of men will be between members of the one body of Christ, who serve one another (I Cor. 12:12). In such daily intercourse among men lies the possibility of the renewal of society.[59]

Wingren emphasizes that recognition of the connection between worship and the life of society strengthens rather than weakens the eschatological dimension of Christian faith. Since eschatology is marked by the tension and unity of death and resurrection, the participant in the Lord's Supper moves toward the future not by dissolving his connection with the things of the world, but by meeting them again as he leaves the Lord's table. "The more earthly and simple a task is, the more it can charge with hope and fulfill a man who lives on the sacraments." [60] When the meaning of worship permeates daily work, the whole of life points toward the ultimate consummation of God's purpose to redeem his creation.

Critique

Values

Wingren's theology combines a fresh, nontraditional reinterpretation of some of the major emphases of Irenaeus and Luther, a critical response to the thought of representative contemporary theologians, and creative insights of his own. Several elements of special strength should be mentioned.

1. His advocacy of two starting points in Christian theology, creation and law as well as redemption and gospel, is persuasively supported and illuminatingly developed. Specifically, his conception of law as rooted in creation itself has the following merits:

a. It accords with the totality of the biblical evidence, recognizing the importance of God's activity as Creator and Judge no less than the distinctive truth of the gospel of forgiveness through Jesus Christ.

b. It provides a valuable supplement to motif research through elaborating in detail the *nomos* theme omitted by Nygren.

c. Through upholding the validity of universal law as a Christian affirmation it supplies an important point of contact between the gospel and secular culture, as well as between Christian faith and some non-Christian religions.

[59] *Ibid.*, pp. 152, 263; *The Living Word*, p. 185.
[60] *Evangelium und Kirche*, p. 24.

Bernhard Erling maintains that Wingren, in pointing out that the Bible and the ancient creeds begin with creation and move on to redemption, fails to distinguish between history as remembered events and faith-oriented interpretation of remembered events. The focal center of the Old Testament is the redemption of Israel. Though the accounts of Israel's history from the Exodus onward are prefaced by the creation narratives and related stories in the first eleven chapters of Genesis, these are interpretations of a faith which is concerned primarily with salvation, not creation. In Erling's view Wingren wrongly assumes that the objective order of the events narrated must take precedence over the cognitive order of man's redemption-centered understanding of them.[61]

The biblical writers, to be sure, view creation from the perspective of a faith focused on salvation. However, they themselves believe that all men are conscious of the gap between what they are and what they ought to be, and so under law. Erling's argument leaves untouched Wingren's central thesis, which is that, biblically understood, man as created by God knows apart from the gospel that he is subject to law, guilt, and judgment. The redemption presupposed in the Old Testament accounts of creation is not the salvation wrought through Jesus Christ. The authors of those accounts wrote without any knowledge of the incarnation. The heart of Wingren's view must therefore be judged to be biblically sound.

2. The importance which Wingren attaches to creation and law does not prevent him from dealing constructively with christological problems. Though he embraces the notion of the self-emptying of Jesus Christ, his strong stress on the real humanity of Christ saves him from the weaknesses of most kenotic theories. "Emptying" for Wingren means primarily Jesus' choice to share fully in the human situation, with its temptation, suffering, and mortality, and to be utterly obedient to God. Not content merely to reaffirm the Chalcedonian two-nature theory, Wingren interprets dynamically the unity of the divine and the human in Christ: the divinity which alone can forgive sins is disclosed in a man who while suffering death prays for his murderers. His modification of Aulén's "classical" atonement theory conserves its major strength—its recognition of the stark reality of man's struggle with sin and the deliverance wrought through God's victorious action in Christ. His insistence on the objective reality of both the cross and the resurrection avoids the errors of subjectivism while asserting the need for the personal experience of faith.

[61] Bernhard Erling, "Swedish Theology from Nygren to Wingren," *Religion in Life*, XXX (1961), 206-8.

3. Wingren makes a profound contribution to the understanding of baptism and its significance for the Christian life. With death and resurrection as the central motif, he perceptively develops the meaning of baptism as participation in the total experience of Jesus Christ, incorporation into the church as the body of Christ, an epitome of the entire life of the Christian, and a constant reminder of the missionary responsibility of the church. He thereby lifts baptism far above the status of a mere formality and restores it to its rightful place as the first sacrament. This he does, however, without depreciating the Lord's Supper. Instead he brings out clearly the underlying unity and the complementary relation between the two sacraments, as well as the essential role played by both, along with the proclamation of the Word, in Christian worship.

4. In his interpretation of worship, particularly the sacraments, Wingren lays firm theological foundations for the practice of self-forgetful love in daily life. Concern for the neighbor is much more than a demand of the law. Since the sacraments bring us into the real presence of him who shares all phases of our earthly life, they thrust us out to participate redemptively in the struggles of our fellow men and to demonstrate there the power of God to crown temptation and struggle with victory. Thus the true praise of God in the assembled congregation leads naturally to the living sacrifice offered in the daily work of his scattered people. This view is reinforced by Wingren's emphasis on the universal priesthood, which sees the ministry of the Word as one of many ministries to which Christians are called. A wide acceptance and practice of Wingren's interpretation would do much to transform sacramentarianism into a healthy sacramentalism, and to end the widespread dichotomy of worship and life. Christians who really "live from their baptism" are strengthened for life in a community of mutual concern.

Difficulties

Among the questions raised by Wingren's thought, three call for brief attention here.

1. Wingren opposes the allegedly Barthian view, based on the primacy of gospel over law, that ethical norms are to be derived solely from the gospel. He argues that this leads to a legalistic use of the New Testament which seeks in the message of God's forgiveness the ethical standards which are ruled out of creation itself. This is hardly a valid conclusion, since strictly speaking Barth finds his norms not in the gospel but in the law seen in the perspective of the gospel.

Wingren's criticism does apply to the degree that the gospel is regarded as the *only* source of ethical enlightenment. However, he seems to imply, beyond this, that there is something inherently legalistic about finding ethical guidance in the gospel, even though it is also sought in the law. This opinion is suggested by his judgment that Barth, in upholding the church's social responsibility, uses the second article as a weapon against collectivist political systems, and opposes an ecclesiastical collective to other collectives.

Why is it legalistic to discover ethical direction in the gospel? The whole Christian life is a grateful response to God's reconciling love manifest in Christ, and inevitably that love becomes a standard for the believer. "We love, because he first loved us" (I John 4:19), and also *as* he loves us— although on the level of our own capacities. On the divine indicative is erected an imperative, which is clearly recognized as such when love of God and love of neighbor are enjoined as the first and second commandments of the law. Moreover, Wingren himself regards the self-sacrifice of Christ which is reenacted in the sacraments as normative for the whole life of the Christian.

With respect to Wingren's view that Barth treats the church as a collective, it is perhaps sufficient to point out that Barth, of all theologians, has been one of the least inclined to espouse anticommunism, and has been more concerned than most of his critics to understand communism and build bridges between East and West.

2. Wingren's tendency to look for ethical guidance in the law more than in the gospel is closely related to his acceptance of Luther's doctrine of the two realms, worldly and spiritual, which are respectively under the jurisdiction of law and gospel. At one point he opposes what he deems a too extreme opposition of the two kingdoms, yet he insists that a sharp separation is necessary.[62] This dichotomy, together with his law-oriented affirmation of culture, disposes him toward acceptance of existing social structures and inadequate recognition of the revolutionary implications of the gospel.

According to Wingren's understanding the Christian must actively and conscientiously participate in the life of society, but as an individual and in nonchurchly groups, within the framework of the existing order, and with no obligation to change unjust social structures. The law provides the constraints and incentives needed for orderly social life, and the gospel

[62] *Evangelium und Kirche*, p. 127.

moves men, within their various callings, to demonstrate the sacrifice and victory of Christ, but neither the law nor the gospel impels the Christian or his church to seek in Christ's name the transformation of situations which blight the lives of persons whom God created and seeks to redeem. In the twentieth century, however, participation in Christ's "death and resurrection" requires Christians and churches to take on themselves the sufferings of their brothers occasioned by racial and economic injustice, and to become agents of social as well as individual reconciliation, change, and renewal.

Relevant in this connection is Wingren's portrayal of a society in which the worldly and spiritual realms intersect in each Christian as he participates in the life of society, so that the secular relationships of men are between members of one body of Christ, who serve one another. This is a noble conception, but is it not quite unrealistic? It presupposes a situation in which the church is established or state supported, where practically all citizens are members and also dedicated participants in its life. But this picture bears no resemblance to the religious pluralism characteristic of the separation of the church and state in America, or the factual pluralism of Sweden and other European lands, where most citizens, though members of the church, are such in name only. In all countries today committed Christians face a society which is at heart hostile or indifferent to the claims of Christian faith, where multitudes are in no genuine sense within the Christian fellowship. Wingren's concept is a laudable goal for the long future, but it can hardly serve as a social policy for the church today.

3. Wingren's objectification of the power of evil, with its assumption that humanity is the scene of a cosmic conflict between God and Satan, raises serious questions, partly perhaps because he does not make his meaning sufficiently plain. His view can claim New Testament support, but the truth of the pertinent passages becomes clearer if they are interpreted metaphorically rather than literally. Two difficulties may be mentioned.

a. Though Wingren probably does not intend to affirm an ultimate dualism, his conception points in that direction. If the struggle between God and the demonic power is really cosmic, it can hardly fail to involve physical nature as well as the life of man—unless we assume a disjunction between the spiritual and material orders which Wingren's doctrine of creation would not allow. But if the conflict rages in nature as well as in man, how can we account for the manifest unity of the cosmos? All evidence that the world is a universe rather than a duoverse speaks against the objective existence of a demonic power which contends with God for mastery over men.

b. The view projects outward tendencies and drives which are better understood if located in human nature itself. The origin of sin lies within man rather than outside him. Temptation and struggle are intense, but the responsibility for disobedience is our own. The supposition of an objective evil tends to diminish our responsibility while adding nothing to our understanding.

PART TWO: ROMAN CATHOLIC THEOLOGY

9. YVES M.-J. CONGAR

The central interest of Yves Congar is indicated by his authorship of a number of substantial volumes on the nature, mission, unity, and renewal of the church, and by his founding of the important collection, *"Unam sanctam."* Since 1957 he has been director of the Dominican monastery in Strasbourg, France. He was long subject to suspicion because of his connection with the *Nouvelle Théologie* [1] opposed by Pope Pius XII in his encyclical *Humani generis*. In 1950 one of his books was condemned, and his activities were restricted. However, he has come through the clouds of mistrust to a position of wide influence and respect. The same breadth of spirit and openness to new approaches which earlier caused difficulty make him now, in a changed ecclesiastical and theological climate, an esteemed interpreter of Roman Catholicism outside of his own church as well as within. He is widely regarded as the leading Catholic ecclesiologist.

---

[1] The "New Theology," strongly influenced by the existentialist emphasis on historicity and subjectivity, and by recent evangelical exegesis, sought to interpret church dogma in contemporary thought forms. It demanded a theological renewal rooted in the Bible, the Church Fathers, and a deepened understanding of the liturgy; openly criticized Thomism and in general the Greek substantialism of scholastic philosophy; and deprecated a narrow juridical conception of the church. Prominent representatives included H. Bouillard, Henri de Lubac, and Jean Daniélou. In *Humani generis* (August 12, 1950) Pius XII denounced such teachings and declared Thomism as obligatory today.

His characteristic attitude is well expressed in his discussion of changing interpretations of Cyprian's famous dictum, "Outside the church there is no salvation." "Catholic theology," writes Congar, "progressively develops resources which it held from the beginning, but concerning which new facts, or a better understanding of facts already ancient, lead it to work out applications or aspects which it did not at first regard in this way. *Nova et vetera. Nova et veteribus.*" [2] For Congar the church is unthinkable apart from Christ, and vice versa. God has acted to save humanity by incarnating himself in Jesus Christ and giving himself in behalf of men, thereby transforming them and drawing them into a new life. This life is lived in the church, and Christ is its source.[3] Christology therefore provides the best starting point for a study of Congar's theology.

Jesus Christ

Congar believes that the basic cause of division between Protestants and Roman Catholics regarding the church and the Virgin Mary is a radical difference in belief regarding the role of humanity in salvation. This in turn is due to an inadequate recognition of the humanity of Christ in Protestant interpretations of the Chalcedonian two-nature doctrine. Both Barth and Luther, for example, assume a wide gap between the two natures, attribute the work of salvation to the divine alone, and empty of value the human action of the Word made flesh. Human nature is little more than a kind of garment for the divine. Afflicted with this error, Protestants in general, and many Roman Catholics as well, are close to monophysitism and monoenergism. They fail to recognize the concrete and intimate relation of God to man in either history in general or Jesus Christ in particular. Hence they are unable to appreciate the parts played by Mary and the church in God's saving action.[4]

The clue to Congar's understanding of the Chalcedonian formula is his distinction between *nature* and *person* as metaphysical principles. The nature of a thing determines its type of existence, "its qualifications, faculties, and structure of activity" which set it off from other types. A human nature is marked by certain physical, psychological, and moral characteristics which are found in all human beings. By contrast, person-

[2] *Sainte Église. Études et approches ecclesiologiques* (*Holy Church. Ecclesiological Studies and Approaches* [Paris: Les Éditions du Cerf, 1963]), p. 144.

[3] *The Mystery of the Temple, or the Manner of God's Presence to His Creatures from Genesis to the Apocalypse,* tr. Reginald F. Trevett (Westminster, Md.: Newman Press, 1961), p. 152.

[4] *Christ, Our Lady, and the Church. A Study in Eirenic Theology,* tr. Henry St. John, O.P. (London: Longmans, Green and Co., 1957), pp. 14 f, 30.

ality is unique and singular; "it is a sheerly existential principle by which the individual is so real that it exists in its own proper being, wholly original, incommunicable, incapable of fusion with another." [5]

Christ partook of a wholly and perfectly human nature, including qualities like intelligence and free will which are common to all men. However, his individuality, his ego, was and is that of the divine Person, the Son of God.

The metaphysical principle of created and incommunicable existence, which permits of saying *I* so exclusively that it cannot be said except of oneself, is, in Christ, supplied from the very beginning by the uncreated principle of which the *I* in this case is the Word. The responsibility for everything done by the man Jesus, prayer, acts of knowledge and love, suffering and death on the cross is ontologically that of the Word.

Congar insists, however, that the existence of the Word as a human personality does not in any way dissolve the reality of the truly human nature of Christ or the movement of his intelligence and will toward God.[6]

God as Word uses the humanity of Christ as his instrument in performing acts which depend on divine power alone, such as the forgiveness of sins, the raising of Lazarus from the dead, or the prediction of future events. The word "instrument" here has a special meaning, for Christ cannot be separated from God, as the bow is separated from the violinist or the interpreter from the speaker. Rather he is united in his very being with the power which works in him. He is *"conjoined* to God in a single existence" as a hand is joined to a man. Nevertheless, he is a living instrument, with human understanding, affections, and will, and God uses his human freedom to the full. Christ's humanity is a perfect agency of his divinity because it is completely in accord with the will of God. In its whole being "it is sanctified and sanctifying, . . . supremely and integrally holy *in itself.*" Being united "with the divinity in the Person of the Word," it is filled with holiness and power. In this way Congar seeks to uphold the part played by Christ's real humanity in the work of salvation, while insisting repeatedly that the power which effects salvation comes from God alone.[7]

[5] *Ibid.*, pp. 47 f., 50.
[6] *Ibid.*, pp. 50 f.
[7] *Ibid.*, pp. 51-54, 31.

Our Lady

As in Christology, so in Mariology and ecclesiology, a crucial consideration for Congar is the extent of human cooperation in the work of salvation. Saving grace is communicated to men because of the union in Christ
of sacred humanity with divinity. Mary, by her intimate connection with
Christ's humanity, brings about the incarnation, while the church communicates it to men and spreads its effects through the world. In a distinctive sense the part played by Our Lady represents the roles of humanity and
the church. Christ was conceived not only by the Holy Spirit, but also by
her. As the bearer of God's gift, she is "the first link in the lifeline which
is Christ's Mystical Body." Though every individual is called to cooperate
with God according to his own situation, Mary is God's partner in the
salvation of others as well as her own. She is therefore involved in a collective cooperation which is universal in scope.[8]

While a clear awareness of the important role of humanity in salvation
makes possible a true appreciation of Our Lady, the lack of such an awareness leads to unjustifiably exalted conceptions of her status. Congar cautions
against two erroneous features often found in Marian literature. One is
the monophysite tendency which stresses the divine nature of Christ at
the expense of the human, thereby leaving a gulf between God and man
which can be bridged only by a more human mediator, Mary. The other
is the related notion which contrasts the tender mercy of Our Lady with
the inflexible sternness of Christ as judge. Congar rejects both views on
scriptural grounds. Though not conscious heresies, they result from "a
spiritual theology" which gives undue weight to religious experiences which
increase fervor, without relating them to the whole structure of faith.
According to the "objective data of revelation" "given in the prophets, in
Christ and by the Apostles," there is only one Mediator, Jesus Christ.[9]

Nevertheless, the church has been right in according special honor to
Mary. The feast of Mary's presentation in the temple and the tradition that
she spent her childhood in the temple are not to be taken literally, but
they symbolize deep truths. God granted to Mary a special gift of grace
which enabled her to be perfectly faithful to God's calling, and thereby to
become the Mother of God. She is thus the true type to be followed by all
Christians; in her dedicated life she expressed superlatively that "presentation" which each Christian is called to make in the service of faith. Indeed,

---

[8] *Ibid.*, pp. 14 f., 17 f., 25, 31.
[9] *Ibid.*, pp. 72, 78 f., 81.

she can be spoken of, figuratively but properly, as herself the temple, the ark of the covenant, and Jacob's ladder. She is the temple of God because she carried Christ in her womb, because of her reception of the exceptional spiritual gifts which prepared her for her divine motherhood and rewarded her for her acceptance of it, and because in her utter obedience to God's will she typifies perfectly the faithful Israel which is the true temple. She is the ark of the new covenant because she bore our Savior in her body and gave him human flesh. She is Jacob's ladder because in her the union of heaven and earth is accomplished. Yet she deserves all of these titles only by reference to Jesus Christ, who alone is the Messianic Temple.[10]

In Congar's interpretation the dogma of the assumption of the Virgin at once affirms her lofty status and provides an antidote to monophysitism. The doctrine asserts the glorification of Mary conferred on her before the general resurrection. Because of her unique personal relation to the Redeemer she becomes the first fruit of redemption and an example and pledge of the glorified humanity to come. Since she is purely human, her exaltation reminds us of the sanctified humanity of Christ through which her humanity becomes victorious over sin and death. It also provides ground for the hope that our humanity will ultimately be glorified like hers.[11]

The Church

Divine-human Character

The church for Congar is the organism which, by conferring divine grace, continues the effect of the work done by Jesus Christ for our salvation. It extends the incarnation throughout history. Like Christ himself, it is a unity of two natures, divine and human. It combines an invisible life, which springs from the Holy Spirit and is fed by him, with a visible structure, the priesthood and the sacraments, through which grace and truth are mediated to men. In the action of each sacrament the same two-fold character is present: God's gift enters and transforms an act of devotion which moves from man to God. In the Eucharist, for example, the sacramental presence of Christ offered for us must be combined with the sacrifice of praise offered by us.[12] The monophysite heresy must be avoided in ecclesiology no less than in Christology.

[10] *The Mystery of the Temple*, pp. 254-61.
[11] *Christ, Our Lady, and the Church*, pp. 54 f., 70 f.
[12] *Ibid.*, pp. 5-7, 82, 63 f.

However, the parallel between Christ and the church is not exact. In Christ a human nature is united with the divine in its very being—in the preexisting Word—whereas in the church the separate human element is joined with the divine only by choice, promise, and covenant. The union is one of alliance, not of substance. Though this bond subserves the holiness of the church, it does not make it sinless or worthy of worship. The church is really human; in it authority is exercised and sacramental grace mediated by weak and fallen human beings who are subject to error, sin, and spatial-temporal limitations. Nevertheless, it is also truly divine, and endowed with infallibility with respect to its basic teaching and its ministry of grace, which are needed for men's salvation. Its power is the power of God himself. "The acts which make up the essential structure of grace and truth within the Church, the valid performance of sacraments, and solemn definitions of the Faith, carry with them God's certain guarantee." [13]

Catholicity

Congar regards as the best brief definition of the church that which describes it as the mystical Body of Christ, in much more than a metaphorical sense. The term accurately portrays the church as a living organism in which members are animated and directed by a head, Jesus Christ, simultaneously by a vital influence from within and by an action utilizing outward, visible forms.[14]

This combination of unity and diversity is basic in catholicity, which Congar defines as that property of the church by which the one and the many, both real, are harmonized. The diversity is grounded in the human nature of the church, while the unity is founded on the fullness of the grace of Christ, the head of a new humanity and a new universe. The manifold expressions and realizations of the church exist "according to the whole," [15] so that the real unity of the organism is one of plenitude rather than poverty.

Catholicity is at once actual and potential. As the universal capacity of the principles of unity it can be said to have been actually given in its very being, since Pentecost. Yet it is still in the process of realization, in that these principles have not found their full expression. Catholicity therefore contains in its very nature a powerful missionary imperative,

---

[13] *The Mystery of the Church*, tr. A. V. Littledale (Baltimore: Helicon Press, 1960), p. 40; *Christ, Our Lady, and the Church*, pp. 56-62, 67 f.

[14] *Sainte Église*, pp. 41-43.

[15] The literal meaning of the Greek words *kata holos*, from which the word *catholic* is derived.

since the possibilities cannot be fully actualized until the whole substance of the first Adam—humanity—has passed into that of the Second Adam by being incorporated into the Body of Christ. At the same time the notion encourages respect for various cultures, languages, religious attitudes, and liturgies—all the diversity involved in being "according to the whole."

The agent of realization of the missionary program thus demanded is the Holy Spirit, or the Spirit of Christ, in liaison with the apostolic body which he has called forth and empowered. At Pentecost the Spirit descended on *each* of the *assembled* apostles in the unity of love, enabling the church to be "of one heart and soul" while speaking many languages. Thus the Holy Spirit today moves those who compose the Body according to an infinite variety of gifts, but still basically according to the whole in living communion.[16]

Particularly significant is the differentiation between the priesthood and the total community. Repeatedly Congar speaks of the association of the hierarchical and the communal principles in the church. Basically they form a single subject of worship, faith, witness, and apostleship, and one Spirit animates them both. Yet clear distinctions must be made between the apostolic hierarchy and the entire community of the faithful. Christ's mediation is exerted through the priesthood for the creation and nurture of a faithful people, and through the whole people for the sake of the world. The former is "the mediation of the means of grace between Christ and the faithful," the latter "a mediation of life between the Body of Christ and the world, and this is also a means of grace in its order." [17] Congar's view of the church needs to be examined from these two points of view.

Apostolicity

Picturing the church as a lake, Congar inquires into the source of its water supply. It might be fed by an invisible spring at its heart, but such immediacy is possible only for the heavenly church. The earthly church must be supplied from an external source, the grace of God; the life which is in Christ must be introduced into it. This may occur in two ways. The water of the incarnation may be evaporated into the sky and fall into the

---

[16] *Sainte Église*, pp. 158-61; *The Mystery of the Church*, pp. viii, 25, 28, 48. See also *Divided Christendom; a Catholic Study of the Problem of Reunion*, tr. M. A. Bousfield (London: Geoffrey Bles, 1939), ch. II.

[17] *Lay People in the Church; a Study for a Theology of the Laity*, tr. Donald Attwater (Westminster, Md.: Newman Press, 1957), pp. iii, 234, 429-33; *Sacerdoce et laïcat; devant leur tâches d'évangélisation et de civilisation* (Paris: Les Éditions du Cerf, 1962), p. 8.

lake; this is the extreme Protestant thesis—that the church is fed by a kind of vertical rain. The other possibility is that the lake be supplied entirely by canalization, with pipes bringing the water from the source; this is the Catholic view, in which the channel is provided by apostolicity. Protestantism underestimates the need for human agency in the transmission of divine grace. The source became a historical reality at a definite point in space and time. Therefore "a continuous conduit from it was needed to convey the sacraments, the priestly succession for their celebration and the grace of truth which the priesthood safeguards." Only by such mediation can men receive the saving grace of God.[18]

It is Christ alone who saves us, not the church. However, since his ascension he has committed the work of salvation to the joint action of the Holy Spirit and his human representatives, the apostles and their successors. To the latter he has entrusted the guardianship over the two chief means of grace, the preaching of the faith and the administration of the sacraments. The sacramental and doctrinal authority of the hierarchy is not delegated by the people; it is a gift imparted by Jesus Christ through apostolic succession.[19] Apostolicity insures the identity of the ministry of the church today with the ministry of the apostles, and through them with that of Christ (Luke 22:29-30; John 20:21). The triple power of teaching, priesthood, and government which the church discharges is the same as that exercised by the twelve, which proceeded finally from Christ, who is himself prophet, priest, and king.[20]

Within the total hierarchy that of the episcopate exercises special authority. The bishops are responsible for (1) mediating the powers conferred on the priesthood by holy orders, (2) insuring that correct doctrine is passed on to us from Christ and the apostles, and (3) judging the conformity to the original deposit of faith of later developments and expressions of it by the faithful, so that the church may speak with one voice.[21] The episcopate thus has magisterial as well as sacramental authority.

In summary, Congar lists three fundamental claims made by the Roman Catholic Church:

To a body of teaching handed down by tradition from Christ and his apostles, safeguarded by the state of grace given to the episcopate; to sacraments as

[18] *Sainte Église*, pp. 66 f.; *Christ, Our Lady, and the Church*, pp. 34 f., 38.
[19] *Lay People in the Church*, pp. 26, 432 f.; *Christ, Our Lady, and the Church*, pp. 7, 111 f.; *The Mystery of the Church*, pp. 15, 186.
[20] *Sainte Église*, pp. 181-85.
[21] *Lay People in the Church*, p. 264.

mysterious channels of the grace which flows from the Cross; to powers of priest-hood inherent in the hierarchy by which both doctrine and sacraments are made effective. These together constitute the content and substance of Apostolicity.[22]

Thus the apostles and those appointed later to carry on their ministry have competences not granted to others. They alone are accorded the gifts of authority and mediation. They alone are the foundation and the master builders of the temple (Eph. 2:20; I Cor. 3:9-17). Others of the faithful are indeed living stones in the temple, but must themselves be built and based. Only the hierarchical priesthood can keep believers in touch with the redemptive presence and action of God as historically embodied in the incarnation.

In fact, Congar insists that the hierarchical functions alone guarantee the existence of the church as the institution of salvation. "They alone are essential to her existence pure and simple." In essential structure the church already existed in the apostles, and therefore it exists in the bishops as their heirs and successors. But Jesus called also the seventy disciples, the holy women, and others to serve side by side with the twelve. Their descendants too are necessary today, not that the church may exist as an institution, but that it may fulfill its mission. Apostolicity is not an end in itself. The master builder exists for the house. The foundation must be related organi-cally to the temple it supports, else it is a truncated stump or ruin. Hence the entire body of the faithful is needed to carry out fully the work of Christ in the world.[23]

The Laity

What, then, is the role of the faithful community as a whole, and par-ticularly of its lay members? Congar emphasizes that since the church is the living, growing organism with Christ as its head, all its members par-ticipate in its communal life, though only its appointed ministers constitute its institutional structure.[24] Three forms of lay activity may be discerned.

1. In two ways laymen may even be said to carry on sacerdotal or priestly activities: they are called on to offer their very lives, making them-selves wholly an offering to God; and they exercise a "baptismal priesthood" by taking part in the celebrations of the church, particularly the Eucharist. In a real sense the whole *congregatio fidelium* joins the hierarchy in the

[22] *Christ, Our Lady, and the Church,* pp. 5 f.
[23] *Lay People in the Church,* pp. 429-31, 174 f.
[24] *The Mystery of the Temple,* p. 172.

offering at the altar. Their sacrifice is consummated in their union with Christ's passion in the Eucharist, and by communing they become the body of their Lord offered to God for the sins of the world. "The life of the organism is properly active only when the community celebrates with its priests. Bismarck was wrong: the Church does not begin and end with her clergy." [25]

2. Laymen are called upon to assist the clergy in various phases of their pastoral, missionary, and teaching activity. Catechetical instruction, for example, is likely to remain academic and artificial if it is carried on by priests alone; it must be supported in the home and by the work of lay teachers. With such activity in mind Pope Pius XI went so far as to define Catholic Action as "the participation of the laity in the hierarchical apostolate"—a formula clarified by the substitution by Pius XII of *cooperation* for *participation*. In this cooperative role laymen do not share the constitutive functions or powers of the bishops, but they do illustrate thereby a new application of the idea of St. John Chrysostom that "the laity form the priestly *pleroma* of the bishop." [26]

3. The most distinctive vocation of lay people is to manifest the saving powers of Christ in the world. They are "to make their way to God while doing this world's work; to live according to the third, vertical dimension while making the stuff of the world and its history, and for that purpose living according to life's horizontal dimensions." The layman's proper contribution to the church's double task—of bringing salvation and advancing God's kingdom—is fulfilled through his involvement in the structures of the world's daily life and in temporal work. According to their varied gifts laymen are responsible for declaring, explaining, and defending their faith amid their day-by-day relationships; and some of them may exert especially significant influence through artistic and literary expression. [27]

Congar quotes an allocution by Pius XII of the twentieth of February, 1946, which urges laymen to be concerned not only to belong to the church but *"to be the church,* the community of the faithful on earth." Congar adds that they are the church insofar as it desires to be the soul of human society. They do not constitute it in its proper being as an institution of salvation; from this perspective it is the mother of the faithful rather than composed of them. But in relation to its second mission of orienting society

[25] *Ibid.,* pp. 185-87; *Lay People in the Church,* p. 216.
[26] *Lay People in the Church,* pp. 346 f., 356-59, 27.
[27] *Ibid.,* pp. 374, 290; *Sainte Église,* p. 340.

toward God, it could be said that they not only make up part of the church but *are* the church.[28] The hierarchical apostolate "generates" the faithful, men whose Christian vocation creates responsibilities appropriate to their secular situation and apportions corresponding spiritual resources. Their proper mission is then that of influencing the structures of civilization "to turn it Christward."

Congar makes plain, however, that authority is vested solely in the clergy, and that "lay people will always be subordinate." The essential being of the church is found in its hierarchical structure, though its well-being and its fullness depend on the faithful community as a whole.[29]

Reform and Renewal

Aware that the empirical church often fails to express adequately its true nature, Congar is full of sympathy with the growing demand for carefully considered reform. He lists two principal aspects of the reformist tendency: *"the desire for authentic actions,* which really correspond with what they claim to signify"; and *"the need for adaptation or revision of certain forms in the life of the church."* The former concerns both worship and doctrine. Masses and vigils, for example, must be far more than mere "rites," "things" complete in their own existence; rather they must become genuinely the acts of *persons* which definitely change the lives of the participants. Beliefs likewise should express not merely abstract truths but living convictions which sustain the actual lives of those who hold them. The latter involves such changes in the structural elements[30] of the church's life as will enable them to manifest the reality of Christian faith and the authentic church of Christ. Instances of needed reforms have to do with the style of preaching and catechetics, the patterns of parish organizations, the use of the vernacular in worship, and the avoidance of pomp and display. Such change must spring from a new scrutiny of sources—biblical, patristic, liturgical, and magisterial.[31]

In this connection Congar is bold enough to call for greater initiative and authority in the responsible leadership of the church over against the papacy. Commenting on the historic tension between pope and church and

---

[28] *Sainte Église*, pp. 340 f.; *Lay People in the Church*, p. 432.

[29] *Lay People in the Church*, pp. xxvii, 42-48, 376 f.

[30] "Structural elements" must be clearly distinguished from the dogma, sacraments, and hierarchical constitution which comprise the essential structure of the church.

[31] *Vraie et fausse réforme dans l'Église* (Paris: Les Éditions du Cerf, 1950), pp. 50-55. The passages directly quoted are from Launcelot C. Sheppard's translation of selections from this book in *Cross Currents*, III (1952-53), 358-65.

the tendency for the former to absorb the latter, as Peter absorbed Paul in the apostolic foundation of the Roman Church, he asks:

Will the Church be the passive recipient of decisions transmitted with authority by its head, or will it again come alive, certainly not cut off from this visible head, but transmitting something to him as well? Will the life of the Church have a structure designed for monologue or one designed for dialogue? [32]

The Salvation of Non-Catholics

Congar has pioneered in exploring the ecclesiological status of dissident communions, and has devoted painstaking attention to the question of the salvation of non-Catholics, or the nonevangelized. He insists on a reinterpretation of Cyprian's declaration, "Outside the Church there is no salvation," which no longer pronounces judgment on concrete persons. It is basically an affirmation that the church of Christ alone is commissioned and qualified by God to convey to *all* men the salvation made possible in Jesus Christ. The ministry is committed exclusively to the Catholic Church. The relation of God with man established in and by Jesus Christ is absolutely perfect, hence incapable of being equaled or surpassed, and the church's hierarchical priesthood is the sole agency, divinely appointed, for bringing men into this relationship.[33]

For any individual, therefore, the crucial question is whether he is related to the church in such a manner as to benefit from its saving ministry. In this respect Congar, in harmony with official Catholic teaching, makes provision for many persons who are not visibly united with the Catholic Church. Those who possess supernatural faith and charity are "related to the mystical Body of the Redeemer," [34] and therefore on the way of salvation. Those whose lives are marked by self-giving rather than self-seeking have at least begun to love God; implicitly they want to do his will. Faith is implicit in them, as the fruit is hidden in the seed, and they have an unconscious and implicit desire for baptism and the church. Thus they are not really strangers to the mystical Body; spiritually they live by the Spirit which informs its existence, and that Spirit moves them toward salvation and grants them encounters with God of which the church is not corporeally the minister. Though they remain outside the visible Body through in-

---

[32] *Sainte Église*, p. 339.

[33] *Ibid.*, pp. 429-32, 444; *The Wide World My Parish*, tr. Donald Attwater (Baltimore: Helicon Press, 1961), pp. 98, 29-31, 112; *Lay People in the Church*, p. 172.

[34] The phrase is that of Pius XII in his encyclical, *Mystici Corporis Christi* (June 29, 1943).

vincible ignorance, they belong to it *voto*—by desire—and are destined to ultimate identification with it.[35]

Congar stresses the saving significance of a righteous life devoted to divine ends. Thus "a sincere Protestant, believing, truly consecrated to God, and living a holy life, [is] more really a member of the church than a baptized Catholic who is slack and sinful or has perhaps lost his faith." [36] Congar even admits the possibility of an "atheism of good faith," in which faith is implied in the intention of moral rectitude and in the end sought. Consecration to a cause which assumes absolute value—justice, truth, fraternity, peace—though a substitute for God, may involve an end which is in fact supernatural, and thus provide a basis for eventual salvation.[37]

Catholic theology insists on the *visible* character of the church. The Body of Christ is fully present only where its underlying substance (*res*) is linked with the visible institution (*sacramentum*). Hence non-Catholics of good faith are not "members" of the Body. Yet the realities of grace which exist in them arise from its substance and tend by nature to incorporate themselves in the visible Body. Thus the salvation ultimately assured to non-Catholics is not given "*extra Ecclesiam*," but is finally attributable to the church.[38]

It remains true, however, that an eschatological relation to the mystical Body is no substitute for effective union with its visible reality on earth. Only persons so united have access to the fullness of the means of grace of which the church is the divinely appointed channel. Thus direct personal participation in the church's sacramental life is the only way to the full reality of present salvation as well as the best guarantee of its final actualization.[39]

Scripture and Tradition

Inevitably Congar's central concern for the church and its unity leads him to examine carefully the relation between Scripture and tradition, for four centuries a major point of difference between Catholics and Protestants. His views illustrate eloquently the *rapprochement* which is now developing on this issue. Scripture and tradition are for him two modes of communication of the apostolic heritage. Neither *is* the active presence of

---

[35] *The Wide World My Parish*, pp. 102 f., 110, 112 f., 136.
[36] *Divided Christendom*, p. 222.
[37] *Sainte Église*, pp. 429-32.
[38] *Ibid.* Here Congar is expounding Pius XII's *Mystici Corporis Christi*.
[39] *The Wide World My Parish*, pp. 102 f., 110.

God, who alone saves and sanctifies. In both, communication occurs through a human agency. However, the two are not equal. In fact,

Scripture is absolutely sovereign: it is of God, even in its form. It is the rule for tradition and church, whereas neither tradition nor church is rule for it. In addition, Scripture is fixed: it conveys today the testimony of missing witnesses in the same form in which they gave it. It lends itself superlatively to playing the role of the "witness" who does not budge. Church and tradition appear thus as subjects of Scripture.[40]

Congar is even willing to accept the historically Protestant principle of *sola Scriptura* if it is taken to mean the *material* sufficiency of the Scriptures, which are regarded as containing in one way or another all truths necessary to salvation. This position he finds in harmony with that of numerous fathers and other ancient and modern theologians, and he points out that even the Council of Trent was content to affirm that the revealed truths and principles of Christian conduct, the whole of which are found in the gospel, have been communicated to us by tradition *as well as* by Scripture. However, Congar goes still farther to affirm that Scripture provides "the primary objective standard of judgment for theology." Every post-Pentecostal experience must be "checked against the *datum* of Revelation given in the prophets, in Christ and by the Apostles; this is the principal objective criterion of the Faith and its theology." [41]

This does not mean that tradition is superfluous. On the contrary, it is indispensable. Three main contributions may be specified.

1. In a profound sense tradition begins with the prophets and the apostles. Their experience lies behind their written witness. The apostles in particular are the "formal reason" for the inspired and normative character of their writings, decisions, and acts. Moreover, the church founded by them preserved and transmitted the writings which bore the stamp of their authority, distinguishing them from others and determining which were canonized—although the fixing of the canon was simply the specific recognition of a normative authority which already existed because it was divinely given. Thus the Scriptures themselves were born and cradled in the church, and are the deposit of its earliest traditions to which they bear witness.[42]

[40] *La Tradition et les traditions* (Paris: Librairie Arthème Fayard, 1963), II, 177 f.
[41] *Ibid.*, pp. 166 f.; *Christ, Our Lady, and the Church*, pp. 72, 81.
[42] *Sainte Église*, pp. 187-200; *Christ, Our Lady, and the Church*, pp. 36 f.; *Lay People in the Church*, p. 307.

2. The Bible needs interpretation, which can be soundly provided by the church alone. Scripture is materially but not formally sufficient. Its meaning is not self-explanatory; even heretics have invoked it, and those who rely on it disagree among themselves. The needed understanding is communicated by the Holy Spirit, and the place of his revelatory action is the church with its rich tradition and teaching authority.[43] "The first conditions of all Bible-reading in any Catholic sense are that it shall be read 'in the Church,' because the Bible is the Church's book; and that it shall be read within the Church's tradition, because the Bible is part of that tradition, its 'head and source,' as St. Cyprian says." [44]

Congar insists that the creation of confessions of faith by Protestant communions constitutes a Protestant admission of the inadequacy of Scripture alone as a rule of faith. If Protestants claim that such confessions only make more precise a faith which is entirely subject to Scripture, he replies that Catholics say nothing other than this respecting the canons of the church councils. If Protestants add that the normative value of their confessions is entirely conditional and subject to revision, he answers that the confessions have been no more revised than the dogmas of the councils. In this respect Congar finds the essential differences between Protestant and Catholic thought in the lack of any genuine ecclesiology in the former.[45]

3. As the Scriptures provide the norm for the *purity* of the apostolic heritage, tradition is needed to assure its *fullness*. There exist traditions not recorded in the writings of the apostles which cannot be a priori excluded from the church's doctrinal articles, because they are presumed or even affirmed in those writings, irrefutably established, and recognized by both Orthodoxy and Roman Catholicism. At least one article of immense dogmatic significance is not found in Scripture—that concerning the canon of Scripture. The norms of canonicity are traceable to the apostles through the church, but they had to be determined by the church, and they are not contained in the Scriptures themselves.[46] In this fashion tradition provides a necessary augmentation of Scripture. The voice of apostolic authority "is echoed by the voice of the faithful people, in such a way that the second voice, while in exact agreement with the first, does not repeat it mechanically: it amplifies it, carries it further, enriches it, and corroborates

---

[43] *La Tradition et les traditions,* II, 140-66, 169 f., 176 f.; *The Wide World My Parish,* p. 48.
[44] *Lay People in the Church,* p. 306.
[45] *La Tradition et les traditions,* II, 176 f.
[46] *Ibid.,* pp. 170-73.

it. And this concerted movement stands foursquare on Scripture and tradition." [47]

The two erstwhile rivals are therefore to be seen as complementary. Far from opposing each other, they imply and support each other. There exists a communion in the gospel under two species—text and ecclesial life—which needs to be recognized and deepened through continual dialogue. For Scripture and tradition "have the same sovereign author, the Holy Spirit, and the same place of existence, the people of God." [48]

Other Themes

If space permitted, a study of other aspects of Congar's theology would be highly desirable. Areas especially worth examining are his affirmative view of man, in whom divine grace rather than sin is victorious; his insistence on the importance of man's cooperation with God in salvation; his conception of salvation as both deliverance and fulfillment, here and hereafter; his view of heaven as the realization of God's purpose and man's destiny in a community of love grounded in direct communion between God and men; his concept of purgatory as the purifying discipline of the Christian in his pilgrimage to the Holy City; his understanding of hell as the consequence of man's refusal to live within God's love; his identification of the kingdom of God on earth with the church; and his demand that Christians work actively for racial justice, international peace, and other social causes, because of the dignity and unity of mankind as created and redeemed by God.

Some of these themes have been dealt with in passing or by implication; others have had to be omitted entirely. However, the investigation undertaken indicates adequately both the primary interests of Congar and the chief directions of his thought. We now turn to a brief critical appraisal.

Critique

Values

1. Congar's acceptance of the obligation to rethink traditional doctrines and restate them in contemporary terms equips him for speaking effectively to critical-minded Catholics as well as for communicating with Protestant and Orthodox Christians and thereby furthering understanding and a sense of unity. His reinterpretations of Mariology, the resurrection of the

[47] *Lay People in the Church*, p. 281.
[48] *La Tradition et les traditions*, II, 63 f., 136, 170, 177-79.

body, heaven and hell, the role of the layman in the church, the authority of the pope, and other doctrines are not only illuminating in themselves; they also disclose areas of agreement between Catholics and non-Catholics which are often ignored.

2. His repeated stress on the humanity of Christ is a sound corrective, in the spirit of Chalcedon, of the one-sided emphasis on the deity which often marks both Protestant and Catholic thought. There is much truth in Charles E. Raven's contention that Apollinarianism, which denies the full humanity of Jesus—since all humanity is fallen—has become "the general Christology." [49] Even the "Basis" of the World Council of Churches errs in this direction when it describes the council as "a fellowship of churches which accept our Lord Jesus Christ as God and Saviour," with no mention of his true manhood. No doubt the humanity is often implied when it is not specifically asserted, but its omission or lack of emphasis encourages the aberration which Congar is rightly concerned to remedy.

3. The prominence which Congar gives to the *congregatio fidelium* in his discussions of the church does much to restore the biblical notion of the faithful people of God which is often underestimated or missing in Catholic theology. By distinguishing the communal principle from the hierarchical in the nature and life of the church, and by identifying the church as a whole with the faithful community, he also provides a crucial point of contact with the Reformation understanding of the church as the "congregation of faithful men." If both western branches of Christianity thus emphasize the community and its faith, there is a firm basis for a closer rapport.

4. Congar's ecclesiology assigns to the laity a distinctive and indispensable role in the apostolate of the church. Laymen are called on not only to assist the clergy in the internal affairs of the church; they have a peculiar responsibility for bearing their Christian witness in the ordinary life and work of the world. Congar's elaboration of this thesis bears in several respects a close similarity to the recent ecumenical emphasis on the ministry of the laity, hence constitutes another bridge of understanding between Catholic and non-Catholic Christians and churches.

5. Congar's christologically founded assertion of the importance of human agency in salvation, in both the individual and the church, may well occasion a reexamination and clarification, in the perspective of the New Testament, of such questions as *sola fides* and the relation of grace to

[49] Raven, *The Theological Basis of Pacifism* (New York: Fellowship Publications, 1951), p. 36.

faith and faith to works. The intense controversies of the sixteenth century drove both sides to a rigid espousal of extreme positions which are no longer defensible. Protestants will properly guard against ascribing saving merit to human acts, and beware of identifying the role of an all-too-human church with that of Jesus Christ. However, they need to recognize, on the one hand, that Catholics like Congar root salvation finally in the un-merited grace of God alone and regard personal trust in divine grace as indispensable; and on the other, that Protestants themselves assume that men must accept or respond to God's offer of forgiveness and that faith must bear fruit in works of love. Congar reminds us that our differences on these questions are not so great as has been traditionally believed.

6. Congar's view of the complementary relation between Scripture and tradition is clearly stated and persuasively developed. He unqualifiedly assigns normative sovereignty to the former, basically concurring with the historic Protestant position that the Scriptures alone contain all things necessary to salvation. At the same time, in emphasizing the important part played by the church in producing, interpreting, and amplifying Scripture in ways consistent with its revelation, he focuses attention on the truths which Protestants have until recently largely overlooked. He therefore pro-vides in this area as in others a firm basis for growing ecumenical under-standing.

Difficulties

1. It may be questioned whether Congar succeeds in fulfilling one of the major intentions of his Christology—that of conserving the real humanity of Jesus Christ. In his view Christ shares with all other men a fully human created nature, but his individuality, the *I* of his personal existence, is that of the uncreated Word, who as Son of God partakes also of the divine nature. Yet this activity of the Logos "in no way dissolves" the reality or the content of Jesus' human intelligence and free will. The question arises, however, as to how intelligence and will can remain truly human if they are exercised solely by the Second Person of the Trinity. If all the acts of the man Jesus are really the responsibility of the divine Word, what place remains for genuinely human responsibility or freedom? Is not human individuality essential to full humanity? Is Jesus then fully human if his unique ego, the singular selfhood which distinguishes him from other human persons, is supplied by the divine Person? In the absence of clear answers to such questions, it is difficult to avoid the conclusion that the real

humanity of Jesus Christ is inadequately safeguarded in Congar's Christology.

2. Inconsistency appears also in Congar's ecclesiology. He maintains that the church, like the Christ whose incarnation it extends, is a union of two natures. Both divine and human poles are "integral" to its "true reality." However, the "essence" of the church is identified only with its divine element. Congar distinguishes "that which belongs to the church as such," which is "absolutely pure and holy," from "that which proceeds from the limitations and faults of the individual exercising the church's authority." [50] To attribute the weaknesses to humanity and the holiness to God accords with the biblical understanding of the church and its historical reality, but this rules out anything approaching a Chalcedonian union of two natures. Congar seems to recognize this when he refers to the divine element alone as the church "as such," but this limitation is out of harmony with the view that the church's "true reality" requires both poles. If the human aspect is not essential to the church as such, how can it belong to its true reality?

3. Congar's subordination of the laity to the clergy is questionable on both logical and biblical grounds. In his interpretation the hierarchical apostolate alone is essential to the church's "existence pure and simple"; it alone constitutes the church "as such," "in its proper being as an institution of salvation." Laymen are necessary to the fullness but not to the essence of the church. But where is the line to be drawn between essence and fullness? Can the church realize its essence apart from those who provide its fullness?

Salvation for Congar includes deliverance from sin and death, victory over the forces which limit and hurt men and separate them from God and one another, the impartation of meaning to the present through a hope grounded in the future, and fulfillment of life through reconciliation with God.[51] Since the church is Christ's agent of salvation, any activity by Christians which is needed for or contributes to the realization of the ends named would seem to belong to its "proper being." The evils from which men need to be saved permeate their daily lives. Hence the living witness to the forgiving, transforming love of God made by dedicated laymen amid the tensions and conflicts of life in the world is not a dispensable addition to the work of the church "as such," but integral to its basic

[50] *Christ, Our Lady, and the Church*, pp. 61 f.
[51] *The Wide World My Parish*, pp. 38-52.

nature and redemptive mission. A church composed only of priests could not be either truly or fully the body of Christ. Nor is it accurate to say that the church is the mother of the faithful rather than composed of them. Faith is "generated" by the faithful community as a whole, not only by the sacramental ministry of its priests, who are often themselves called into the priesthood through the sacrificial ministry of their families and other lay members of the community of faith.

The New Testament writings identify different gifts and functions among members of the *laos tou theou*, the people or laity of God, but they offer no warrant for restricting the church as institution of salvation to the ordained clergy. Precisely the opposite is the case. According to Paul all who have been reconciled to God through Christ have been given a ministry of reconciliation (II Cor. 5:18-20). In Ephesians apostles, prophets, evangelists, pastors, and teachers are responsible for equipping God's people "for work in his service, to the building up of the body of Christ"—a task which they all share (Eph. 4:12 NEB). Similarly, it is the whole community which is commissioned in I Peter as "a royal priesthood, a holy nation, God's own people," to proclaim the redemptive acts of him who called them "out of darkness into his marvelous light" (I Pet. 2:9-10).

4. The considerations just urged are equally relevant to the Roman Catholic claim, supported by Congar, that authority and truth are transmitted by apostolic succession through the historic episcopate. It can be readily admitted that God uses horizontal as well as vertical channels to call and empower his people for their ministry. As Congar insists, the church is human as well as divine, and illumination, faith, and spiritual power are transmitted partially through human agency. But the restriction of this agency to a special class of persons given their authority by Christ himself through the apostles is no more justified than the limitation of the church per se to the clergy.

Obviously the problem is much too complex to be discussed adequately in the present context, which may do no more than reveal a Protestant bias. Yet brief mention must be made of three difficulties involved in Congar's interpretation of apostolic succession: (a) it lacks convincing scriptural foundations;[52] (b) the historical evidence discloses serious breaks in the supposed line of succession; (c) the view assigns to a self-perpetuat-

---

[52] Congar cites Luke 22:29-30 and John 20:21 in support of his view. In the former Jesus appoints his apostles to share his table in the kingdom to which his Father has appointed him, and to judge the twelve tribes of Israel. In the latter he sends his followers as the Father has sent him.

ing hierarchy an authority and responsibility which should belong to the whole church.

As we have seen, in New Testament times the entire Christian community was called to proclaim the gospel of salvation and minister in Christ's name. The whole church succeeded to the apostolic ministry, and the whole church is given that ministry today. The service of those who preach the Word or administer the sacraments is part of the total ministry to which all of the people of God are summoned. Genuinely apostolic succession is thus to be found in the ongoing faith and life of the apostolic church, re-created and renewed in each generation by the indwelling Spirit of the living God.

Leaving aside important historical-critical questions, four observations may be made here: 1. The Lucan passage is highly figurative in nature, and refers to the twelve tribes, not the church. 2. The Johannine commission is addressed to the disciples—an inclusive term—and there is no indication that only apostles were present. 3. Neither passage mentions any transfer of authority to the successors of those addressed. 4. Both must be related to other passages in which the whole church is given a similar mission (cf. above, pp. 203 f.).

10. KARL RAHNER

One of the most profound and influential among contemporary Roman Catholic theologians is the Jesuit Karl Rahner, university professor in the Institute for Christian World View and Philosophy of Religion of the University of Munich. His massive scholarship has produced almost three hundred essays, seventy-seven of which have been assembled in the five volumes of his *Schriften zur Theologie.*[1] He edited the revision of Denzinger's *Enchiridion Symbolorum* (1953), classic compendium of official Catholic teaching, and is coeditor of the second edition of the multivolume *Lexikon für Theologie und Kirche* and the collection *Quaestiones disputatae*, which includes a number of his own writings. Though he has been condemned by opponents as the purveyor of unorthodox ideas, at the Second Vatican Council he was personal theologian to both Franziskus Cardinal König of Vienna and Julius Cardinal Döpfer of Munich.

Permeating all of Rahner's thought is a spirit of adventurous questioning to which no area of doctrine or life is closed. At one point he describes dogmatics as "the understanding and appropriating science of listening,"[2]

---

[1] Einsiedeln, Zürich, Köln: Benziger Verlag, 1957-62. The first two volumes have been published in English by Taplinger (Helicon) Press, Baltimore, with the title *Theological Investigations* (I: *God, Christ, Mary and Grace*, tr. Cornelius Ernst, 1961; II: *Man in the Church*, tr. Karl H. Kruger, 1963).

[2] *Theological Investigations*, I, 17. In later references this work will be cited as *Investigations*.

and listening for him means earnestly probing for the living meaning of the faith of the church. This requires us to deal forthrightly with the questions which today's intellectuals are asking. Such inquiry is a difficult and dangerous procedure, since it demands a willingness to reformulate old questions, to raise new ones, and to explore untried solutions whose agreement or disagreement with the established doctrine of the church cannot be known in advance. Yet rigid adherence to accepted formulas can be even more dangerous. Doctrinal statements which are orthodox but unintelligible, suffused with "the graveyard calm of weariness and boredom," cannot support an effective Christian witness in our time.[3]

Christian truth must be expressed in precise formulations. However, these are by nature self-transcending; they are beginnings as well as ends of searching thought. Even the clearest and most hallowed condensations of the long struggle of the church to understand the mysteries of God are more means than goals, statements of truth which open the path to *the* truth, which is always greater. For example, the Chalcedonian "formula" is—a formula; it is marked by an incompleteness which it "does not resolve but in fact preserves." What is merely conserved or handed down without a fresh, personal effort to understand it, in relation to the source of revelation, "rots as the manna did." We can really preserve the past "in its purity" only by relating it responsibly to the present and the future.[4]

Closely related to Rahner's demand for new approaches is his partially existentialist orientation. The influence of Martin Heidegger, with whom he studied at Freiburg from 1934 to 1936, is apparent in his anthropological approach to theology. Human nature as he sees it is a mystery which cannot be neatly defined; it is known best in the decisions and actions of concrete existence. Man can be understood only in his wholeness as a being who, aware of being questioned by existence, needs to respond in passionate commitment as well as reflection. Our clearest thought of God and Christ is related to the salvation-event in man. Divine grace can be understood adequately only when it is personally experienced at the point of one's own present need. Christian ethical decisions must take full account of the concrete singularity of the individual in the existing situation.

Nevertheless, Catholic theology in Rahner's view must also be a theology of essence. Though human "nature" is a "remainder concept," it is necessary and objectively justified. There are intrinsic and continuing structures

---

[3] *Schriften zur Theologie*, IV, 104-7; *Investigations*, I, viii f., 2-7, 11, 13. In later references the *Schriften zur Theologie* will be cited as *Schriften*.

[4] *Investigations*, I, 149 f., 7, 10.

and connections in reality which can in some measure be known and elucidated. Unlike Bultmann, for instance, Rahner believes it is possible to make
true statements about the real God whose grace man encounters in salvation, and even about life after death. Likewise ethical decisions, though
singular, refer to universal norms which they attempt to relate to particular
situations.

Rahner's deep concern for a theology which speaks effectively to men
today leads him to take the entire world of ideas and their practical meaning as his theological parish. Systematic theology is the servant of the
effective proclamation of the gospel in and through the church; it is therefore concerned with pastoral and moral theology, the spiritual life, and the
Christian witness in the world as well as with the more basically doctrinal
issues which claim his chief attention. Both types of questions receive at
Rahner's hands the same rigorous and penetrating treatment. The discussion below will necessarily omit many of his themes. However, those considered represent major emphases, and together they disclose the quality
and trend of his thought.

Christology

History is "a becoming new which preserves the old." Therefore doctrinal formulas which are historical embodiments of Christian truth should
be neither abandoned nor passed on in petrified form. Rahner follows this
principle in considering the incarnation, presupposing but not simply re-
peating the Chalcedonian declaration.[5] Since the church's christological
dogma has never claimed to be an adequate distillation of biblical teaching, there is need for a fresh examination of biblical Christology. Such
study would, for one thing, produce a renewed recognition of the humanity
of Christ. Rahner finds in the current understanding of the Chalcedonian
formula an implicit if unconscious monophysite tendency which fails to
do justice to the New Testament portrayal of the historical Jesus and his
role as Messiah and Mediator. Thus the incarnation becomes "almost a
transient episode in God's activity in his world," and the continuing manhood of Christ strongly affirmed at Chalcedon is overlooked. Jesus becomes
God among us, but the Jesus who in human freedom becomes our Mediator
is left in question. Freedom subjected to the divine nature cannot be the
intrinsic personal freedom which is essential to human personality. The
real humanity of Christ must therefore be clearly and explicitly asserted.[6]

[5] *Investigations*, I, 150, 154; *Schriften*, IV, 137.
[6] *Investigations*, I, 155-61, 188 f., 198.

The Incarnation

Rahner devotes major attention to the meaning of the incarnation, examining it both metaphysically and existentially. One of his most profound and difficult essays deals successively with the questions: What does it mean (1) that God has become *man,* and (2) that he has *become* man? In approaching the former, he endeavors to formulate the ontological counterpart to the ontic statements of orthodox Christology, asking how the nature of real being should be conceived to correspond to the church's assertions regarding God, man, and Christ. Which account of ultimate reality is necessarily adapted to these statements? Rahner believes that a sound answer to this question will prevent the mythological impression, often made by the traditional affirmations, that God has clothed himself in the garment of a human nature which only externally envelops him.

Rahner's basic conviction is that true being, represented by both man and God, is Spirit as such. Man cannot be defined in any way which would specify limits to his nature. All that can be said is that his existence is referred to the incomparable God. Our nature is self-transcendence, limitless reference to the "mystery of fullness." We exist in the decision of accepting or rejecting our own mystery, and the larger mystery to which it refers. The transcendence "which we are and act" makes up our existence and God's, and both as mystery. However, this mystery is not something concealed and to be disclosed, standing next to something already known. Rather it is simply what is there, the given. It is the ultimate horizon of all conceiving, in terms of which we conceive other reality. It is the uniqueness which always distinguishes God, and because of him ourselves.

The reality which is human nature comes to itself by losing itself. This occurs most radically when, yielding itself utterly to the mystery of fullness, it is so expropriated that it becomes the mystery of God himself. It is accepted by God as *his* reality, thus arriving at the point toward which according to its essence it is always moving. This occurs in the incarnation. Man *is* in the degree to which he gives himself away. His nature is his potentiality for obedience. The Word of God "assumes" human nature, therefore, when this potentiality is most fully developed. Found thus by infinity, man becomes what he is. His being finds supreme fulfillment when a true man gives himself to God so fully that in him the mystery toward which man's questions point, the question beyond question, becomes present as final answer.

When we ask who fits this description in earthly history—who therefore is the one to whom we can bring the mystery of our own nature—we can turn only to Jesus of Nazareth. Such an event took place and eternally takes place only in him. We others are too far from God, thinking that we alone understand ourselves. But Jesus knew that only the Father knew his mystery, and therein he understood that only he knew the Father.[7]

What, then, does it mean for God to *become* man? Rahner finds the answer primarily in the concept of *kenosis*. The Word can become flesh because the Absolute has in his infinite unrelatedness the possibility of divesting himself of himself to become the finite other. By giving himself away, God posits the other as his own reality, without having to undergo becoming in his own original essence. Differentiation is implicit in God as love; since he wills to have the other as his own, he constitutes it in its genuine reality. As the fullness which gives itself away, he externalizes himself and becomes historical. This original capacity for divine differentiation is the ultimate source of the possibility of creation, in which God gives reality to the other without giving up himself. Therefore rooted in the deepest ground of creation itself is the possibility of its being "assumed" by God, the basis for his possible self-objectification in human history. The immanent self-utterance of God in his eternal fullness is the condition of the self-utterance and self-projection of God in both creation and incarnation.[8]

In Rahner's view the relation of creation and incarnation extends still further, the latter being seen as the goal of the former. The incarnation of the Word is indeed a unique event in real history. However, it is not merely a subsequent occurrence in a world already finished, a kind of divine afterthought occasioned by human sin and the need of redemption. Ontologically it is the "unambiguous goal of creation as a whole," to which everything prior is preparatory, pointing to the event in which God, while giving being to what is other than he, once for all achieves both the greatest proximity to it and the greatest distance from it. In radically objectifying himself God appears in utmost truth. The history of what he has created thus becomes profoundly his own, and it finds its center and fulfillment in Christ.[9]

Though Rahner devotes his full intellectual powers to christological speculation, he maintains that a person who misunderstands and therefore rejects the orthodox formulas may nevertheless consummate faith in the

---

[7] *Schriften*, IV, 140-45.
[8] *Schriften*, IV, 145-49.
[9] *Investigations*, I, 164 f.

incarnation existentially. Many a man, looking at Jesus and his cross, confesses that therein the living God has spoken to him the last and decisive Word, and thus has delivered him from all those factors in his existence which hold him captive to guilt and death. Such a person derives from Jesus the final truth of his life. But his belief is true only if Jesus really is the one whom the faith of the church confesses. Therefore this person believes, whether or not he knows it reflectively, in the incarnation of the Word of God. Indeed, Christ has been met by many who were unaware that they had encountered the one whose life and death held the secret of their redemption. The grace of the incarnate God is present in every reality worth choosing, as its hidden essence. When therefore a man accepts his existence in quiet patience, in faith, hope, and love *as* the mystery contained in the mystery of eternal love and life, he says yes to something which is what it is because God has actually filled it with the Unmeasured—himself—since the Word became flesh. Such a person entrusts himself to Christ without knowing it. "Whoever wholly accepts his manhood . . . has accepted the Son of man, because in him God has accepted man." We do fulfill the law and love God when we love our neighbor, for God has become this neighbor.[10]

Christology and Anthropology

It should now be apparent that for Rahner the incarnation is the clue to a true understanding of man no less than of God. The fact that God has become man means that Christology is the beginning and end of Christian anthropology, and that such anthropology is inevitably theo-logy. Humanity is not something added on to God, a mere form of appearance; it is his very presence in the world. In Christ's human life we see what our human life really means. Our finitude is that of the Word of God himself. Most profoundly understood, man is seen to *be* because God himself *ek-sists*—projects himself outward, externalizes himself in the other. Through this self-emptying God's existence "receives its value, strength, and reality." Man arises when God, willing to be non-God, lovingly speaks himself out into the godless nothing. "He has spoken his Word as our flesh into the emptiness of the not-divine and sinful." Man is the abbreviation of the divine Word, the image of God himself. He is the expression of the bottomless mystery of his ground, in which he eternally participates. Through the incarnation the finite itself has been given an infinite depth. It is no longer an antithesis to the infinite, but that which the infinite has become in order to open to the finite a door into the infinite. Man is there-

[10] *Schriften*, IV, 152-54.

fore forbidden to think poorly of himself, for he would then think poorly of God.[11]

Nature and Grace

According to the usual textbook distinction, nature and grace represent two sharply circumscribed strata in man. The former is a self-enclosed, finished system which includes everything man can learn about himself independently of revelation, whereas grace is a pure superstructure which leaves unchanged the nature beneath, and which lies completely beyond consciousness. Human nature is thought to contain potentialities—for example, of knowing God or obeying the moral law—which can become realities without grace, though they may be somewhat heightened, without man's conscious awareness, by the objective imposition of supernatural grace from above. The two sectors are related chiefly negatively, by the absence of mutual contradiction. Rahner rejects this compartmentalization, tracing partly to it the contemporary lack of interest, even among Catholics, in the supernatural. If grace is not to be experienced where man himself is, and has nothing to do with the fulfillment of his present spiritual existence, why should he be concerned with it? Practical if not philosophical naturalism is often a not surprising result.[12]

Though Rahner preserves the distinction between nature and grace, he sees them as interpenetrating. Implicit in human existence are fundamental orientations which he calls "existentials." Like the "categories" of traditional ontology, these are the a priori conditions which make possible particular phenomena, the modes or forms comprising the structure of human existence. Among these is the "supernatural existential," man's longing for or unconditional ordination to God's love and eternal blessedness. This is experienced as unexacted, unowed, unearned (*ungeschuldet*) grace. It cannot be considered a part of man's nature, since then the God who created man with this yearning would be *obliged* to fulfill it, whereas existentially man is free to accept or reject the beatitude offered him by God's free decision. Man's concrete existence may therefore be differentiated into the supernatural existential and the "remainder," which is his nature. This nature cannot be precisely defined, but it is the synthesis of all the

[11] *Investigations*, I, 183-85, 190-92; *Schriften*, IV, 150-52.

[12] *Nature and Grace; Dilemmas in the Modern Church*, tr. Dinah Wharton and G. Richard Dimler (New York: Sheed and Ward, 1964), p. 123; *Investigations*, I, 298-300; *Schriften*, IV, 210-19; "Natur und Gnade nach der Lehre der Katholischen Kirche," *Theologie heute*, ed. Leonhard Reinisch (München: Verlag C. H. Beck, 1959), p. 98. The last mentioned essay will be cited hereafter as "Natur und Gnade."

capacities and powers which identify man as a created spiritual being, make possible his earthly accomplishments, and enable him to respond to supernatural grace. Grace, then, is the justifying, sanctifying, divinizing action by which God communicates himself to man and empowers him to participate freely in God's own life. Nature is man's potentiality for the divine life, while grace is the divine action through which alone this nature finds absolute fulfillment.[13]

So conceived, grace is "existentialistic, actualistic, personalistic" for both God and man. From the divine standpoint it is not a power or a substance other than God which he imparts to man; rather it is God himself, his free act of forgiving love. It is God communicating himself to man. On the human side, grace is not medicinally ingested into a substratum of man's being, but personally experienced as the deed of love that calls for decision. It is realized in man's experience of himself as made new in the cleansing, strengthening, illumination, and life-transformation which occur in his concrete existence.[14]

For Rahner, therefore, there is no such thing as a purely "natural" man. Man's life as we know it is already "graced." All human events occur within a supernatural order, and no one—not even the worst sinner—can escape from it. Man's whole spiritual-intellectual existence is rooted in what traditional theology has called the uncreated or prevenient grace of God, which no one can require of God or deserve, but which can become created or actualized grace for anyone who chooses to accept it.

This conception has two important corollaries. First, grace is operative outside the church and its sacraments, for example, in the freedom of man to live an ethical life. Every good act is positively related to and made possible by the saving will of God. We must therefore admit the possibility of a saving history outside churchly Christianity. Who can dismiss the intellectual endeavors of secular philosophers or the thought and practice of non-Christian religions as only the voice of nature, and perhaps of its guilt? May they not also unwittingly represent the sighing of creation, already in hidden ways moved by the grace of the Holy Spirit, for the glory of the sons of God? [15] Secondly, this understanding of the relation of grace to nature enables Catholics to approach agreement with the Reformation in affirming that "the grace of God is everything." Ultimately man depends

---

[13] *Investigations*, I, 301-4, 312-15; *Schriften*, IV, 232; "Natur und Gnade," pp. 93 f.; *Nature and Grace*, pp. 140 f.

[14] *Schriften*, IV, 219, 221-26; *Nature and Grace*, pp. 135 f.

[15] *Schriften*, IV, 219, 226-32, 235.

utterly on God. He has no autonomous goodness on which to base a claim to salvation. Even when in faith and love he freely accepts God's mercy, he must praise this appropriation as God's gift. God gives us himself, and also makes possible our acceptance of his self-communication. When the disobedient servant responds, he does so because even in his sin he has been the object of the seeking love of God.[16]

In another respect, however, Rahner's doctrine of grace opposes that of the Reformers. He cannot agree that the recipient of grace remains "at the same time sinful and righteous." God's action produces a real change in man, so that he really becomes righteous rather than being only declared righteous. God's grace is healing and safeguarding as well as forgiving. It enables the justified person to keep God's commandments; "if he falls again into sin he falls although he could have stood firm and he himself is the responsible, guilty cause." Catholic theology does not forget that the redeemed man is still on the way between Adam and Christ, needing always to pray for new forgiveness; his present righteousness is that of walking in a holy adventure of Christian existence toward the time when God's final judgment will pronounce him righteous. Yet though still a sinner he is really sanctified by God's grace; in the hidden depths of his nature he actually is already holy and righteous, and does not merely hope to become so. As one to whom God has communicated himself he partakes on his limited level of the holiness of God.[17]

Church, Word, and Sacrament

The saving grace embodied in Christ is communicated to men in all times in and through the agency founded by Christ himself—the church. Though grace is everywhere operative, only in the church can it be experienced in the fullness that makes salvation a present reality. Rahner therefore devotes major attention to the church and the means of grace which it alone supplies.

The church is essentially the continuing presence of Christ and his redemption in the world. It is "the visible, socially composed communion of men with Jesus, the source of sanctifying grace," "the community which, in its historico-social form, its tangible liturgical actions, its word of truth and its life, is the continuation of the historically tangible reality of Christ." [18] Hence it has the same function as that which Christ performed

---

[16] "Natur und Gnade," pp. 96 f.; Investigations, I, 302.
[17] "Natur und Gnade," pp. 99 f.; Nature and Grace, pp. 48 f., 60.
[18] Investigations, II, 96.

—that of making effective in men the freedom of God, delivering them from guilt, law, and death. By its very existence the church symbolizes "the eschatologically triumphant grace of God." In the genuine holiness of the faithful congregation this grace is already demonstrably real. True, individual members may be fallible and lacking in faith, but the church as a whole is always a hearing and believing church, the visible reality of the victorious Word which puts itself into effect.[19]

On the authority of God the church is empowered to proclaim the Word of God and to administer the sacraments to men. These two basic powers constitute its essence. Initially, God's Word is uttered in creative and redemptive acts and events which primarily disclose God himself rather than doctrinal propositions about him. This dynamic view of revelation provides the background for six cumulative theses on the relation between Word and sacrament.

1. The Word is spoken by the church, in and through which Christ makes his message contemporary with all times. 2. This Word in the church is an inner moment in the saving action by which God communicates himself to man and inwardly transforms him. 3. As in God's action in Christ and the church, the inner Word of grace is combined with the external, historical Word of revelation. 4. This Word actually brings to pass the salvation-event which it announces. 5. This eventful, exhibitive Word occurs in the church with different levels of intensity, calling forth varying degrees of faith and acceptance. 6. Its highest actualization in the "radical engagement" of the church takes place in the sacrament, and only there. The sacramental Word is the supreme form of the effective Word; spoken in the church in the authority of Christ, it is the decisive event in which God communicates himself to man as the salvation which both justifies and sanctifies him.[20]

Rahner strongly emphasizes that the Word as sacrament, like Christ and the church, is *opus operatum*, the work wrought, salvation actually achieved. This becomes fully clear only when we understand the church itself as the primal sacrament. In its concrete nature it is the abiding sign that God not only *offers* to the world the grace of his self-communication, but powerfully *accomplishes* the acceptance of this offer. The world not only *can* be rescued if it will; it actually *is* rescued, because God in Christ *brings about that it will*. It is the redeemed, not merely the redeemable

---

[19] *Investigations*, II, 96-98; *Schriften*, IV, 353; *The Church and the Sacraments*, tr. W. J. O'Hara (New York: Herder and Herder, 1963), pp. 19, 39, 41.
[20] *Schriften*, IV, 314-36.

world. To be sure, the destiny of the individual is still open, but that of the world as a whole is already positively decided. Of this victory the church is the historically tangible and audible sign. It is itself *opus operatum,* the consummation of God's saving action, "the historical, eschatological Presence of redemptive grace." The sacraments, then, are the actualization of the church's nature with reference to individual men in the decisive situations of their lives.[21]

Several corollaries of this basic view may be very briefly stated. First, since the church itself is the primal sacrament, a churchly action does not have to be explicitly established by the historical Jesus to be a true sacrament. He founded the church and gave it its sacramental nature. Therefore any act of the church which truly actualizes for the individual its nature as the concrete historical presence of God's saving grace is *ipso facto* a sacrament.[22] Secondly, grace is conferred without the subjective merit of the minister or the recipient. But this does not mean that human faith is ignored; rather, grace imparts faith, love, and the power to accomplish.[23] Thirdly, the operation of the Word of God is not restricted to the sacraments. There are other forms of its utterance in the mouth of the church which precede, accompany, and follow its sacramental expression. However, all these diversified words are inwardly connected with the one whole of meaning from which they derive their strength and value, and which finds fulfillment in the historically tangible Word. Ultimately God utters only himself—as eternal salvation in the Spirit of the incarnate Logos.[24]

All sacraments come to a focus in the Eucharist. It is "in all truth the sacrament of the Word absolutely, the absolute instance of the Word in general." It is the center of meaning of all churchly reality, making most victoriously present not only the redemptive grace of Christ but the source of grace itself. All other sacramental words are only expositions and applications, preparations and echoes, of this Word. All words of teaching, admonition, and command have but one aim—that men faithfully and lovingly accept what in this holy celebration becomes wholly real and present, the gift of God to man in him who has given himself for us. In the Eucharist the Lord is present through and under the effective Word

---

[21] *Ibid.,* pp. 337-44; *The Church and the Sacraments,* p. 39.

[22] *The Church and the Sacraments,* pp. 41, 57 f.

[23] *Ibid.,* pp. 32-34. Rahner asserts that to deny that what is signified or pointed to in gestures, rites, and figurative representations is in fact present is to overlook "the primarily ontological nature of symbol." What is signified is really present precisely because it is "represented." *Ibid.,* p. 36.

[24] *Schriften,* IV, 345-47.

which has two constituents: the barely material species of bread and wine, and the more spiritual, formal, unequivocal species of the explanatory words of the Lord, which make the Word understandable and determine it. Only the two species together form the one sign of this sacrament which makes present what it signifies.[25]

Also involved in Rahner's doctrine of the church are his discussions of the relation between the hierarchy and the whole community of believers, the apostolate of the laity, and the relation between Scripture and the church's tradition. If space allowed, an examination of his views on these issues would be rewarding. However, since they very closely parallel those of Yves Congar, which have been treated in the preceding chapter, they are omitted here in order to permit closer attention to Rahner's more distinctive contributions.[26]

The Meaning of Death

A striking example of the probing quality of Rahner's thought is his theology of death. Starting with the teachings of the church, he relates them to other types of knowledge and critically examines the concepts involved, dealing successively with death as an event common to all men, as a consequence of sin, and as a dying with Christ.

1. Though the meaning and the outcome of death are vastly different for different persons, it is an unavoidable and universal event. According to Christian faith all men must die, not because of any discernible biological necessity, but because all are sinners, because of "the moral tragedy of mankind through its first parents." The traditional view that at death the soul is separated from the body rightly affirms that the spiritual life-principle of man assumes a different relation to what is usually called the body, and does not perish when the physical structure of the body is dissolved. But it by no means provides an adequate definition of death. For example, it obscures the fact that death concerns man as a whole person. Questions must be raised also about another traditional conception—that the soul at death becomes acosmic, out of all relation to the world. Rahner suggests that the reverse is more likely to be true—that the human spirit becomes "all-cosmic," open to the "all" in a way which its limited bodily structure makes impossible, and somehow able to exert an ontological influence on the universe as the ground of existence of other spiritual-

[25] Ibid., pp. 348-53.
[26] See Investigations, II, 319-52; Schriften, III, 285-328; V, 303-55; Inspiration in the Bible, tr. Charles H. Henkey (New York: Herder and Herder, 1961); Nature and Grace, pp. 83-113.

corporeal beings. As an event common to all men, death is both the conclusion and the consummation of our earthly pilgrimage. It is the end of
man's biological life, which is demolished from without; it is also his active
personal fulfillment from within, the ripe result of what he has freely made
of himself during his temporal existence.[27]

2. The declaration that death is the expression and consequence of
human guilt does not mean that apart from sin the first man would have
lived endlessly on earth. His life would certainly have come to an end, but
in a manner which would have permitted the perfect consummation of his
personal life in bodily form without the violent dissolution of his physical
constitution through an external power. His end would have been "a death
without dying," the pure, active affirmation of the whole man from within,
including that openness to the cosmos in its totality which is now possible
only for the redeemed. According to its original essence, therefore, death
was and is a natural event, the necessary consequence of man's nature as
body and spirit. But actually man has sinned, losing the divine life that
was rooted in his union with God by grace, and thereby causing the disin-
tegration of his earthly existence. Hence death as we now confront it is
both a natural event and a result of sin.[28] Yet since it retains its proper,
natural essence, it contains for man two possibilities: the death of Adam
in punishment for sin, or the death of Christ and entrance to eternal life.
Which alternative is actualized depends on the personal attitude with which
man sustains this essence in the many acts that make up the course of his
life. He may die sinfully, by autonomously willing the rejection of God,
or rightly, by repeated decisions of loving surrender to him.[29]

Death with its darkness and horror is the decisive event in which man's
sinful self-centeredness reaches its complete expression. It is the consequence and manifestation of man's estrangement from God which has
marked all dimensions of his life since Adam's fall. It is likewise the expression and penal consequence of grave personal sins that remain unfor-
given—the individual's own affirmation of the sins of Adam. The
"righteous," those who have appropriated the redemption offered in Christ,
must also die, but they experience a very different death. Death is not
merely a passively suffered occurrence which is identical for all men. Its
meaning varies greatly. In a profound sense a man's death is his own act,

---

[27] *On the Theology of Death*, tr. Charles H. Henkey (New York: Herder and Herder, 1961),
pp. 21-40, 71.
[28] *Ibid.*, pp. 41-43, 50.
[29] *Ibid.*, pp. 44, 45 f., 51 f.; *Schriften*, IV, 434.

since the *kind* of death he dies is the culmination of the kind of life he has lived. Existentially death is widely different for the sinner and the righteous, though externally the event may be the same. The death "done" in a life of thoughts and deeds opposed to or indifferent to God leads to the empty end of a death suffered—"mortal sin" in the full, proper sense of the term.[30]

3. At the other extreme, death may be the climactic act of mortal man's appropriation of the salvation based on the redemptive death of Christ. For those who respond to Christ in faith and love and who die "in the Lord," death is completely transformed. Primarily, the death of Christ has saving efficacy because it established "an ontological order of salvation" for all spiritual beings related to this world by their bodily nature. Through his death "his spiritual reality, which he possessed from the beginning, enacted in his life, and brought to consummation in his death, becomes open to the whole world and is inserted into this world as a permanent destiny of a real-ontological kind." [31] This conception Rahner finds implicit in the church's teaching concerning Christ's descent into hell. When the reality of Christ is consummated through his death and grafted into the oneness of the world in its ultimate depths, he enters intimately into the existential foundations of all personal action in the world. Thus the world as the ground of personal life becomes quite different from what it would have been if Christ had not died, and the way is opened for other men to a similar relation to its basic oneness, in which each can make his contribution to the whole.[32]

For the Christian, therefore, death becomes a dying with Christ and a sharing of his victory. He still encounters it as darkness, the bitterness of guilt, and remoteness from God. Yet through the grace of Christ he is given that faith in God's mercy, hope for life in God, and love for God which transform it into an act of resigning obedience and a trustful commitment into the hands of God. As such, death crowns a life of daily dying with Christ. This occurs centrally in the sacramental life of the Christian. In particular, our participation in the death of Christ begins with baptism and faith, is repeatedly enacted in the Eucharist, and reaches its climax in extreme unction. Thus that which happens mystically and sacramentally in our earthly Christian existence—our assimilation to the death of our

---

[30] *On the Theology of Death*, pp. 54-58, 89-94.
[31] *Ibid.*, p. 71.
[32] *Ibid.*, pp. 71-75.

Lord—occurs really and finally in our death, through which we are freed to eternal life.[33]

Rahner's belief in a deep inner connection between the spiritual life of man and the material order finds expression in his interpretation of the resurrection of the body.[34] This article of the church's faith means for him belief in the persistence of the whole reality and meaning of man in dependence on the living reality of God. The one God has created both spirit and matter, and both participate in some way in the perfection of the human person made real in death. Personal spirit is the meaning and goal of the entire reality of the world, and it is far more real than matter or energy, but precisely as human spirit it is "material, worldly, embodied." Therefore the world remains beyond history "the connatural environment of the perfected spirit," which reaches its own consummation and that of the world in fellowship with God. To believe in the resurrection of the body means to believe that we shall be alive, whole, perfected in all dimensions of our existence. In some manner not completely comprehensible, the material is a part of reality itself, and thus shares in the consummation of man's personal life. Paul's paradoxical reference to a "spiritual body" (I Cor. 15:44) points to a bodiliness which gives the spirit real expression without occasioning its limitation or abasement, and which instead of canceling the freedom from the here and now won in death, brings it to its full manifestation.[35]

Ethical Thought

One of the best instances of Rahner's synthesis of existentialist and essentialist tendencies is found in his ethical thought. He explores favorably the possibility of a "formal existential ethic," but rejects the "situation ethic" which is often grounded in existentialist philosophy. Situational or contextual ethics asserts the radical particularity of human existence, which leaves no place for an abiding essence or nature in man or for ethical principles normative for all men. The Christian must simply answer before God, in faith, the peculiar demands of each situation as it confronts him. Rahner regards this view as quite impossible for a Catholic. He affirms the reality of an enduring human nature and of universal ethical norms to which specific choices should be related as far as possible. The command-

[33] *Ibid.*, pp. 75-88.
[34] See his essays, "The Resurrection of the Body," *Investigations*, II, 203-16; and "Das Leben der Toten," *Schriften*, IV, 429-37.
[35] *Investigations*, II, 212-16.

ments of God proclaimed by the church are objectively valid, demanding obedience.[36]

Nevertheless, Rahner raises serious questions about the "average Catholic" attempt to deduce syllogistically from general norms the action required in a specific situation. He admits that this deductive procedure may be sufficient for many decisions. Yet the question always remains whether the concrete situation facing the individual is identical with that which the universal norm is concerned. For the Christian all ethical norms are grounded in the will of God. The individual is subject not to abstract laws but to the personal God who has spoken to men concretely in Jesus Christ.[37] His will relates to particular situations, and it cannot always be expressed in universal terms. The concrete moral act is more than an instance of the application of a general principle or the realization at a particular place and time of a universal idea. Rather it is a reality with a positive content all its own, fundamentally and absolutely unique. Likewise the man who makes ethical decisions is not simply an instance of the general class "man"; he is rather a spiritual individual, a singular person whom God calls by name—a name which is his alone.

Christian ethics must take full account of this positively individual element in men's moral acts. There are "individual norms" as well as universal ones, and they, no less than general laws, must be referred to the obligating will of God—a will directed to the concrete in all its uniqueness. We therefore need an existential ethic of a formal kind to investigate the fundamental structure of the individual aspects of ethical conduct, the ways in which individual norms may be known and applied, and the functioning of conscience and obligation in the person making specific moral choices.[38]

Though Rahner does not himself undertake to develop such an ethic, he discusses briefly several practical implications of his theory which would, for example, modify our ordinary understanding of sin. Instead of limiting sin to violations of universal moral standards, it would show that sin is also and equally a singular offense against an individual imperative rooted in God's individual will. It would thus enable us to see sin more clearly as failure to trust the personal-individual love of God. It is also relevant to the place of the individual in the church. If there is truly an existential ethic, then there is a sphere of individual choice which the command of

[36] *Investigations*, II, 217-20, 222; *Nature and Grace*, pp. 42-44.
[37] *Investigations*, II, 220-23; *Nature and Grace*, pp. 58 f.
[38] *Investigations*, II, 225-31, 233 f., 103-5.

ecclesiastical authorities may not take away. There is in the moral decisions of the Christian a concrete, personal dimension which cannot be directly or officially governed by the church. As a unique spirit-person he has the right and responsibility to make his own conscientious decisions. Beyond all the commandments of the church he must still ask in each situation, "Lord, what do you want me to do?" [39]

Critique

Values

1. Rahner combines profound respect for the historic positions of the church with enthusiasm for raising unexplored questions and reexamining accepted truths in new contexts. He asserts that the individual theologian must begin with doctrine as proposed by the *magisterium*; when this is determined—often in itself a rugged task—it becomes the unquestionable basis for all further investigation. But wide latitude remains for the elaboration and interpretation of official doctrine and the exploration of unresolved issues. Denzinger's definitions should never be used to conceal mental laziness! Rahner has mastered the history of dogma and honors the conclusions reached, but is equally at home on the growing edge of Christian thought, investigating disputed questions, offering and testing new hypotheses, and inviting the critical responses of other theologians to his proposals, while ready to withdraw them if better answers are found. In his explorations he makes constructive use of the methods, theories, and insights of other disciplines, notably philosophy and the sciences. His combination of regard for the old and openness to the new and different has invigorated Roman Catholic thought, advanced Catholic-Protestant understanding, and provided a valuable point of contact between Christian faith and secular culture.

2. Rahner's theology derives great power likewise from its synthesis of existentialist and essentialist features. He is concerned that certain truths of God's revelation so often become unexistential in the day-to-day life of the Christian, but never seriously doubts the objective reference and grounding of such truths. He insists as strenuously as Bultmann that Jesus Christ must be known personally in his power to transform actual existence, but just as firmly contends that such an experience implies that Jesus truly *is* the Christ, whose capacity to save springs from his relation to ultimate reality. He is sensitively aware of the emotional impact of death on the

[39] *Investigations,* II, 105, 232-34; *Nature and Grace,* pp. 27 f.

finite individual, yet seeks the truth concerning death "by way of disinterested elaboration." [40] He recognizes both the singularity of moral decisions and the universality of ethical norms. Interwoven emphases like these are in fundamental accord with biblical faith; they also point the Christian today toward a faith which has personal vitality, concrete relevance, and objective support.

3. At a number of important points Rahner's thought opens the way to a closer Protestant-Catholic *rapprochement*. Like Congar, he maintains that the church's teaching authority can never supersede that of the canonical Scriptures or the historically verifiable norm of faith and morals which they provide. He moves far in the direction of Luther and Calvin in declaring that ultimately God's grace is "everything," and in repeatedly stressing the importance of faith in man's acceptance of salvation. In his contention that grace operates in all men, whether they are conscious of it or not, he approximates the teaching of John Wesley that no man is without prevenient grace. Such views help appreciably to lower the barriers which divide Catholics and Protestants, especially when on the Protestant side there are emerging a heightened appreciation of tradition and an increased recognition of the indispensability of works of righteousness and love as the expression and accompaniment of saving faith. Likewise, Rahner's conception that the church is itself the fundamental sacrament, so that its sacraments flow from its nature as the enduring presence of the grace of Christ in the world, tends to reduce to a subordinate status the dispute over the number of sacraments instituted by Christ himself.

4. Rahner's strong insistence that God's grace is healing and sanctifying as well as forgiving and his incisive criticism of the "mystique of sin" are convincing, biblically grounded assertions of the positive possibilities of the Spirit-led life. The God proclaimed in the New Testament is Creator as well as Redeemer, and those whom he redeems become new creations. The apostle Paul is utterly realistic about the power of sin, but he specifically refutes those who justify continuing in sin "that grace may abound." Actually, in their baptism they have died to sin so that they "might walk in newness of life." Christians are called on to be "transformed by the renewal of their minds," to be "imitators of God," to be "made perfect in love." [41] Such is the New Testament portrayal of the life which is centered in God and empowered by him. Rahner's position is a valuable corrective

---

[40] *On the Theology of Death*, p. 17.
[41] II Cor. 5:17; Rom. 6:1-4; 12:2; Eph. 5:1; I John 4:17, 18; cf. Gal. 5:25; 6:15; Eph. 1:4; 4:24.

for all theologies, Catholic or Protestant, which in the name of biblical realism stress so one-sidedly the sinfulness of man that they doubt or overlook the life-changing power of the grace of God proclaimed by the gospel.

5. At first sight one might easily dismiss as empty speculation Rahner's suggestion that the individual person, rendered "all-cosmic" by death, may come to exert a real ontological influence on the universe. However, further reflection is more likely to elicit approval. Rahner believes that when a man is freed from the finite restrictions of his present life he is integrated into the world as a whole and able to affect it. The personal reality achieved in his earthly life and consummated in his death is now introduced as his contribution into the abiding reality of the universe and so enabled to influence other beings. Such an expectation is consistent with the interrelatedness of reality as we now know it, and in the context of Christian faith in life eternal therefore becomes a reasonable possibility. It adds concrete content to belief in the communion of saints and also imparts dignity and significance to life here and now. If each human life is to contribute to the whole of reality something permanent which would not be there otherwise, there is added reason why it should be lived on earth in faith, love, and complete devotion to the enduring purposes of God.

Difficulties

1. It is questionable whether Rahner's kenotic view of the ultimate relation between God and the finite creation preserves the distinct identities of God and man. He ventures the profound hypothesis that the Absolute, while retaining his own infinite unrelatedness, may freely divest himself of himself, or give himself away, thereby positing the finite other as his own reality. In this sense God may become the other without having to "become" in his own original essence. Both creation and incarnation spring from this possibility. Creation is the loving self-projection or self-differentiation of God's eternal fullness, and the Word made flesh brings this divine self-emptying to its supreme fulfillment.

This theory is not subject to the fatal objections raised to the nineteenth-century Protestant kenotic Christologies, since Rahner conceives God as giving reality to the finite without surrendering his divinity. However, the similarity between his conception and Hegel's personalistic pantheism suggests another difficulty. In Hegel's dialectical "notion of religion," the subjective, undifferentiated unity of God objectifies itself to produce its finite other, but returns to and fulfills itself in a higher unity which includes differentiation.[42] The question is whether Rahner's view is not ultimately as monistic as Hegel's. Is he any more successful than Hegel in maintaining the full metaphysical identity of man? If the finite is that which the infinite has become, if in its genuine reality it is "constituted" by God, if man is truly God's "own reality," [43] is not man ultimately a part of God rather than possessing individual identity as a creature of God? Rahner's language seems to imply an affirmative answer, which would in turn raise serious questions regarding the relation of human sin and error to the divine perfection. Further clarification of this issue by Rahner himself is much to be desired.

2. At several points it is difficult to reconcile Rahner's interpretation of the effective operation of divine grace with his emphasis on human freedom. He regards freedom of decision as essential to personality, and declares that man is finally what he makes of himself in exercising his liberty. On the other hand, he maintains that God's grace sometimes forces a man to see what he may not want to see, and may suppress an emerging insight. He asserts that grace is personally experienced as a deed of love calling for decision, not medicinally introduced into a substratum of the self. Yet he seems to contradict this when he insists that one who is still a sinner may be through grace already holy and righteous in the hidden depths of his life. The same problem appears less sharply in Rahner's discussion of the sacraments. He regards the belief that grace is conferred apart from the subjective merit of the recipient as simply the negative counterpart of the positive *opus operatum,* God's unambiguous, irrevocable promise of grace for the individual person. The person must respond in faith, but his answer is "only an answer." God gives this faith out of pure grace—"a grace of faith and love, the grace to be able and to accomplish, a grace which is realized in the loving faith of men." [44] Where sacramental grace is involved, therefore, the answer of faith seems inevitable. But this eliminates real freedom in the recipient.

3. As we have seen, Rahner takes issue with the Reformers' view that the justified person is "at once sinful and righteous." He contends that through God's action man actually becomes righteous rather than only being declared so; the believer really partakes on his level of the holiness of God. However, the difference is not so great as Rahner assumes. He overlooks the fact that both Luther and Melanchthon affirm an actual righteous-

---

[42] G. W. F. Hegel, *Der Begriff der Religion* (Leipzig: Felix Meiner, 1925), p. 188.
[43] *Schriften,* IV, 148 f.
[44] *The Church and the Sacraments,* pp. 32-34.

ness in the believer. Furthermore, Rahner himself cautions that the Christian continues on the way from Adam to Christ, carrying the treasure of grace in an earthen vessel, constantly needing to pray for the forgiveness of his guilt as a sinner, and looking for that righteousness which will come only at the end. Such words, taken at their face value, involve as much recognition of continuing sin as the Reformation formula which Rahner attacks.

4. Rahner's judgment that death is the consequence of sin requires careful scrutiny. He deals directly with one objection to this view when he indicates that even apart from sin man would not have lived endlessly on earth, but would have experienced "a death without dying," the consummation of his life on earth without the fear-ridden dissolution of physical existence involved in death as we know it. This is an intriguing hypothesis which can be neither proved nor disproved. However, in the absence of discoverable foundations, either scriptural or empirical, it can hardly be accepted as definitive. Indeed, what evidence there is suggests that man's biological death is implicit in his participation in a created, finite, natural order. All life is marked by a movement from birth to death. The mortality of the lower animals, which apparently know nothing of God or responsibility to him, is not traceable to sin. They also instinctively fear death and seek to avoid it, with no guilt to cause such a reaction. Man's physical death, therefore, is best understood as an inevitable resultant of his involvement in physical nature. His attitude toward it is, of course, a very different thing. In his advance awareness of its certainty, in the fears and hopes he entertains regarding it, and in his capacity to relate it to his faith in God or the lack of such faith, man is unique among created beings. He can know spiritual death with all its horror of separation from God and his fellows, and he can know eternal life with its supreme blessedness. All in all, the inner import of the biblical passages which attribute death to sin—Gen. 3:3, 19, 22-24; I Cor. 15:22—is best conserved if we take them to mean the existentially experienced lostness, the forfeiture of any truly personal life which is the inevitable lot of those who flout their responsibilities to their fellow men and persist in centering their lives in their own impoverished selves instead of in the love of God.

PART THREE: EASTERN ORTHODOX THEOLOGY

11. NIKOS A. NISSIOTIS

Though Nikos Nissiotis is the youngest of the theologians considered in these chapters, he is exerting a wide and growing influence on the Continent and elsewhere. As associate director of the Ecumenical Institute at Bossey, he is a constant and leading participant in the ecumenical dialogue. He is the author of numerous substantial theological essays in German, English, and French as well as Greek. His address on "Christ the Light of the World" made a deep impression on the delegates to the Third Assembly of the World Council of Churches in New Delhi in 1961. He is firmly rooted in his own Greek Orthodox tradition, yet critically open to new interpretations, while appreciative of Protestant and Roman Catholic positions.

Nissiotis makes plain that the frequent identification of "orthodoxy" with barren institutionalism or hardened biblicism is quite different from the understanding of the term in the Eastern Church. "*Orthodoxia* means the wholeness of the people sharing the right conviction concerning the Event of God in Christ and His Church and the right expression of this faith." [1] The term applies not only to members of Eastern Orthodox bodies, but also to all who profess their spiritual kinship with the one Spirit and

[1] "Interpreting Orthodoxy," *The Ecumenical Review,* XIV (1961-62), 25.

recognize the one calling to be genuinely orthodox in faith and life. It excludes only those who willingly separate themselves from the historical life of the one church. Eastern Orthodoxy represents in all its weakness "the line of unbroken continuity of the One Apostolic and Catholic Church." However, instead of implying judgment on non-Orthodox churches this statement is intended to serve the cause of unity, which depends basically on a shared communion of God with man in the life of the whole church, and which is expressed in united evangelistic action.[2] An examination of some of the "right" convictions and expressions of faith stressed by Nissiotis will make possible an understanding of both his own theological position and that of the Orthodoxy he represents.

The Mystery of the Triune God

Characteristic of all Orthodox thought is an emphasis on "mystery." In contrast to the tendency of Western scholasticism to seek precise definitions of all aspects of belief, it often prefers to suggest or enact liturgically its deepest convictions, with a minimum of exact verbalization. Mystery, however, does not connote either obscurity or a hidden reality revealed only to the initiated. In the New Testament a mystery is a truth surpassing human understanding but disclosed in Jesus Christ and proclaimed in the gospel. The fundamental mystery or paradox of Christian faith is that of the incomprehensibility of the trinitarian God who yet wills to make himself known to man in Jesus Christ. "God is incomprehensible because He has communicated Himself to man, and without man's knowledge He has achieved for man His highest goal, which is the knowledge of Himself in man." [3] The category of mystery thus affirms both the incapacity of human reason to fathom God and the reality of communion between God and man.

The basic dogma of Orthodoxy is that of the Trinity. When we speak of Father, Son, and Holy Spirit as hypostases or persons, we are using tentative human expressions for the active existence of God as he is revealed to us in creation, redemption, and regeneration. The three Persons are through their essence united in One, yet they realize a communal, corporate relation, a *koinonia*. In this sense God may be spoken of as personal, though not as a person; he is a plurality of reciprocal movement motivated

[2] *Ibid.*, p. 26.
[3] *Ibid.*, p. 5.

by love. To be a person means to exist in living relation with a vis-à-vis which is identical in essence but different in its function of existence. Such is the nature of God as known to Christian faith. The relation within the personal God is a communion, a perfect union of three Persons. This union is the ground of his communion with man and of the communion between men in the church.[4]

Though Nissiotis insists on the full equality of the Persons of the Trinity, he devotes particular attention to the Holy Spirit. This emphasis probably represents in part an effort to counteract the subordination of the Spirit to the Son which Orthodoxy historically associates with the Western addition to the Nicene-Constantinopolitan Creed of the *filioque* clause, which asserts that the Holy Spirit "proceeds from the Father and the Son" rather than simply from the Father, as originally stated. Nissiotis specifically criticizes the Roman Church for the omission of Pentecost and the Holy Spirit in its "christomonistic" view of the priest as the direct vicar of Christ via Peter and the apostles, and also for the neglect of the Holy Spirit in the schema *de ecclesia* of the Second Vatican Council. Nevertheless, he cautions against the isolation of the pneumatological aspect of Christian faith, which easily leads to a sectarian ecclesiology founded on emotion.[5]

It remains true that for Nissiotis pneumatology is the heart of the Christian religion, touching all aspects of our faith in Christ. It is the Holy Spirit who accomplishes the salvation made possible by Jesus Christ. Only after Pentecost, through the action of the Spirit, does the redemptive work of Christ become effective in man, the church, and history, opening the way to the transformation of sinful man and the restoration of the world as a new creation. Throughout history the Holy Spirit bears witness to the Son and seals the work of the Redeemer. Through his action the Word incarnate becomes the Word communicated in preaching, the Eucharist, and the *koinonia* of the Body of Christ.[6]

It is therefore in the church that the distinctive work of God as Holy Spirit occurs. Conversely, no ecclesiology is possible without a full under-

[4] *Ibid.*, p. 6; "Spirit, Church, and Ministry," *Theology Today,* XIX (1962-63), 485 f.; "Le sacerdoce charismatique, le laïcat et l'autorité pastorale," *Verbum Caro,* XIV (1960), 227 f.

[5] "Pneumatologie orthodoxe," *Le Saint Esprit,* Faculty of Theology, University of Geneva (Geneva: Labor et Fides, 1963), pp. 89, 92, 100; "Is the Vatican Council Really Ecumenical?" *The Ecumenical Review,* XVI (1963-64), 365; "Die Ekklesiologie des Zweiten Vatikanischen Konzils in orthodoxer Sicht und ihre oekumenische Bedeutung," *Kerygma und Dogma,* X (1964), 156 f.

[6] "Pneumatologie orthodoxe," pp. 85, 91, 93 f., 105; "Interpreting Orthodoxy," p. 6.

standing of the Spirit's activity. Since the triune God is himself a communion, a necessary condition of the reception of his grace is a community of persons. This community was established in time and space by the Holy Spirit at Pentecost, thereby fulfilling the reconciliation made manifest in Jesus and realizing the communion of God with his people. Since Pentecost, the culminating point of history, the Spirit continues to act as the permanent presence in the church of the uncreated power of trinitarian grace. "When the Spirit acts, he acts with the Father and the Son, but it is through his act only in the church that the love of the Father is manifest and the grace of the Son is given." The Spirit is constantly creating anew and empowering the personal-corporate reality of the church, which in its living *koinonia* is an image of the hypostatic union in God himself.[7]

Christ, the Holy Spirit, and the Restoration of Man

The union between God and man founded in creation has been broken by man's sin. However, in the incarnation and the Pentecost-event the triune God has acted to reestablish this communion with his creature and thus confirm and fulfill creation. This reunion was made possible by the redemptive action of Christ, who joins divine and human natures in one Person, but it is brought to fulfillment by the grace of the Holy Spirit who dwells in men through the church.[8]

The revelation of this created, broken, and restored relationship is the central meaning of Christ as the Light of the world—a conception which must be understood pneumatologically and anthropologically as well as christologically. The "light" with which God begins his creation (Gen. 1:3) is not the physical, natural light created on the "fourth day." It is rather the fundamental principle of his creative action, the first presupposition of existence of everything that is connected with him. God does not create the world for "emancipation"—separate, independent existence; instead he creates life in his trinitarian image for fellowship with himself, and it can truly exist only in this relationship. "Light" is therefore the life-strength, the life-principle, the life-purpose of the creature formed by God to abide in communion with him, and the divine power to preserve and perfect this living fellowship.[9]

Christ is the Light of the world because through him the restoration of the broken fellowship becomes possible. Uniting the divine and the human

---

[7] "Pneumatologie othodoxe," pp. 89-91, 101; "Spirit, Church, and Ministry," pp. 485-89.
[8] "Interpreting Orthodoxy," pp. 7-9.
[9] "Christus, das Licht der Welt," *Kyrios* (Neue Folge [New Series]), I (1960-61), 13 f.

in one Person, he is the living revelation of true man as well as the true God, and equally of the deep communion which God purposes between Creator and creature. In his divine-human existence he discloses that man exists from the beginning in, through, and with God. Through the light of Christ man becomes aware of his underlying unity with God and of God's call to him to accept through personal decision the redemption offered in Christ. Through the Holy Spirit man is born again in the truth of Christ, given strength to experience the life of Christ, and enabled in spite of his mortality to participate now in eternal life. In the incarnation and the Pentecost-event God's energy redeems man, renews the ruptured fellowship, and fulfills the goal of creation.[10]

In this context it becomes apparent why Nissiotis considers anthropology "the chief concern of all true theology." [11] His own anthropology, like that of Orthodoxy in general, comes to a focus in the concept of the "theosis" or "christification" of man, formulated classically in the affirmation of Athanasius that "Christ became man in order that we might become divine." [12] Nissiotis avoids terms like "deification" and "divinization" because of the false connotations of such expressions which he finds in Western theology. Though "theosis" cannot be precisely defined, it points primarily to three realities:

1. The reestablishment of communion between God and man through the union in Jesus Christ of God with humanity, as a whole and in a distinctive Person, without confusion of the two natures.

2. The communication of the grace of God to man through the Holy Spirit, who actualizes in men the consequences of the union realized in Christ.

3. The genuine transformation and re-creation of human nature by the power of God, the reaffirmation of man's real humanity, which as the direct creation of God originally partook of the divine. The ultimate goal of the revelation of God in Christ is the restoration of humanity to the condition it enjoyed before the fall.[13]

Through the present and continuing activity of the Holy Spirit man may become that which he is intended to be and which in his deepest nature he

[10] Ibid., pp. 12, 14-16.
[11] Ibid., p. 19.
[12] J.-P. Migne, Patrologiae cursus completus, Series Graeca, XXV (Paris: Garnier Fratres Editores, et J.-P. Migne Successores, 1884), 192. This idea appears frequently in the writings of the fathers. Cf. Irenaeus, Gregory of Nyssa, Gregory of Nazianzus, and John of Damascus; and Nissiotis' discussion in "Christus, das Licht der Welt," pp. 17 f.
[13] "Interpreting Orthodoxy," p. 8.

is. When pneumatology is added to Christology—and only then—we can recognize fully the reality of the new creation, turning from academic questions about the *imago dei* to the restored image and the regeneration of man in Christ. Man faces forward, not backward, and his future is to be seen in terms of his Regenerator. Christ is the type of what we can also become. Through the theosis wrought by the Holy Spirit, sinful man is even now on the way to becoming man without sin, a new creation. By grace he may be the subject of a continual spiritual ascension.

The world, says Nissiotis, is properly tired of a church which preaches only death and the cross. It needs to see also the light of the resurrection. The center of the evangelical message, jubilant and triumphant, is the promise that life can be re-created and bring forth the fruits of the Spirit. The new birth may be and is a living, existential, personal reality.[14]

The Church and Its Ministry

Nissiotis emphasizes that for Orthodoxy the restoration of man is not an individualistic matter; it depends on the church, the mutual strengthening of its members, and the energy of the Spirit which flows through its sacraments. The Holy Spirit acts only "through a corporate body of distinct persons."[15]

The essence of the church cannot be defined, but it can be broadly described. It far transcends every local congregation, every confessional or denominational grouping, and even its entire earthly manifestation. "The Church is the realization in time of the divine economy decided before the foundation of the world through the election in Christ of all those who would believe in Him. It is a transhistorical event in Creation which unites its origin, its actual state and its fulfillment."[16] The church is thus the kernel or microcosm of creation. In its being is summed up the purpose of the entire universe. This intimate connection safeguards the continuity of the action by which God creates, saves, and regenerates his world. It also underlines the fact that the nature and purpose of creation are communicated to man through the reestablishment in the church of his communion with God.

The church, therefore, is neither a purely historical reality nor a merely supernatural, spiritual, eschatological entity. It is both earthly and heavenly, historical and supernatural. The visible church is the locus in time of

---

[14] "Pneumatologie orthodoxe," pp. 102-6; "Christus, das Licht der Welt," pp. 17-19.
[15] "Spirit, Church, and Ministry," p. 487; "Christus, das Licht der Welt," p. 18.
[16] "Interpreting Orthodoxy," p. 11.

the one church which in its wholeness transcends time. The local congregation, with all its limitations and defects, is an expression of the whole which is hidden beyond its limits, because in its preaching and sacramental life it represents and realizes the divine-human communion accomplished in Jesus Christ. As the channel of God's regenerating power in the world it bears the fullness of truth, the action by which God redeems the humanity which he has created for fellowship with himself. The world as a whole is embraced by the reconciling act of God, and all men are potentially saved by the Word incarnated in Jesus Christ, proclaimed in the church, and mystically shared in its eucharistic life.[17]

Here is the clue to the Orthodox understanding of the catholicity of the church. The church is catholic not simply in the geographical sense of worldwide extension, but primarily in a qualitative sense. Catholicity connotes fundamentally the wholeness of the salvation effected in Christ and its availability to the entire world. The church is catholic in that it is the steward of this wholeness and mediates the fullness of God's truth and grace. In it is realized and completed the saving action of the triune God comprised in creation, redemption, and fulfillment and perfection. Within its life man and the whole world become new creations. In its Word and sacraments the catholic energy of God as Father, Son, and Holy Spirit moves to restore men to full fellowship with himself.[18]

Being catholic, the church is inevitably one. However, its unity consists not in its institutional or hierarchical structure, but in the fullness of its charismatic life, in which men receive the gifts and fruits of the Holy Spirit. Its oneness is therefore the eucharistic unity of the mystical Body of Christ. The institution and the ministry do not constitute the church; rather they result from the eucharistic community which they serve. The new community began when the redemption fulfilled in the incarnation was perfected at Pentecost through its personal actualization in the apostles. It was continued and extended in others who through the apostles likewise realized the transforming power of the Spirit of God. Thus apostolicity was given by the Holy Spirit to the totality of the church, all of whose members, the people of God, are called to be priests.[19]

This means that in the personal fullness of the church, as disclosed and

---

[17] *Ibid.*, pp. 11 f.; "Spirit, Church, and Ministry," pp. 490 f.

[18] "The Ecclesiological Foundation of Mission from the Orthodox Point of View," *Greek Orthodox Theological Review*, VII (1961-62), 44; "Die qualitative Bedeutung der Katholizität," *Theologische Zeitschrift* (der Universität Basel), XVII (1961), 260 f., 271; "Interpreting Orthodoxy," p. 12; "Spirit, Church, and Ministry," p. 491.

[19] "Die qualitative Bedeutung . . . ," pp. 276 f.; "Pneumatologie orthodoxe," p. 95.

experienced in its eucharistic center, there are no ontological or qualitative differences. The sharp distinction between laity and clergy, between a general and a special priesthood, is a recent invention which is theologically dangerous. In the Orthodox view the authority of the church resides in its sacerdotal, charismatic, personal, and communitarian unity, and this unity permits no separation between clergy and laity which would elevate the hierarchy above the fullness of the whole body of Christ. There is no superior juridical order or tribe in the church, but only a charismatic order in which all are involved as participants in the gathered company of the Holy Spirit. Laymen are responsible members of the church; their function is not merely to aid the clergy to fulfill their parish duties in a better manner. As recipients of the grace of God they become with their fellow members—not privately—new creatures, and together they are equally called to be a light in the world, transmitting the divine grace to others.

Truly understood, however, the communitarian, "ecclesial," or qualitatively catholic conception of the Christian faith maintains, even while it surmounts, the differentiation between clergy and laity. Since apostolicity is a personal gift of the Holy Spirit, it is manifested and expressed not by the church in general, but in a personal manner by bishops and priests chosen by the community under the guidance of the Spirit. There is no office of bishop or priest apart from the totality of the body of Christ, nor is there any subordination of the lay Christian to the hierarchy. Nevertheless, the church's eucharistic ministry requires the selection and consecration of persons whose special function is the discharge of this ministry. They perform the liturgical or priestly work of Christ in and for the community of the faithful. It is thus through them that the unity and catholicity of the total body of Christ find their deepest expression and reach their fullest realization. In this way Orthodoxy avoids both the qualitative exaltation of the hierarchy over the rest of the faithful and the total negation of the personal priesthood.[20]

The bishop—and the priest who represents him—is a concrete and personal channel of the transmission of divine grace to all who believe. Through him the new life in Christ through the Spirit flows into the whole community of the faithful. He is therefore "its charismatic center and constitutes at the same time the pivot of the two principal elements of ecclesial life: the personal and the communitarian. Through him the trinitarian life

[20] "Die qualitative Bedeutung . . . ," pp. 277 f.; "Le sacerdoce charismatique . . . ," pp. 221 f., 229, 236; "Wort Gottes und Liturgie in der Ostkirche," Der Remter, VII (1961), p. 37; "Spirit, Church, and Ministry," pp. 495-97; "Pneumatologie orthodoxe," pp. 94 f.

is incarnated in personal communion among men." [21] The interpersonal nature of the communication of grace is well exemplified in the role of pastoral authority in the confession of sins. Confession is made personally to a priest, not to an impersonal institution, and the pardon which follows is not the announcement of automatic absolution, but rather the repentant believer's existential awareness of forgiveness and his total submission to the divine will, within the charismatic community. The confessing Christian does not subject himself to the hierarchy; rather he submits himself to the Holy Spirit personally through the priest. Thus the grace of the Spirit is personified. Pastoral authority is incarnated in the person of "my" confessor, yet it is transindividual because the confessor is the instrumentality of the Holy Spirit who unites me with other believers in the church.[22]

Nissiotis finds a definitive statement of the meaning of the church, and particularly of the relation between clergy and laity, in Acts 20:28: "Take heed to yourselves and to all the flock, in which the Holy Spirit has made you guardians, to feed the church of the Lord which he obtained with his own blood." Addressed to the elders of the church at Ephesus, these words constitute for Nissiotis the "establishment of a hierarchical order." The bishop or the elder unites in himself the two poles of person and community. Rather than a legalistic authority with a chiefly disciplinary function, he is a "guardian" whose task is to "feed" the flock of Christ. His guardianship and his pastoral function are two "moments"—the institutional and the dynamic—inseparably joined in the same person. The first expresses itself in the second: the institution becomes action, and authority becomes pastoral responsibility. The priest celebrates the eucharistic communion on behalf of, but only *with,* the people, and the pastoral relationship includes provision for the mutual admonition of priests and other believers who together comprise the gathered community of the Holy Spirit.[23]

In Nissiotis' view pneumatology saves Orthodox ecclesiology from the error of tracing authority lineally from Christ through the apostles to bishops and priests, with other believers playing only a subordinate and receptive role. In contrast, Orthodoxy, taking Pentecost seriously, conceives the life of the church more as a series of concentric circles. In the center is the activity of the Holy Spirit, who in relation to the sacrifice of

---

[21] "Le sacerdoce charismatique . . . ," p. 230.
[22] "Spirit, Church, and Ministry," pp. 236-38.
[23] "Le sacerdoce charismatique . . . ," pp. 231 f.; "Interpreting Orthodoxy," p. 12; "Die Ekklesiologie des Zweiten Vatikanischen Konzils . . . ," pp. 161 f., 164.

Christ transfuses his grace personally through priests and pastors to the whole body of the faithful. This body precedes and conditions the selection and ordination of bishops and priests. The church lives through both its royal or ontological priesthood, composed of all baptized persons, and its personal or functional priesthood, those set apart to offer the eucharistic sacrifice. The latter are the necessary channels of sacramental grace, but their ministry is both authorized and fulfilled by that of the total community of believers.[24] Together they constitute the pleroma which enables the church to realize its supreme end, which is "the new birth and the transfiguration of man by the Spirit in the house of God, and the diffusion of this grace in the entire world." [25]

Eucharistic Worship

Running through all of Nissiotis' writings is a lofty conception of worship as the center of the church's life. Using earthly symbols, the liturgy moves in a cosmic and eschatological dimension in which the entire temporal life of man and the whole material order are related to the eternal and transformed by it. The worshiping congregation takes with full seriousness the reality and dignity of bodily existence, yet already lives in the end. Worship recapitulates "the incarnation, cross, and resurrection of Christ; it is an offering of the Body of the Church, as an organic whole, taking part in a universal event, through which the whole of creation is rejoicing at its redemption and restoration." Worship is "the pivot of history" in which the celestial and the terrestrial are inseparably united.[26]

Orthodox worship broadly conceived includes the following aspects: (1) the redemptive action of God which calls man to offer back what God has offered through Christ and continues to offer through his Spirit; (2) an ecclesial act of participation in the Body of Christ manifested as an immediate reality; (3) an acknowledgment by man in repentance and faith of God's action among men; (4) man's response in dynamic personal commitment within the communal effort of all members of the Body; (5) the reorientation of man's whole life in the light of the victory of the resurrected Christ over death and sin; (6) the proclamation in preaching and sacrament of the saving act of God and the glory of his coming kingdom;

---

[24] "Pneumatologie orthodoxe," p. 96; "Spirit, Church, and Ministry," pp. 495-97.
[25] "Le sacerdoce charismatique . . . ," p. 223.
[26] "Worship, Eucharist and 'Intercommunion': An Orthodox Reflection," *Studia Liturgica*, II (1963), p. 194; "Wort Gottes und Liturgie . . . ," pp. 35 f.

and (7) preparation for the living sacrifice to be offered daily in mission and service to the world.[27]

Orthodox worship culminates in two main actions: the preaching of the Word and the celebration of the Lord's Supper. The former is the proclamation and exposition of the reconciliation of men with God, while the latter is the realization of this reconciliation. The two belong together. The preached Word is an inseparable element in the eucharistic liturgy, the necessary presupposition and preparation for the actualized presence of the Christ. However, the Word is not merely the spoken Word which is conveyed in intellectual teaching; it is even more a mystical Word which brings the divine life with itself, planting the seed of that life deeply within the hearers. It is in turn incomplete without the Eucharist; indeed, there is no real preaching in the worship of the new community if it is not followed by the eucharistic sacrifice, which makes real God's loving fellowship with men.[28]

The Eucharist is therefore the center of Orthodox worship, the climax toward which all else points.[29] Nissiotis rejects what he terms the two extremist interpretations which regard Holy Communion on the one hand as a repetition of the sacrifice of Jesus and on the other as a mere remembrance. The Lord's Supper roots in the transhistorical event of "the Lamb slain before the foundation of the world" (Rev. 13:8). It actualizes this event here and now by representing symbolically its historical fulfillment in the crucifixion of Christ. Because of the union preserved by the Holy Spirit between the members of the Body of Christ and their head, each ecclesial community in celebrating the Eucharist shares in this same event, "communicating in His sacrificial body and blood" and thus receiving the grace of redemption. Jesus' sacrifice occurred once-and-for-all, but through its concentrated representation in the Holy Communion all men in all times may participate in the grace which it makes available. In the presence of the Lamb of God, forgiven sinners within the Body of Christ offer back to God the same sacrifice, but in bloodless, spiritual form. The words of the celebrant preceding the *epiklesis* of the Holy Spirit express clearly this double movement: "Thine own, out of thine own, we offer to thee entirely

---

[27] "Worship, Eucharist and 'Intercommunion' . . . ," pp. 201-3.

[28] "Wort Gottes und Liturgie . . . ," pp. 34 f.; "Die Liturgie und das geistliche Leben," *Kyrios* (Neue Folge [New Series]), I (1960-61), 156.

[29] "Wort Gottes und Liturgie . . . ," p. 30; "Worship, Eucharist and 'Intercommunion' . . . ," p. 203; "Interpreting Orthodoxy," p. 15; "Spirit, Church, and Ministry," p. 494.

and on behalf of all." Both distinction and continuity exist between the one-time sacrifice of Jesus and the repeated offering of his church.[30]

Orthodox theology affirms that the risen Lord is truly present in the eucharistic sacrifice, which because of this is also a memorial of his past coming and a sharing in the promise of his return as Lord of all. However, the words "This is my body" refer not only to the elements, but to the real presence of Christ's sacrificial body in his gathered community. It is the reality of that presence in the whole Body of Christ "which enables the elements, by the invocation of the Holy Spirit, to be the sacrificial body and blood of Jesus." In the *epiklesis* the celebrant implores God to send his Holy Spirit "upon us and upon the gifts here set forth," making them the body and blood of Christ. The words assume the presence of Christ as head in the midst of the unbroken communion of his Body. Therefore Orthodoxy refuses to focus attention on efforts to explain the new quality of the material objects as such by theories of transubstantiation or consubstantiation. It prefers to think instead of the total process of "change" which, occurring in the liturgy as a whole, profoundly transforms the entire life of the Body. Within this Body "the elements become the transfused, sacrificial, spiritual body and blood of Jesus for us members," who through the real presence of our Head become new creatures. Through sharing in his sacrifice, we experience a foretaste of his coming kingdom. The miracle of change in the elements is a mystery which belongs inseparably to the mystery of the church itself; attempts to conceptualize the how and what implicitly deny the mystery. No explanation can say more than the simple assertions, "This is my body" or "This is my blood." The meaning of these words can be comprehended by faith alone.[31]

The strong stress on the eucharistic sacrifice as an act of the whole church calls attention to an important difference between the Orthodox and the Roman Catholic Churches. According to Orthodox theology the offering is made by the community of believer-priests, who have elected one of their number for the special function of representing the real celebrant, Jesus Christ. He is the center because he is endowed by the Holy Spirit to discharge this personal priesthood for the entire church, "with the laity and in their presence." Though he voices the invocation, it is always in the first person *plural*. Since Christ makes his offering *in the midst of* his church, the priest who represents him can never conduct the liturgy

---

[30] "Worship, Eucharist and 'Intercommunion' . . . ," pp. 205-7.

[31] *Ibid.*, pp. 208-15; "Pneumatologie orthodoxe," pp. 97-100; "Die Liturgie und das geistliche Leben," p. 152.

alone or for himself. It is "impossible for one priest to celebrate alone a service of Holy Communion as 'his mass,' and no Communion service can be valid with only one communicant."[32]

According to Nissiotis all Orthodox worship aims to relate man in this spatial and temporal world to God and eternity. Through historical elements grounded in the incarnation it prepares the historical-eschatological community for its transhistorical destiny. Here is the clue to the frequent use of icons, colors, movements, and set forms in Orthodox worship. Such symbols are not ends in themselves, nor are they essential. They represent "a legitimate use of nature which in an eschatological perspective is already restored, in order that the worshipping community may receive the real presence of the Lord coming in His glory." They are windows through which the faithful may glimpse hidden spiritual realities. In no sense are icons and similar objects worshiped or superstitiously revered as sacred; rather every object helpful in worship is respected because it is material selected from God's creation to make his immediate presence more real.[33]

The Church's Mission to the World

Centrally, the liturgy is a foretaste of the absolute rule of Christ and the life of the coming age. We therefore fulfill its meaning best when we live in such a manner as to realize the presence of Christ now. We must let the liturgy come to lordship in the whole life of man in the whole world, making our everyday life a continuing thanksgiving and liturgical offering. Such existential demonstration is the best proof of the claim of the liturgy to relate men directly to God as living reality.[34] Orthodox worship

in its realistic combination of history and eschatology thus becomes the springboard from which its faithful members may leap up renewed for action and service in this world. . . . Every historical event stands in direct relationship to its final fulfillment through its sanctification by the eucharistic offering of the Church.[35]

By the very nature of its worship, therefore, the church is thrust into the world in *diakonia* (service) and *martyria* (witness or mission). The

---

[32] "Worship, Eucharist and 'Intercommunion' . . . ," pp. 214 f.; "Pneumatologie orthodoxe," p. 101.
[33] "Interpreting Orthodoxy," pp. 14 f.
[34] "Die Liturgie und das geistliche Leben," pp. 153-58.
[35] "Interpreting Orthodoxy," p. 15; cf. p. 25.

CONTEMPORARY CONTINENTAL THEOLOGIANS

church is responsible for alleviating the suffering of people outside its membership and for finding answers to the personal, domestic, economic, and political problems of men. However, the care of the church for human social needs is not primarily philanthropic, humanitarian, or even compassionate in nature. Rather it is ecclesial—an overflowing of the grace which informs and moves its inner life. The church's outreach in service is the counterpart in the world of the Word of God which is already accomplished within its own charismatic life. It expresses the work (*ergon*) of the Spirit of God through the accompanying work (*parergon*) of man in and for the world. *Diakonia* is "the Eucharist *incognito,* represented in another way." [36] Basically, therefore, it is an expression of the saving and sanctifying purpose of the church in the world, which by the sacrifice of Christ is already potentially saved. The church approaches the life of the world not in terms of its political or other institutions, but in terms of persons whom God seeks to save. Hence there is no danger of a fusion of the political and ecclesial realms. Although the church does have formally and externally an institutional character, it disposes of the grace which comprises its existence always "at a distance, free from any kind of state pressure, above and beyond all temporal political directions and parties." The church functions in the world as the steward of the mysteries of God, the channel of the grace by which the whole life of states and societies is reborn and sanctified. It is thus enabled to transcend and overcome political authorities while in no sense corresponding or competing with them on the same level. [37]

Basically, therefore, the church's practical *diakonia* is an aspect of its total mission, the proclamation of the divine salvation and the transmission of divine grace. At heart the church is a dynamic process of regeneration; to be true to its nature it must offer the new life in Christ to the whole world. "The life of the Church is salvation, communion with God, oneness, mission and evangelism." It is therefore commissioned to preach the gospel to those outside, calling on them to be converted and to become baptized participants of the eucharistic community. Actually, the liturgy itself is "the missionary force *par excellence.*" Together with preaching and the sacraments, it mediates the abiding presence of the glorified Christ; cele-

[36] "The Ecclesiological Significance of Inter-Church Diakonia," *The Ecumenical Review,* XIII (1960-61), 191-93.
[37] "Interpreting Orthodoxy," pp. 19-21, 25.

brated by the whole church on behalf of the whole world, it is a concrete, visible witness to God's saving power and a call to men to acceptance of the new life of the Holy Spirit.[38]

Nissiotis insists that a church may not be judged as nonmissionary simply because it has no organized foreign mission or, as in the case of Orthodoxy, no missionary societies. A real missionary is one who goes "where the gospel has not yet been preached or is not being truly lived." [39] The principal mark of a missionary church is its capacity to produce from its inner life members who spontaneously feel impelled by the Spirit to preach the gospel. This is regarded by Nissiotis as both the biblical understanding of true mission and the means by which the church has won most of its converts throughout history. Such evangelism by devoted individuals, originally independent of the church's institutional structures but within the pastoral authority of the hierarchy, has created strong evangelistic lay movements. Often the Christian witness of these laymen has combined with direct preaching an educational approach to social questions similar to that of the German lay academies. In such ways they have become channels through which the life of the church has flowed into the world. Frequently their action has led to the formation of new, indigenous local churches.[40]

Orthodox Uniqueness and Christian Unity

In Nissiotis' view the mission of the one undivided historical church affords the best clue to the uniqueness of Eastern Orthodoxy and its contribution to Christian unity. Mission means "sharing directly in the grace of God the Holy Trinity in his Church," and therefore implies oneness. Unity is the very life of the church, not a mere attribute. It is the essence of God's creative, redemptive, and life-renewing action which culminated at Pentecost and which continues in all ages in the life of the Body of Christ. Without it the redemptive community cannot exist. Therefore the church witnesses to God's saving work far more authoritatively by the unbroken continuity of its own historical existence, which perpetuates Pentecost, than by the Roman See's exclusivistic claims to primacy and obedience or by the confessional statements of particular churches attempting to ex-

---

[38] "The Ecclesiological Foundation of Mission . . . ," pp. 30-33, 52; "Interpreting Orthodoxy," p. 23.

[39] "Interpreting Orthodoxy," p. 23.

[40] "The Ecclesiological Foundation of Mission . . . ," pp. 41 f.; "Interpreting Orthodoxy," pp. 22 f.

plain and justify their separateness.[41] Authentic unity is found in the shared life in the "historic churches"—those which in terms of the Nicene Creed confess their faith in the whole revelation of God and believe in the continuation of this event by the action of the Holy Spirit in Word and sacrament.

Here is the basis for the claim of Orthodoxy to be "the one true church." That claim "is founded on the faith and the continuity of the one church, in that it upholds the apostolic faith in its fullness and holds high the traditions as gifts of the Holy Spirit to all generations." [42] However, "Orthodox" here does not connote one church or even all of the Eastern Orthodox Churches. Synonymous with "catholic" and "apostolic," it is an inclusive rather than an exclusive term. It extends beyond the bodies called Orthodox to include "all those churches and believers who seek to offer an honest confession and achieve a life which is untouched by heresies and schisms and to arrive at the wholeness of the divine revelation in Christ." [43] Nissiotis echoes Georges Florovsky's interpretation of Orthodoxy as meaning centrally "right glory," and infers that all those are Orthodox who would join in glorifying God in thanksgiving in and through the unseparated church.

Precisely because Eastern Orthodoxy has in a distinctive way preserved true continuity in its undivided "mysterious" life, it has a pivotal contribution to make to the reunion of the church. However, it must offer itself in humility. Even as in New Testament times an effective *martyria* often meant martyrdom, so amid today's division and sin an effective witness to the unity of God's saving act may involve suffering. Orthodoxy must therefore renounce its narrowly confessional, defensive attitude, emulate the self-offering of Jesus, and become a channel of the reconciling, victorious power of the Holy Spirit. Instead of saying, "Come back to us," or "Let us return to the first eight centuries," it must be ready to sacrifice its self-sufficiency, practice tolerance in difficult situations, and share its privileges with other churches. Its right course would be to declare: "The presence and witness of the Eastern Orthodox Churches and their witness to the unbroken Orthodox tradition can help all the other historical churches to recover their own true life." For example, it should invite the churches which resulted from the Reformation to see themselves not mere-

---

[41] "The Witness and the Service of Eastern Orthodoxy to the One Undivided Church," *The Ecumenical Review*, XIV (1961-62), pp. 193-95, 198, 201 f.; "Die Ekklesiologie des Zweiten Vatikanischen Konzils . . . ," pp. 164-66.

[42] "Die Ekklesiologie des Zweiten Vatikanischen Konzils . . . ," pp. 164 f.

[43] "The Witness and the Service of Eastern Orthodoxy . . . ," p. 198.

ly as collections of local congregations, but as participants in the charismatic life and unbroken communion of the one universal church sustained by the indwelling Spirit of God. The Orthodox should also encourage closer relations with the Roman Catholic Church by rethinking their conception of the primacy of the Bishop of Rome, recognizing in it a valuable instrument in the calling of pan-Christian councils and an important unifying link between the churches. Through such inclusiveness and dynamic openness Orthodoxy can serve as a genuine pivot-church in the movement toward the reunion of the church and the fulfillment of its mission.[44]

The breadth of Nissiotis' interpretation of Orthodoxy may seem to imply a willingness on his part to modify the traditional Orthodox refusal to join with other Christians in the Eucharist. However, his insistence on the undivided unity of the true church leads him to oppose "intercommunion" between separated churches. Communion at the same table must be simply *communion* of those who compose one church. The very prefix *inter* denies the reality of one church, and is thus inconsistent with Orthodox ecclesiology. True communion presupposes an already existing spiritual oneness. In the movement toward full fellowship it should therefore be the crowning event rather than a stage on the way or a means toward the end.

Nissiotis specifies three main reasons for the Orthodox opposition to intercommunion:

1. There now exist deep schisms which separate the totality of professing Christians into different spiritual communions and prevent them from being of one accord in the undivided Body of Christ. Even some churches which hold the same doctrine of the Eucharist are thus divided.

2. Many Christians are not committed to one unbroken ecclesial communion, and regard separation as normal even in a church which is undergoing spiritual renewal. For the Orthodox, however, such a commitment of life is an indispensable prerequisite to full communion in the Eucharist.

3. Commitment to the one ecclesia involves far more than mere good will and superficial emotion shown at ecumenical meetings in order to practice intercommunion, while local churches and denominations continue their schismatic isolation. Real commitment is rooted in the one faith and concerns the church's whole life. It requires acknowledgment of a charismatic order embodied in persons and acceptance of definite "links," permanent, visible elements which express concretely and functionally the

[44] *Ibid.*, pp. 196-200.

spiritual discipline and mutual obedience of the one Body. Without such commitment intercommunion would be an empty pretense.[45]

Nissiotis insists that this attitude does not represent an antiecumenical exclusivism. It is rather for the Orthodox a consistent position which they hope will lead to a sound ecumenism and a real *koinonia* expressed in common participation in the Eucharist. From this standpoint the Orthodox practice of closed communion is a gift of God to the ecumenical movement, since it poses graphically the basic problem of unity and "demands drastic measures and communal conversion to the one spiritual communion of the One Body of Christ." [46]

Critique

The Protestant interpreter must be particularly careful in evaluating Eastern Orthodox theology, lest his criticism reflect little more than a pro-Protestant bias against Orthodoxy or an anti-Roman Catholic bias in favor of Orthodoxy. It is therefore imperative that as far as possible Nissiotis' thought be evaluated from within his own perspective, and that comparisons pay major attention to biblical evidence and early church tradition. When this approach is followed, elements of both strength and weakness will emerge.

Values

1. Nissiotis' strong emphasis on Pentecost and the Holy Spirit corrects the subordination of the Spirit which for many centuries has characterized much Western theology. His exposition of Orthodox pneumatology recognizes fully the important place of the Holy Spirit in the New Testament church, but does not minimize the significance of either the Father or the Son. God the Spirit makes effective in men in all ages the redemptive work of God the Redeemer, and through the reality of the new creation fulfills the purpose of God the Creator. This balanced trinitarianism saves Nissiotis from the narrowly christocentric doctrine of apostolic succession, which grounds the authority of the priest in his linear connection with Christ via Peter and the apostles and diminishes the importance of the new community called into being by the Holy Spirit. The greater relative significance accorded the Spirit also has weighty implications for the Christian doctrine of man.

2. Nissiotis' anthropology, while quite realistic regarding man's sinfulness

---

[45] *Ibid.*, pp. 215-19.
[46] *Ibid.*, pp. 216, 221.

and need of redemption, soundly stresses the possibility of the renewal of man through the grace of God. The concept of theosis conserves the proclamation of the New Testament writers that sinful man can be both forgiven and transformed. Though it recognizes that even redeemed man is beset by temptation and sin, it focuses central attention on the good news that he can by the power of the Spirit become a new creature. This is, as Nissiotis maintains, the heart of the gospel message, and it needs to be strongly accented in a time when psychological, sociological, and theological influences are combining to give man a dismal picture of himself and his possibilities. With the early church, Orthodoxy preaches the new birth as a joyous personal reality.

3. In full accord with the New Testament accounts, Nissiotis accents the wholeness of the church as the charismatic community of the Holy Spirit, treating hierarchical structure as consequential to its eucharistic life rather than constitutive of it. This conception grounds the authority of the church in its communitarian unity, and excludes any qualitative subordination of laity to clergy. It preserves the priesthood of all baptized persons no less than the functional priesthood of those chosen by the Spirit-guided community for a personal eucharistic ministry. It identifies apostolic succession with the ongoing life of the whole body of the faithful. It guards Orthodoxy against the incongruity of Communion celebrated by a priest without other communicants. It contributes to an illuminating interpretation of the Eucharist, according to which the transformation of the elements expresses the deeper change wrought by the real presence of Christ in his living Body, the church. The stress on oneness and qualitative catholicity can also help Protestants to avoid atomistic notions which see the church as little more than a loose association of human individuals helping one another in their religious quest.

4. In Nissiotis' thought Christian worship and missionary and social concern are related in profound manner. As in primitive Christianity, Christian witness and service in the world follow directly from the nature of the church and its worship. As the channel of divine grace and the locus of God's regenerating action, the church cannot truly be itself unless it proclaims and offers to all who are outside its ranks the new life it has found in Christ. Similarly, its acceptance of responsibility for meeting men's personal and social needs asserts the universal lordship of the God who is glorified in the liturgy, recognizes the degree to which material things may manifest spiritual and eternal realities, and makes the whole of

life a joyous eucharistic offering. Nissiotis' view has the added virtue of making unmistakably plain the obligation of every Christian to be an evangelist and a witness to the divine will in society.

5. The openness and inclusiveness which mark Nissiotis' understanding of Orthodoxy are an encouragement to non-Orthodox Christians to engage with him in active exploration of the meaning of church unity. He broadens the term "Orthodox" to include all who, recognizing their kinship in the one Spirit, sincerely wish to share the faith and life of the one unseparated church. He calls on his own church, even while it witnesses to its own unbroken tradition, to cease urging others merely to "come back," to renounce its feelings of self-sufficiency, to attempt to understand the positions held by Protestants and Roman Catholics, and to work positively to help other churches to fulfill their true life. Such a spirit fosters genuine encounter and the mutual respect which are essential to real ecumenicity.

Difficulties

1. Nissiotis' portrayal of the church according to the analogy of the Trinity raises questions regarding the true individuality of members of the church. The three divine "Persons," though one in essence, exist vis-à-vis one another in *koinonia*; this communion of the triune God within himself is the model for that of the community of human persons who compose the church. Conversely, the living *koinonia* which marks the true church is "an image of the hypostatic union in God himself." If this analogy is taken with full seriousness, it points toward an ecclesial monism which threatens the concrete singularity of individual Christians. It is true that the persons who make up the Christian community are "one body in Christ," and that Jesus' High-Priestly Prayer in John 17 asks that they may be one as the Father and the Son are one. Possibly this metaphorical oneness is all that Nissiotis has in mind, and the implication here mentioned may ascribe to the language of an Orthodox theologian greater literalness and precision than he would allow. Nevertheless, if we take the unity of God as seriously as Nissiotis does, it is difficult to understand how the relationship between the differentiations of the Trinity can be a genuine model for that between finite persons who in spite of their interdependence retain their separate identities. Therefore the question naturally arises whether he actually does conceive the organic wholeness of the church in the ultimately monistic terms which would make his analogy consistent.

2. Two problems appear in Nissiotis' doctrine of the theosis of man, which he interprets to mean in part the action by which humanity is re-

united with God and restored to the condition it enjoyed before the fall. First, is not the restoration of man to his "original" situation patently impossible? Whether "before the fall" is understood chronologically or mythically, it implies a state of innocence which can never become a reality to one who has succumbed to temptation. As long as memory remains man can never become as though he had never sinned. Paradise regained can never duplicate Paradise lost. Secondly, Nissiotis' view seems to underestimate the continuing sinfulness of the believer and overoptimistically to anticipate man's heavenly state. However, these difficulties do not affect the central truth which Nissiotis is concerned to assert—the reality of the re-creation and renewal of human nature by the power of God.

3. Ambiguity, if not inconsistency, appears in connection with Nissiotis' view of the church's service in the world, particularly the relation between church and state. Since the church seeks the sanctification of society by the divine grace which it mediates, it seeks to maintain friendly contact with the state within which it exists. It therefore avoids intervention in politics and asks freedom from state pressure. In relation to the state it always acts "at a distance," transcending political directions and parties. Nissiotis rightly opposes any effort by the institutional church to compete with the political authorities for domination over the secular life of man, as well as the fusion of church and state which victory by the church in such a struggle might bring. He also avoids the grave dangers involved in the endorsement by the church of any political party and its identification with any particular governmental or economic system. But it is not clear why the church, in order to serve as the channel of God's saving grace, must always "act at a distance" in relation to political affairs.

Indeed, Nissiotis calls on Christians to extend the scope of worship by making their daily lives a liturgical offering, thereby demonstrating the claim of the liturgy to relate men directly to the living reality of God. He sees the liturgy as a springboard projecting men into the life of the world. He also emphasizes the degree to which material realities may embody and express the life of the spirit. If the church is to act in harmony with these ideas, it can hardly avoid asking how it can best mediate the presence of God *in the midst of* the political and social life of men, rather than at a distance. This requires the church on occasion to deal with public issues in the light of the gospel of God's reconciling love, and to bring to bear in concrete situations what it knows of his righteous will. It is certain that social conditions often hinder the salvation which the church is called to proclaim. If men are to be saved, it must be in relation to the complexities of daily life, not in separation from them.

4. There is some ambiguity in Nissiotis' "inclusive" interpretation of Orthodoxy. He insists that the term "Orthodox" can be properly applied not only to certain Eastern Orthodox bodies, but also to all those churches and believers who seek the wholeness of the faith and life of one unbroken church. This seems not to require that such churches be structurally one with the Eastern Orthodox Church. Yet he insists that commitment to the one ecclesia demands recognition of a charismatic order embodied in persons, visible "links" expressing concretely the disciplined interdependence which marks the Body of Christ. This language seems to imply acceptance of the Orthodox conception of the priesthood, and the position affirmed is the basis for a rejection of intercommunion. Thus the inclusive openness advocated by Nissiotis appears to be qualified by exclusivistic elements. He does not say that other churches can "recover their own true life" only by merging with some Eastern Orthodox body, but it is not clear how the conditions he mentions can be fulfilled short of such action. On the other hand, if the Orthodox really include all who are devoted to the wholeness of the church and earnestly seek its fulfillment in the life of one unbroken community, should not all such Christians be welcome at the Lord's table whether or not they belong to officially Orthodox bodies? Do they not already represent the reality of the *koinonia* which for Nissiotis should precede rather than follow a shared Eucharist? His implicitly negative answer suggests that in this respect he is departing from his own rather broad definition of Orthodoxy in favor of a more restrictive view.

PART FOUR: CURRENT MOVEMENTS
IN PERSPECTIVE

12. CONVERGING AND DIVERGING PATHS

In order to understand the contemporary situation in Continental theology it is necessary to examine not only individual thinkers and movements, but also their relation to one another. The net impression yielded by careful comparison of the eleven thinkers investigated is one of sharp diversity against a background containing many common features. The terrain is varied, but the country is one. Those engaged in its exploration seem often to journey in opposite directions, far out of hailing distance, only to meet unexpectedly and find themselves traveling the same trail. In accord with the plan of the volume thus far, we shall first relate the Protestant theologians to one another, then bring them into dialogue with their Roman Catholic and Orthodox colleagues.

Protestant Theology

Similarities

A number of characteristics are present in greater or less degree in all three of the Protestant movements studied. Specifically, the eight thinkers are in essential agreement on the following emphases.

1. The basis of all human knowledge of God and salvation is God's self-revelation recorded and mediated by the Scriptures. Divine revelation is our final authority in matters of faith. It is differently conceived, but whether interpreted objectively or existentially it needs no grounding other than itself. Faith-illumined reason is needed to understand revelation, but is not qualified to pass judgment on it. There is therefore no place for natural theology as a way to religious truth, except in limited measure for Wingren, who maintains that man as created by God knows apart from the gospel that he is subject to law, guilt, and judgment.

2. Jesus Christ is central for Christian faith and Christian theology alike. Marked differences emerge over the very possibility of Christology in the historic sense, yet all the theologians investigated agree that Jesus Christ or the New Testament message concerning him is the fundamental datum for Christian faith. The revelation which is seen as alone authoritative is the divine self-disclosure which centers in Christ.

3. Salvation is wrought not by human works, whether ceremonial, legal, or ethical, but by grace appropriated through faith. A difference appears in this respect between the Barthians and the confessional Lutherans, who strongly stress the sovereignty of the God whose grace calls forth faith, and the existentially oriented theologians, whose rejection of the subject-object scheme leads them to say little of grace per se. Nevertheless, the latter emphasize as staunchly as the former the element of uncertainty and the absence of all guarantees in saving faith, hence implicitly recognize man's utter dependence for salvation on the God who is not at his disposal and whose favor he cannot earn or deserve. All agree in affirming the Reformation doctrine of justification through faith alone.

4. The gospel which systematic theology is called on to interpret is primarily the preached word. The concern of Bultmann and Gogarten for the Christian kerygma which calls men to decision is matched by the kerygmatic theology of Barth, which integrally relates the Word of God to the concrete preaching of the church, and by Diem's view of the New Testament proclamation of Jesus as the Christ, based on Jesus' self-proclamation, as the basis of all Christian theology. Belonging in the same frame of reference are Ebeling's close attention to the gospel as language-event, Wingren's concern for the living Word, and Schlink's insistence that the purpose of the Confessions, like that of the Scriptures, is the proclamation of the good news of salvation. In this context it is striking, though not surprising, that the men investigated are themselves preachers as well as

systematic theologians, and that a number of them have published substantial volumes of sermons.[1]

5. The church has a central role in both the proclamation of the Christian message and the critical exposition of its meaning. This recognition appears most clearly in Barth, who stresses that dogmatics is a function of the church as a whole rather than simply of individual Christians; and in Schlink, for whom the church's interpretation of Scripture in its confessional writings is the starting point of dogmatic theology, and who is deeply concerned for church unity. Less attention is devoted to the church by the theologians who are most influenced by existentialist thought forms, since they tend to emphasize the faith response of the individual to the kerygma. Nevertheless, Bultmann never forgets that the message which calls men to decision was originally and is now proclaimed by the church. Ebeling likewise presupposes this when he wrestles with the problem of the historical character of the church and its proclamation.[2] For him the church not only voices but constitutes the summons of faith. It is a fellowship of men who have been called together by the gospel into a unified community which is commissioned to summon others to faith. It is therefore indispensable. Even Gogarten, who devotes little attention to the church as such, has written one book on the role of the church in the world.[3]

6. Since the gospel has to do with redemption, a basic concern of theology must be the nature or existence of man. Barth's christocentric approach leads him to see man—even sinful man—as the being whom God wills to be his covenant partner. For Hromádka, too, the incarnation discloses the nature of man as well as of God; in its light we perceive man's dignity and destiny no less than his misery and corruption. Bultmann, Gogarten, and Ebeling insist that we cannot speak intelligibly of God apart from man, and they emphasize that the gospel calls the whole man to authentic existence. Wingren points out that the Christian doctrine of creation places man, not nature, in the center. Created by God, man is called to righteousness and love, thus already "destined for Christ," and in spite of his sinful

---

[1] See, for example, Barth, *Deliverance to the Captives*, tr. Marguerite Wieser (New York: Harper & Row, 1961); Bultmann, *This World and the Beyond* (New York: Charles Scribner's Sons, 1960); Ebeling, *Vom Gebet: Predigten über das Unser-Vater* (*Concerning Prayer: Sermons on the "Our Father"* [Tübingen: J. C. B. Mohr, 1963]); Gogarten, *Der Schatz in irdenen Gefässen* (*The Treasure in Earthen Vessels* [Stuttgart: Friedrich Vorwerk Verlag, 1960]). Gogarten's sermons comprise a large volume of 364 pages.

[2] *Die Geschichtlichkeit der Kirche und ihrer Verkündigung als theologisches Problem* (Tübingen: J. C. B. Mohr [Paul Siebeck], 1954).

[3] *Die Kirche in der Welt* (Heidelberg: L. Schneider, 1948).

rebellion he is enabled through God's reconciling action to become a new creation. In varying ways, all of the theologians considered stress the positive possibilities opened to man by divine grace received in faith.

7. Truly Christian faith involves concern for the problems which confront men in their daily existence and responsible participation in the life of society. Thus Barth sees humanity as basically fellow humanity, and calls on Christians to recognize their solidarity with all men. Hromádka emphasizes that every aspect of life is related to the purpose of the God who became man; this means for Christians and the church love for those whom God loves and concrete action for a better social order. Gogarten appeals in the name of faith for the secularization which gives man both freedom from the world and lordship over it, while Ebeling advocates a "worldly speaking of God" which finds fullest expression in the Christian's life in the world, the proper sphere of faith. Schlink insists that Christians, living in eschatological perspective and preaching a God who sustains as well as creates and redeems his world, must accept responsibility for the just ordering of historical society. Wingren grounds Christian ethics in the doctrines of both creation and redemption, and shows how true worship implicates the worshiper in the struggles and sufferings of men in society. Though Bultmann calls on the church to avoid all social and political programs, and though he denies that faith affords any principles for the guidance of ethical life, he affirms emphatically the duty of the Christian to act responsibly in all his social relationships, listening in each situation for the claims of the "thou" and acting accordingly.

8. Since theology is the work of finite men whose understanding is limited, it must be seen as an approximation toward truth rather than as its final expression. It is always the theology of pilgrims who are on the way to the goal but have not arrived. It is therefore constantly subject to change and improvement through critical discussion. Hromádka sees the church itself as a congregation of pilgrims; it must proclaim an enduring gospel in changing situations which raise new problems and require new expressions and understandings. Barth declares that theologians are called on to understand and learn from one another in order that all may make their best contributions—within the church rather than in a theological "school." [4] Schlink demands constant checking of the confessional writings by the Scriptures. Ebeling emphasizes that because of the inwardly his-

[4] Foreword to Otto Weber, *Karl Barth's Church Dogmatics,* tr. Arthur C. Cochrane (Philadelphia: The Westminster Press, 1953), p. 9.

torical (*geschichtlich*) character of the Word of the Scriptures which includes both the preaching of that Word and the man to whom it is preached, exegesis and preaching must be carried out ever anew.[5] This circumstance is recognized equally by the hermeneutical observations of thinkers who otherwise differ as widely as do Diem and Bultmann. There can be no perennial theology, but only a pilgrim theology.

Differences

Mingled with agreements like those noted are differences so deep-seated that they sometimes jeopardize communication and mutual understanding. Major disagreements concern the relation between human self-understanding and the ontological reality of God, faith and history, hermeneutics, the nature of man, the relation of law and gospel, the nature and mission of the church, Christian social responsibility, and eschatology.

1. Probably the most fundamental divergence of all—a kind of continental divide which largely determines the direction of thought on other issues—pertains to the question whether priority in theological inquiry belongs to the givenness of the revelation of God or to man's personal understanding of existence. Does theology deal with the objective nature and activity of God himself, the ontological reality disclosed in Jesus Christ, or is its proper concern limited to the existential relation of man and God and the faith-events which bring men to authentic existence? The basic difference between Barth and Bultmann, for example, has been described as the opposition between ontology and personalism.[6]

Barth recognizes that the reconciliation accomplished in Jesus Christ must be realized in men; nevertheless, he emphasizes that God's self-revelation recorded in Scripture imparts true knowledge of the real God, and that dogmatics is concerned with his nature and redemptive action. Diem likewise asserts that though saving truth must be actualized in particular men, God is always prior to and the objective ground of the response which transforms human existence, and theology based on sound exegesis yields truth concerning his ultimate being. For Hromádka, too, the sovereign God has been embodied in Jesus of Nazareth. Schlink is no less emphatic in declaring that when dogmatics proceeds rightly it formulates true knowledge of God as he actually is. In similar vein Wingren maintains that in both law and gospel we have to do with one who actually is the Redeemer and

---

[5] *Die Geschichtlichkeit der Kirche*, p. 24.

[6] Hans-Horst Schrey in the *Weltkirchenlexikon* (*World Church Dictionary*), ed. Franklin H. Littell and Hans Hermann Walz (Stuttgart: Kreuz-Verlag, 1960), col. 293.

Creator encountered in Christian faith, while the Chalcedonian decree expresses objective truth regarding the person of Christ.

In sharp contrast to these views, Bultmann insists that it is impossible and misleading to interpret the Christ-event in terms of objective reality. New Testament faith excludes all grounding or authentication, hence the character of Christian preaching would be drastically altered if knowledge were supposed to be conveyed which had no direct reference to man's existence. I can speak of God not in terms of what he is in himself, but only in terms of his Word which confronts me. I cannot discuss either his nature or his actions without myself being involved as acted upon. To believe in God means to respond to my meeting with him in the personal decision of faith, not to acknowledge his objective existence. Theology therefore cannot make statements regarding the nature or attributes of God, the person or work of Jesus Christ, or the objective content of any Christian belief.

Gogarten is equally emphatic in repudiating the subject-object schema which sets man over against the divine object and seeks to ground faith in the objectivity of the God believed in. The reality with which authentic Christian faith is concerned is that of the Word of God which man encounters, never an objective reality which provides external support or validation. The objectification of God and his Word is equivalent to their denial. Ebeling likewise warns against the dangers of objectification. God is not a superbeing whose existence can somehow be verified apart from faith. He meets us as the Word of faith made flesh in Jesus Christ and communicated in the gospel. Therefore we can speak of him appropriately only in personal commitment, not in objectifying statements.

Various attempts have been made to reconcile the differences noted. Diem, for example, observes that both sides use humanly conditioned means of expression when they speak of the action of God. He also asks whether, in view of the trinitarian activity of God witnessed to in the Bible, the whole opposition of ontology to personalism is not false. Nils A. Dahl suggests that Barth's point of departure is essentially the situation of the preacher concerned to proclaim the Word of God, whereas Bultmann's is that of the modern hearer who needs a new understanding of the Word, and that these two approaches may be seen as complementary rather than antithetical.[7] Similarly, Heinrich Ott seeks a synthesis based

---

[7] Review of Bultmann's *Theologie des Neuen Testaments, Theologische Rundschau* (Neue Folge [New Series]), XXII (1945), 23.

on a common presupposition of the two tendencies, the first commandment as a "theological axiom":

Barth seeks to maintain Jesus Christ in his intrinsic selfhood and God's sovereignty revealed in him. Bultmann uses existentialist interpretation to show the relevance of the living Word of God to man's existence. He does it scientifically, yet always in the service of the Church's proclamation. In my opinion these two concerns are in the last resort not contradictory, but complementary.[8]

The truth of these observations seems self-evident. Nevertheless, the opposition is so deep-rooted, complex, and related to differing presuppositions that no efforts to bridge the gap have been very fruitful.

2. The question of objectivity appears in another form in the problem of the relation between faith and history, especially that between the Christ of faith and the historical Jesus. What does it mean for the church to declare that God's revelation occurred in the historical event of the coming of Christ? What is the connection between the proclamation and its factual source or basis? What bearing do the past events witnessed to in the kerygma have on the present faith of the believer?

Barth is unambiguous in declaring that the eternal God actually became man in Jesus Christ, entering human history in concrete actuality. The events set in motion by the incarnation are of course salvation-history, which we share in faith, and which cannot be substantiated or authenticated by ordinary historical inquiry. Also, the revelation occurs when man encounters Jesus Christ. However, it is really Christ who is confronted, and the subject and content of the revelation are not the man who receives it, but the incarnate Word himself who mediates and establishes it. "The reconciliation of the world to God is in every respect history." [9]

In Diem's view likewise the Jesus Christ who acts in the church's post-Easter preaching about him, and who therefore meets us through the proclamation, is identical with the earthly Jesus. In proclaiming Jesus as the Christ the church transmitted the essential message of Jesus himself. However, this identification cannot be scientifically demonstrated; its chief value is that it opens the way for a new encounter in which men like ourselves may in faith meet the Jesus of the Scriptures as the living and present Christ. Hromádka is equally opposed to the reduction of man's encounter

---

[8] Hans Werner Bartsch (ed.), *Kerygma and Myth. A Theological Debate*, II, tr. Reginald H. Fuller (London: S. P. C. K., 1962), 334 f.

[9] CD IV/3, 211; cf. IV/3, 182.

with Christ to a faith-event. It is rather the answer to the objective action in human history of God himself, who in the life, cross, and victory of Jesus of Nazareth actually took on himself men's sin, suffering, and finitude, and wrought their redemption. The events of this history are discernible only to faith, but they represent real deeds in time.

Schlink and Wingren take basically the same position, interpreting the Scriptures as upholding the factual nature of both the cross and the resurrection. Wingren, for instance, believes that without such factuality there would be no valid ground for the Christian message. The preaching of the gospel assumes that the events it proclaims really took place independently of their acceptance in faith—though such faith is necessary, and it radically changes the meaning of the events.

In contrast to the position just outlined, Bultmann believes that the historical factuality of Jesus' life and death has no important bearing on the revelatory and redemptive meaning of the Christ-event proclaimed by the church. Exegesis cannot get behind the kerygma to Jesus' own message; it discloses the *that* but not the *what* of Jesus. Jesus' life and work did occur in history. However, the real significance of Jesus must be apprehended by faith and cannot be discovered by detached historical inquiry. The real coming of Jesus was not a spatial-temporal occurrence, but an eschatological event in which men, responding to the kerygma in faith, entered a new and authentic existence. Thus Jesus comes whenever he is encountered in the word of preaching, and this encounter is not contingent on information regarding Jesus' earthly life. Concern for the historical origins of the kerygma would imply that such information could establish its validity, and would make faith dependent on the outcome of historical research. In complete harmony with Bultmann, Gogarten maintains that attention to the historical reality of the so-called facts of salvation is a form of objectification as misleading and dangerous as the attempt to objectify the ultimate ground of faith. Faith is properly concerned only with the reality of the Word of God as encountered.

Ebeling stands in a somewhat mediating position. He recognizes that our New Testament accounts are powerfully influenced by the faith of the writers, who sought to communicate not facts about Jesus or even past impressions of him, but his meaning for them as a present reality and the way in which he may now be understood in faith. The purpose of their writings is that the faith they proclaim may become ours. Nevertheless, he is quite critical of Bultmann's separation between the *that* and the *what*, and insists that the historical Jesus is directly relevant to and positively connected with our understanding of the kerygma. If Jesus never lived, if he made no contribution to the kerygma, or if faith in him misconstrued what he historically was, Christian faith would be undermined. Faith in Jesus must be based on Jesus as he actually was.[10]

3. Closely interwoven with the foregoing issues is the hermeneutical question, which for some theologians is the most basic of all. Which method should we follow in interpreting the biblical texts which make known the gospel? Which principles should guide our exposition? On what basis are we to understand and communicate the New Testament message? How is faith itself to be understood? Answers to these questions disclose essentially the same division of opinion as that noted in regard to the problems of objectivity and faith and history.

In Bultmann's view, since the biblical writings are expressions of life, the presupposition for understanding is the interpreter's relationship in his own life to the subject expressed in a given text. This relation constitutes a kind of prior understanding of the subject. It prompts the questions which the interpreter brings to the text and evokes the answers he obtains. Admittedly we cannot approach the New Testament with an advance understanding of the God revealed in Jesus Christ. However, we are already related to God because the question about our own personal existence, which consciously or unconsciously moves us all, is a form of the search for God. Therefore the key hermeneutical question is: How is man's existence understood in this passage? How does this text help me to relate myself to my own being? Answering these questions in the light of the concepts which arise from my prior understanding of existence, I can understand a word of the New Testament as the Word of God addressed to me.

Gogarten agrees completely. According to him the biblical writings must be interpreted not from the outside, but from within the interpreter's own self-understanding, that is, existentially. The believer himself is involved in every apostolic statement about Jesus Christ and in every affirmation of the Apostles' Creed. Only when he assumes the insertion of *for us* after each can he truly apprehend in faith the event called Christ. Such interpretation in turn heightens self-understanding.

Ebeling sees hermeneutics as primarily the investigation of how the

---

[10] Along with other former students of Bultmann, notably Günther Bornkamm, Ernst Fuchs, and Ernst Käsemann, Ebeling is representative of what James M. Robinson calls *A New Quest of the Historical Jesus* (London: SCM Press, 1959). Käsemann, for instance, insists on the identity of the exalted Lord and the earthly Lord. "Das Problem des historischen Jesus," *Zeitschrift für Theologie und Kirche*, LI (1954), 125-53.

Word of God comes to understanding. This requires a recognition of the meaning of *word* itself, and of the language-character of reality. Basically, word means self-expressing, happening content. On the human level it is the communication of a person—his existence, the man himself, not simply information about him. The Word of God therefore means God's self-communication, his address to man. Understanding is possible because being itself has linguisticality or language-character. Hence reality is oriented toward historical encounter. Language by nature mediates understanding, and the divine utterance personally encountered becomes the basic hermeneutical principle, the ultimate ground of understanding.

Man's existence is a word-event which originates in the Word of God and is called on to respond to that Word. But man fails to utter the word he owes to men and God. He therefore needs the saving, healing, justifying word which comes from God and is proclaimed in the Christian gospel.

The function of exegesis is to make each new communication of the gospel what the passage in question originally was—a coming-to-expression of the word-event. It is less concerned with understanding *of* the text than with understanding of present experience *through* the text. Preaching is thus enabled to fulfill the intention of the text by bringing to life now the reality with which the text has to do—the Word of God. The proclamation which occurred in the past thus becomes *occurring* proclamation. In this sense the word-event itself is the hermeneutical principle.

Wingren and Schlink find in the Scriptures themselves the best guide to understanding. God himself has spoken in the Word of the Bible, and his meaning can be best perceived when we listen to the biblical witnesses on their own terms. This position finds considerable common ground with Ebeling, and even some with Bultmann, but it rejects the basic presuppositions of existentialist hermeneutics. For example, Wingren stresses the importance of the Scriptures for present Christian faith, hence the inadequacy of purely historical exegesis. Yet he opposes the use of the hearer's understanding of his own existence as the main principle of interpretation. Partly because of this, Wingren believes, New Testament references to God, Christ, and eternity in Bultmann's thought refer to experiences of man rather than to objective realities, while the death and resurrection of Christ become simply the spiritual death and resurrection of the hearer of the gospel.

Barth is even more sharply opposed to Bultmannian hermeneutics. According to him we begin with God's Word itself as found in the canonical Scriptures. The primary task of theology is to confront, confirm, and declare that Word. The Word calls forth, constitutes, and regulates theology, and therefore takes precedence over all interpretation. A text is to be understood and expounded only in the light of its theme, although it must be related to other texts with the same theme. Thus Scripture dictates its own method of interpretation. In the light of God's self-revelation in Jesus Christ our human language can be confidently applied to God. To rely instead on alien philosophical presuppositions is to distort or dilute the gospel, and to deny the lordship of Christ.

Diem proceeds from primarily Barthian premises, but also utilizes existentialist insights. Basic is his concept of proclamation-history, which connects Jesus' self-proclamation, the apostolic preaching of Jesus as the Christ, and the continuing proclamation of the church. Jesus Christ is thus at once initiator, object, and continuing subject of the proclamation. According to the principle of concordance hearing, the different biblical witnesses are allowed to speak on their own terms, yet they are seen to complement each other and protect each other's varying emphases, which *intend* to testify to the one reality of God's saving action.

Diem offers for our guidance in interpreting Scripture three "hermeneutical circles," each marked by the reciprocal influence of two associated realities. First, the witness (apostolic preaching) is to be interpreted only by what is witnessed (Jesus Christ), though this in turn can be known only through the witness. This circle can be opened only from within: the Scriptures interpret themselves. This conception contrasts sharply with Bultmann's circle which links scriptural understanding with man's self-understanding. Secondly, church dogma must be tested by the Scriptures, but in turn serves to disclose their meaning. The doctrine of the Trinity, for example, is an interpretation by the church of the biblical revelation of God, but it in turn illuminates the scriptural witness to God's manifold activity. Thirdly, the testimony of Scripture, proclaimed ever anew, evokes through the living, self-disclosing activity of God the responsive, obedient hearing which confirms it and gives it meaning. In this dynamic present event the biblical message is reenacted, authenticated, and elucidated. This stress on the hermeneutical function of responsive listening in the present provides an important point of contact for the otherwise divergent views of Diem and Ebeling, for Diem's obedient hearing is quite similar to Ebeling's occurring proclamation.

4. In the main, the differences so far considered divide theologians who stress the objective Word of God from those most influenced by existentialist thought. When we return to the relation of law and gospel, we

encounter a radically altered alignment. Here conservative and existenialistic Lutherans are largely united against Barth and his associates.

The Lutherans regard the law as the indispensable background of the gospel. For Wingren the law with its compulsion is inherent in the nature of man's corporate life as created by God. It is also God's sovereign will as disclosed in his conflict with human sin. It is thus grounded in the total life of man as a disobedient creature of God. Quite apart from the gospel, man knows that he is subject to law, guilt, and judgment. However, he becomes fully and personally aware of the true depth of his need only when he hears the gospel, with its vivid disclosure of his radical alienation from God and its promise of forgiveness and a new life through Jesus Christ. Schlink finds at the heart of Christian doctrine the double Word of God which brings together the antitheses of sin and grace, judgment and mercy, demand and assurance. The law demands, the gospel gives. Yet both are acts of the love of one triune God, and ultimately the supremacy of the gospel must be recognized. It, not law, is God's "proper" Word; we are justified by grace through faith.

This long-held Lutheran view has come under vigorous attack by Karl Barth, who on christocentric premises replaces the opposition and order of law-gospel with the synthesis gospel and law. For him the latter can be understood only in the light of the former, as its concrete expression. Thus the law itself partakes of the nature of the grace which is the content of the gospel. It is basically a promise of the action to which we are freed and led by the gospel. The priority of gospel over law means that the obedience commanded by God is itself his gift. Further, the law portrayed by the New Testament as brought to an end by Christ is not God's real law but the law as legalistically misunderstood by man.

Wingren charges that Barth's christocentric depreciation of creation and law results in the derivation of ethical norms solely from the gospel, and thus a legalistic misuse of the New Testament. Actually, the "you shall" of God's command is contained in the law itself, before and apart from the incarnation. Yet Barth insists that the redemptive encounter with Jesus Christ does provide ethical guidance for both the individual and the church. Hromádka, too, finds in the incarnation the Christian's ultimate basis for ethical and social concern. Since God has entered human life redemptively as well as creatively, to worship and love him is to find ourselves in the presence of men, and to hear his call to love those whom he loves. Christ in his lordship both releases and commands us to act righteously toward our neighbors.

On this issue Bultmann, much closer to his conservative Lutheran colleagues than to Barth, asserts that grace can be understood only by the man who knows the pressure of the law. All men are aware of being subject to ethical demands which they cannot fulfill. This precedence of our status under the law over the preaching of grace is an *essential* priority, though not necessarily temporal. To maintain that we discover the full meaning of sin only through the gospel is only to confirm the reference of grace to law. Whereas the law requires freedom, the gospel confers it. In freeing man to live for the future, released from himself and his past, Christ is the "end" of the actual law, not merely of the law as misunderstood. However, Bultmann agrees with Barth that the man under grace perceives the law as a commandment to the life which God himself offers.

Though Ebeling is a Lutheran strongly influenced by Bultmann, on the problem of gospel and law he is closer to Barth. He fully agrees with Barth that the unity of gospel and law is to be defined in the light of the gospel. Likewise, the fact that the law is the law of God—not merely human precepts—can be recognized in its full depth only in the light of the gospel of Christ as the end of the law. Further, the law which accuses man of sin must be included in the preaching of the gospel, in order that the gospel itself may not be misunderstood as law. However, Ebeling is Lutheran rather than Barthian in regarding Christ as the end of the law as willed by God rather than simply as misinterpreted by man. He is both Lutheran and Barthian in his affirmation that the abrogation of the law occurs not through the fulfillment of its divine precepts, but through the gospel which calls forth faith and frees men's consciences.[11]

5. A pressing question is that of the nature and extent of the ethical and social responsibility of the Christian and the church. Here a three-way division of thought is evident. All the theologians studied stress the close connection between Christian faith and life in the world, but they differ widely regarding the ground of that relation and the kinds of guidance found in the gospel for concrete decisions.

Barth's ethics, like the remainder of his theology, is christocentric. In the light of the incarnation, every man's existence belongs to God; therefore the man who is called to become God's covenant-partner is directed also to his fellow man. Humanity is fellow-humanity, since Christ is every man's brother and God is every man's Father. Further, God calls men into the Christian community, which is commissioned to witness in word and

---

[11] Ebeling, *Word and Faith*, pp. 268, 270.

deed to his love for men, hence to act responsibly against social injustice. The gospel does not offer specific rules for human relations, but it does provide indispensable indirect guidance. For example, in the relationships of man and woman, parent and child, and the larger community of near and distant neighbors, man is called upon to affirm and honor human life— his own and that of every other man—recognizing it as a loan from God, and securing it against caprice so that it may be used in God's service. On this basis Barth finds justification for taking definite positions on ethical and social issues, including legislation.

Hromádka's ethics is also rooted in Christology. The Word made flesh shows human life to be the sphere of the creative and redemptive life of God himself. Hence every aspect of life is related to the divine purpose. Love for God involves love for all men, to whom God has given himself in infinite love. This requires concrete action for a better social order. The lordship of Christ over all earthly existence commands and releases us to act in repentant obedience and love in behalf of the inward and outward freedom of all men. The church is therefore called to rise above all divisions of class, race, nationality, and political power blocs to reconcile man to man and to work for the just ordering of society. This requires it to maintain communication with Communists and others outside the church, sharing their concern for righteousness while seeking to minister to their deepest spiritual needs.[12]

In opposition to Barth, Wingren grounds Christian ethics in creation and law as well as in the gospel and redemption. Operative in the nature of man as created by God are norms which make possible orderly corporate life and which all men, quite apart from the gospel, are called upon to obey. However, the gospel itself has profound ethical and social significance. Fellowship with Christ cannot be genuine if pursued in isolation from the world he came to redeem. The sacraments, for example, celebrate the present action of the Christ who shares the whole range of our earthly experience; they therefore move the recipient to offer himself as a living sacrifice among men in the events of every day. The Christian's vocation is to stand uprightly and lovingly beside his neighbor and live in obedience to God in all secular relationships. This requires him to be critical of earthly institutions, including government. The spiritual and worldly realms must remain separate, but individual believers are involved in both,

---

[12] Diem's ethical and social orientation is also Barthian. He has not been so directly involved in social questions as have Barth and Hromádka, but has written a number of short treatises relating the gospel to contemporary problems.

CONVERGING AND DIVERGING PATHS

and they are sent out by the church to participate in the life of society as those who "live from their baptism," thus opening the way to social renewal. The church as such, however, has no responsibility for social reform. Adhering closely in this respect to Luther's doctrine of the two realms, Wingren holds that the church must respect existing social relationships as divinely appointed and not attempt to regulate them. To assign an initiative to the church on the political level, as Barth does, is to make the church a collective against other collectives and artificially to separate Christians from their non-Christian neighbors.

In Schlink's view the church has two main tasks: to unite its members in worship and fellowship and to send them out to proclaim the gospel and serve their fellow men. His major theological grounding for social concern is the doctrine of God as Sustainer. Such a God demands that his worshipers accept the obligation to preserve all human life and to act responsibly in behalf of freedom, justice, and peace for all men. However, Christians should not mistake peace on earth for peace with God, a just social order with Christ's kingdom or the new creation. The command of God the Sustainer to seek the establishment of earthly justice is secondary to, and contributory to the fulfillment of, the command of God the Redeemer to proclaim to a world under judgment the way of redemption.

Helmut Gollwitzer has commented penetratingly[13] on what he finds to be a significant, though paradoxical, difference between the functioning of the Barthian and Lutheran conceptions of Christian social responsibility. Because of the two-realm doctrine, Lutherans find in the gospel no directions for conduct in political questions, whereas Barthians with their christocentric approach do find indirect guidance. However, Lutherans in Germany take much the same political position—essentially the conservative anticommunist one of the West—while Barthians represent various positions, asking what God wills but differing in their answers. This observation is a realistic reminder that the ethical and social attitudes of Christians—not only those of Barthians and Lutherans—are not the simple resultant of theological beliefs, but may be decisively affected by cultural and other nontheological factors.

A third position appears with the theologians most influenced by existentialist thinking. In Bultmann's view the man who responds trustfully to God's address to him in the Christ-event is freed from himself to a life of devotion to others in faith and love. Ethical living is therefore expected

---

[13] In a conversation in Berlin in June, 1960.

of the Christian. However, faith offers no prescriptions or principles. The believer knows only that he is commanded to love; as one who loves he listens in each moment for the claims of the "thou" who confronts him, and tries to act accordingly. His chief duty is to live responsibly, making use in his decisions of the same moral insights and resources which are available to all men. The church must proclaim the Word of God, call men to decision, and point them toward authentic, responsible existence. But it must not provide answers to political or social questions, since to do so would be to judge as unchristian positions differing from those it upholds.

In Gogarten's view faith deprives works of saving significance but preserves their earthly meaning, secularizing them by making them an affair of the world. This gives man both freedom from the world and lordship over it, while enabling him to discharge his secular responsibilities as a divine trust. However, it does not offer him ethical knowledge grounded in ultimate reality. Such knowledge would rob faith of its questioning uncertainty and its unconditional openness to the future. True faith faces the obscurity and precariousness of the future trusting in the salvation wrought by God, making its decisions as each new situation arises.

Ebeling likewise portrays faith as "de-divinizing" the world and at the same time giving man true freedom for responsible participation in politics, art, morals, science, and philosophy. Such activities constitute history, which is the sphere of faith. The church summons Christians to serve in the freedom of sonship to God, which is freedom for brotherly love for their fellow men. However, Christian faith does not provide ethical norms, nor is the church commissioned to change social structures. Sin is basically unbelief, and its remedy is faith. Therefore the church must go beyond symptoms to causes, fulfilling its primary responsibility as the summons to faith. Its chief social significance is that those who respond to its call are freed from self-love to love for God and neighbor.

6. All eight of the Protestant theologians agree that the ethical-social life of the Christian must be seen in eschatological perspective. However, they represent two sharply different conceptions of eschatological existence. For Barth the eschatological event is the real coming again of Jesus Christ which brings the entire temporal process to its ultimate goal. According to the New Testament this is a single occurrence, but it takes place in three forms: the resurrection, the impartation of the Holy Spirit at Pentecost and throughout history, and the final return of Christ. The church, the eschatological community, is called into existence to proclaim the living

Lord and call men to repentance and service in anticipation of the judgment and glory to come.

Hromádka's eschatology is similar. In a world moving toward the end disclosed in Christ, the church is the pilgrim people of God called to witness to the sovereign grace of the Lord of history and share the struggles of men in Christ's name, sustained constantly by the confident expectation of his final victory. Schlink likewise maintains that history must be seen in the light of its end, when Christ will return to judge both the church and the world. Actually the world is already subject to him as its Lord. We are now living in the last days, the time of God's patience, when he is preserving the world in order that the gospel may be preached and new multitudes brought to salvation. Fulfillment of this responsibility, however, requires the church to seek also to establish justice and peace here and now. A similar transhistorical perspective is influential in Wingren; developing particularly the eschatological dimension of the sacraments, with their celebration of the overcoming of death in resurrection, he finds them pointing the whole of life toward the ultimate consummation of God's purpose to redeem his creation.

In contrast to these theologians, Bultmann interprets the end not chronologically, as the terminus of historical time, but qualitatively, as the end of the worldliness of man. For the apostles the Easter-event meant the rise of faith in the risen Lord, which completed their faith in the redemptive efficacy of the cross and made them new persons. Proclaiming this faith, they summoned other men to understand themselves as crucified and risen with Christ. Thus the resurrection of Jesus Christ is the eschatological event, signifying the newness of life opened to those who respond in faith to the preaching of God's grace. The event is individual rather than cosmic. It occurs again and again. It is the end of the old world of the believer and his entrance into a transformed life. His "old man," torn by anxiety, rebellion, and guilt, is freed to become a new creation, belonging to a different order. Eschatological existence is nonworldly existence within the present world, the life of those who have renounced concern for self and security and live by faith working through love, in complete openness to God's future.

Obviously this understanding of the eschatological event, which is shared by Gogarten, may also be held by nonexistentialistic theologians. Thus Barth speaks of the event of being crucified and therefore living with Christ as the overcoming of death, "the end of time, the last day" for those who experience it. However, for the Barthians and conservative

Lutherans this individual occurrence of redemption and renewal is only one aspect of a process to be consummated by divine action at the end of world history—a conception which Bultmann rejects as indefensible objectification.

Protestant, Roman Catholic, and Orthodox Theology

The complexity of the current theological situation becomes even more evident when we compare the Protestant theologians investigated with their Roman Catholic and Orthodox counterparts. Serious differences among the representatives of the three confessions may be readily identified. Nevertheless, they stand on a common foundation of Christian conviction which is far more extensive than the disparities in the superstructures which they have erected. In some respects, indeed, both the Roman Catholics and Nissiotis are closer to particular Protestant thinkers than some of the latter are to each other, while some aspects of Nissiotis' Orthodox thought have more in common with Protestant than with Catholic emphases.

Similarities

1. Something akin to the "pilgrim theology" noted among the Protestants is discernible in the Roman Catholics and Nissiotis. They are willing to reexamine old formulas, to raise new questions, to listen seriously to ideas different from their own, and to modify previous positions. Notable examples are Congar's reinterpretation of Mariology, his creative thinking on the lay apostolate, and his breadth regarding the salvation of non-Catholics; Rahner's relentless questioning, his earnest probing for the living meaning of the church's faith, and his utilization of existentialist insights; and the inclusiveness of Nissiotis' view of the church, his fresh and illuminating treatment of the work of the Holy Spirit, and his understanding appreciation of Roman Catholic and Protestant positions.

2. A genuine *rapprochement* between Catholics and Protestants is apparent in reference to the historically divisive issue of the relation between Scripture and tradition. On the one side Rahner and Congar agree that the church's teaching authority in matters of faith and morals can never equal or supersede that of the canonical Scriptures, and Congar even accepts the Reformation principle of *sola Scriptura* with respect to the *material* sufficiency of the Bible. On the other hand, the works of Protestants like Barth, Diem, Wingren, and Schlink reveal a high appreciation of the indispensable role of the historic Christian community in producing, trans-

mitting, and canonizing the Scriptures and interpreting them in each generation.

3. The Reformers' insistence on the primacy of the unmerited grace of God in salvation is of course implicitly or explicitly affirmed by all of the Protestant theologians, but hardly more unambiguously than by Rahner, Congar, and Nissiotis. For example, Rahner agrees that "the grace of God is everything," and that ultimately man depends utterly on God, while Nissiotis attributes to the grace of the Holy Spirit the transformation and re-creation of human nature which the Orthodox call theosis.

4. With regard to the human response to divine grace, the traditional opposition between the Protestant principle of faith alone and Catholic insistence of faith and works (and the Orthodox accent on love) is considerably diminished in most of these theologians. While Barth, Wingren, and Schlink insist that man cannot earn forgiveness, they clearly acknowledge that saving faith must produce and find completion in works of righteousness and love. On the Catholic side, Rahner stresses repeatedly the necessity of faith in man's acceptance of salvation, while Nissiotis brings out the importance in Orthodox worship of the repentance, trust, and commitment with which man responds to God's redemptive act.

5. The essential agreement among the Protestants on the centrality of Jesus Christ is echoed in the thought of Congar and Rahner. Both devote major attention to Christology; while they accept fully the Chalcedonian two-nature doctrine, they seek to correct oversights they find in Protestantism, and somewhat in Catholicism, by stressing the part played in the work of salvation by Christ's real humanity. Significantly, this emphasis is equally strong in Wingren. Nissiotis emphasizes that the reunion of man with God is made possible by the union in Jesus Christ of God with humanity, though it is fulfilled by the Holy Spirit in the church.

6. Congar, Rahner, and Nissiotis share a major tendency among the Protestants in devoting serious attention to man and in stressing the renewal of life opened to him by the grace of God. Like Barth, Rahner finds in the incarnation the clue to a true understanding of man. In Christ's human life finite man is seen to possess an infinite depth. Humanity is the very presence of God in the world; man *is* because God has projected himself outward. Man is therefore forbidden to think poorly of himself, for he would then think poorly of God. Nissiotis' anthropology, which is grounded also in the incarnation, comes to a focus in the concept of the theosis or christification of man. The gracious activity of the Holy Spirit actualizes in man the consequences of the union realized in Christ, re-

creating humanity in the image of God, and enabling man to fulfill the intent of his deepest nature. Congar likewise upholds a view of man in which divine grace rather than sin is victorious. All three of these theologians emphasize more than do most of the Protestants that salvation involves the real transformation and renewal of man as well as his forgiveness.

7. Further three-way agreement is evident in ecclesiology. For example, Schlink and other Protestants join Rahner and Congar in supporting in essence Nissiotis' belief in the qualitative catholicity of the church, which connotes not merely worldwide extension but basically the wholeness or fullness of the salvation accomplished in Christ and its availability to all men. Several of the Protestants assert as strongly as Orthodox and Catholic thinkers the basic oneness of the church, while Nissiotis and Rahner join with them in locating its essence in the proclamation of the Word and the administration of the sacraments, indissolubly related. Congar's identification of the church as a whole with the faithful community—a view essentially supported by Rahner and Nissiotis—approaches the Reformation view of the church as the "congregation of faithful men." Closer rapport is also made possible by Congar's recognition that non-Catholics who have supernatural faith and charity are related to the Redeemer's mystical body, hence on the way to salvation, and by Nissiotis' extension of the term Orthodox to all who profess their kinship with the one Spirit and sincerely wish to share the faith and life of the one unseparated church.

8. *Rapprochement* is also seen in the emphasis of Protestants like Hromádka, Barth, Wingren, and Ebeling on the lay ministry and the recognition by Congar, Rahner, and Nissiotis of the distinctiveness and indispensability of the lay apostolate. The Catholics assert particularly the vocation of laymen to witness to their faith and manifest the saving power of Christ in the world; in relation to the secondary mission of the church— to orient society toward God—laymen *are* the church. Similarly, Nissiotis asserts that eucharistic worship by its very nature thrusts believers out into the world in witness and service, which is "the Eucharist incognito."

9. Implicit in support of the lay apostolate is agreement that Christian faith involves acceptance of ethical and social responsibility. In Congar's view the dignity and unity of humanity as created and redeemed by God demand that Christians work actively for world peace, racial justice, and other social causes. Rahner affirms the reality of both universal and individual ethical norms grounded in the obligating will of God and the duty of the Christian to relate these norms to particular situations in a way

which fully recognizes the personal dimension in moral decisions. Nissiotis sees the main social function of the church in its sanctification of society through the mediation of divine grace, and he believes it must always "act at a distance" in relation to political affairs. However, he calls on Christians to make their daily lives a liturgical offering, thus relating men directly to the living reality of God, and he affirms the church's responsibility to alleviate human suffering and to find answers to domestic, economic, and political as well as personal problems.

10. Finally, it is worth noting that Rahner and, to a lesser degree, Nissiotis are in accord with some Protestant existentialistic emphases. Though Rahner affirms the enduring reality of both divine and human nature, he believes that man is known best in his concrete decisions and actions as he responds in passionate commitment to the questions put to him by existence. Such response must take account of the singularity of each situation. Likewise, our clearest thought of God is related to the salvation-event in man, and grace can be understood only when personally experienced. Nissiotis' assertion that anthropology is the chief concern of theology calls to mind the insistence of Bultmann and Ebeling that we cannot talk of God without at the same time talking of man. Moreover, the theosis of man emphasized by Nissiotis, though it is essential as well as existential, bears genuine resemblance to the authentic existence stressed by Bultmann. For Nissiotis also the new birth must be a personal, existential reality. In this regard he is expressing a conviction shared by all the Protestants discussed.

Differences

Intermingled with similarities like the above are pronounced contrasts, most of which reflect historic differences between the traditions represented. The total theological situation will come into clearer focus if we briefly examine some of these areas of disagreement.

1. With the partial exception of Wingren, the Protestant thinkers investigated reject natural theology. For them there can be no knowledge of God apart from the Christian revelation. In Barth's view, for example, only the mind consciously enlightened by God's disclosure of himself in Jesus Christ is capable of discerning religious truth. In contrast, Rahner sees human nature as so permeated by divine grace that there is no such thing as a purely natural man. Man's whole existence is rooted—whether or not he is conscious of it—in the uncreated or prevenient grace of God, which becomes created or actualized grace to the degree that man responds

to it. Hence the intellectual endeavors of secular philosophers and the thought and practice of non-Christian religions cannot be dismissed as only the voice of nature; they may also be an unwitting response to the hidden action of the Holy Spirit. From a similar perspective Congar finds a basis for the ultimate salvation of persons of good faith who, though technically atheists, are dedicated to causes like justice, truth, peace, and brotherhood which assume absolute value and involve ends which are in fact supernatural.

2. Pronounced differences remain with regard to the roles of Scripture and tradition. Though the Protestants would agree that the Scriptures must be interpreted within the church, they accept nothing approaching the binding authority of the Catholic teaching office, and they refuse to recognize the church's right to promulgate doctrines not clearly founded on Scripture. Schlink, for example, insists that the Confessions only make more precise a faith which is wholly subject to Scripture. Congar attributes such restrictions on the authority of tradition to Protestantism's lack of any genuine ecclesiology. However that may be, it is clear that Protestant-Catholic differences on this question do reflect divergent doctrines of the church. Still a third position, represented by Nissiotis, is an integral part of his ecclesiology. In his view authority is located neither in the Bible nor in institutions or officials, but in the fullness of the life of the church, both clergy and laity—its mysteries, worship, preaching, theology, and evangelism. The primary reality, which cannot be more precisely defined, is the event of Christ perpetuated in the "mysterious" life of the church, which is the grace of the triune God in action. The Bible, written within this divine-human event, is its authentic reflection but not its judge.

3. Worthy of note is the difference between the primarily christological approach of Rahner, Congar, and most of the Protestants and the more pneumatological orientation of Nissiotis. The former of course recognize the continuing activity of God as Spirit, and the latter refuses to isolate the Spirit from the Father and the Son. Nevertheless, unlike the others Nissiotis regards pneumatology as the heart of the Christian religion, and he devotes much greater attention to Pentecost and the Holy Spirit than do any of the other theologians. Though he affirms with them the importance of the incarnation, he stresses repeatedly that it is only through the renewing and transforming action of the Spirit that the salvation made possible in Christ becomes effective in man, the church, and history.

4. Further differences in emphasis appear with regard to the bearing of salvation on the persistence of sin in the redeemed person. The Lutherans

share the familiar Reformation view that justification means the imputation to man of the righteousness of Christ, so that the recipient of saving grace remains "at the same time sinful and righteous." Rahner admits the continued presence of sin, but insists that man really becomes righteous rather than being only declared righteous. God's grace is healing and sanctifying as well as forgiving; it actually enables the justified man to keep God's commandments. Nissiotis goes even further in affirming the theosis of man, the spiritual ascension by which man through the Holy Spirit is on the way to becoming what he is intended to be, man without sin. Schlink and Wingren also rejoice in God's re-creating activity: the Christian experiences daily the death of the old through temptation and self-discipline and the birth of the new in trust and joy. The Barthians and the existentialist Protestants speak likewise, with varying meanings, of God's renewal of man, but none of these interpret so radically as do the Orthodox and Catholic thinkers the extent of the change wrought in redeemed humanity by divine grace.

5. The historic Protestant-Catholic opposition between justification by grace through faith, and salvation by faith and works appears in new though qualified forms. Though these Catholics declare that grace is ultimately everything and the Protestants assert the necessity of deeds of love, they differ considerably on the place and value of human cooperation. Thus Congar traces the divisions regarding the church and the Virgin Mary to a radical difference in belief regarding the role of humanity in salvation. In his view Protestant interpretations of the two-nature doctrine do not recognize fully the real humanity of Christ. Similarly, Protestants fail to see that Mary, as the mother of Jesus, represents the collective role of humanity in the appropriation of salvation, and that the church also, human as well as divine, combines with God's gift in the Eucharist an act of sacrificial devotion which moves from man to God. Further, a righteous life devoted to divine ends, implicitly a life of faith, has saving significance. None of the Protestants would accept these intimations of error or agree that man is redeemed by a combination of divine and human action. Instead, they ascribe salvation solely to the grace of God, while admitting that man empowered by God must respond in faith which bears fruit in deeds of love.

6. The most profound differences of all concern the nature of the church and its ministry and sacraments. In general, the representatives of Catholicism and Orthodoxy agree with each other and differ from the Protestants in upholding a deeply organic, mystical, and predominantly sacramental

ecclesiology. Other relationships of similarity and difference are more complex.

Congar claims for the Roman Church a body of doctrine transmitted from Christ and the apostles and kept safe by the episcopate, the sacraments as channels of the grace which issues from the cross, and a priesthood with power to make effective both teaching and sacraments. The church includes the entire community of the faithful. Therefore laymen also have their apostleship, that of mediating life from the Body of Christ to the world, which they are called to turn toward Christ. However, the clergy mediate the grace of Christ to the faithful, and only the clergy constitute the church in its proper being as an institution of salvation. They, alone exercise authority, and the role of the laity is definitely subordinate.

By contrast, in Nissiotis' view apostolicity was given to the whole church and is transmitted by it. The gathered company of the Holy Spirit is a sacerdotal, charismatic, personal, and communal unity in which there are no qualitative differences. The whole body of the faithful precedes and conditions the selection and ordination of bishops and priests. The latter are the necessary personal channels of divine grace, but their ministry is both authorized and fulfilled by that of the total community of believers.

On these issues the Protestants broadly agree with Orthodoxy. The basic reality of the church is the whole company of the faithful who are gathered for worship and fellowship and commissioned to preach the Word of life and give themselves in service to men. All are called to minister according to their spiritual gifts, though some with special capacities are designated and ordained by the community for a special ministry of Word and sacrament. The authority of the latter is derived wholly from the gospel entrusted to them, not from the laying on of hands. Genuine apostolic succession means that ministers and laymen alike share in the faith, teaching, fellowship, witness, and service of the apostles and the Christian community which they founded.

With respect to the number and efficacy of the sacraments, Rahner, Congar, and Nissiotis are in basic agreement on positions which are unacceptable to Protestants. All three recognize seven sacraments, and agree that they confer grace by the very nature of the act performed. All likewise assert that a real transformation of the elements occurs in the eucharistic action, although Nissiotis' sense of mystery prevents him from formulating this so precisely as does the Roman doctrine of transubstantiation. Rahner speaks of the church itself as the primal sacrament—a conception essentially in harmony with Nissiotis' view that the change of the elements expresses a deeper transformation wrought by the real presence of Christ in his living Body, the church. A different alignment appears with regard to the nature of the sacrifice offered in the Eucharist. In Catholic doctrine the offering is made by the priest on behalf of the people, and its purpose is fulfilled whether or not other worshipers are present. In the thought of Nissiotis and the Protestants, on the contrary, the offering is made by the whole community of believer-priests through the celebrant, and private celebrations are excluded because of the incongruity of communion without communicants.

Congar asserts that the Catholic Church alone is commissioned by God to convey to all men the salvation wrought by Jesus Christ. In this sense there is no salvation outside the Catholic Church; nevertheless, persons who through invincible ignorance remain outside the visible body really belong to it by desire. Nissiotis declares that the Orthodox constitute "the one true church," though the Orthodox for him include all, whether members of Orthodox bodies or not, who wish to confess their faith in the whole revelation of God through the worship and life of the undivided church. However, his opposition to intercommunion limits the inclusiveness which he seeks to uphold. None of the Protestants claims sole authority for his church. Even Schlink's commitment to the Lutheran Confessions does not lead him to assert the supremacy of Lutheranism; he is more concerned that all Christians accept the authority of the one Lord proclaimed in the Scriptures which the Confessions interpret. The Protestant theologians are unwilling to treat any ecclesial body as the true church; for them Christ alone is the truth that saves.

INDEX OF PERSONS

279

INDEX OF SUBJECTS